I0153312

MORE THAN A SONG

THE PUBLIC WITNESS OF PENTECOSTAL WORSHIP

MORE THAN A SONG

THE PUBLIC WITNESS OF PENTECOSTAL WORSHIP

EDITED BY MARCIA CLARKE
& STEVEN FÉLIX-JÄGER

CPT PRESS
Cleveland, Tennessee

More Than a Song
The Public Witness of Pentecostal Worship

Published by CPT Press
900 Walker ST NE
Cleveland, TN 37311
USA
email: cptpress@pentecostaltheology.org
website: www.cptpress.com

ISBN: 9781953358738

Copyright © 2026 CPT Press

All rights reserved. No part of this book may be reproduced or translated in any form, by print, photoprint, microfilm, microfiche, electronic database, internet database, or any other means without written permission from the publisher.

Dedicated to
the Society for Pentecostal Studies

CONTENTS

ACKNOWLEDGEMENTS

This volume was made possible through the generous support of a Vital Worship, Vital Preaching Grant from the Calvin Institute of Christian Worship, Grand Rapids, Michigan, with funds provided by Lilly Endowment Inc.

The editors extend heartfelt thanks to the 'More than a Song' project participants: Selwyn Arnold, Kellen Brooks, Betsey Christensen, Nate Glasper, Laura Payne, Melaine Rochford, Phillip Struyk, Wes Tuttle, Andy Wingate, and Isaias Zarazua. While space constraints did not allow for the full inclusion of everyone's individual reflections, the essay by Philip Struyk stands as a representative voice for the group's collective insights and shared work.

INTRODUCTION

MARCIA CLARKE & STEVEN FÉLIX-JÄGER*

Introduction

It was a normal youth practice, our (Marcia's) choir practice took place at least once per week in the sanctuary of our church. About twenty of us gathered to practice for some upcoming event, or it may have been Sunday service, I don't remember. We were practicing the song 'Jesus is Love' made popular by Lionel Richie. We had the soprano, alto, descant, and tenor parts down. We were singing the song through again to consolidate our parts, I remember looking at my fellow choir members and I noticed that there was a shift in their composure. '*He's got the power, He's got the glory, forever*'.[1] Along with the ad libs '*Who can heal you (Jesus), who can save you (Jesus) … O yeah*'. As we sang, there came a point when practice had stopped and something else began. The words filled the room in perfect harmony; tears began to stream down faces; some people continued to sing; others fell to their knees on the altar; still others stopped singing with faces turned up to heaven.[2] Practice had opened a portal through which heaven connected to earth.

---

* Marcia Clarke (PhD, University of Birmingham, UK) serves as the Pastor for Spiritual Formation and Discipleship at New Beginnings Church in Simi Valley, California, and as adjunct faculty at Vanguard University.

Steven Félix-Jäger (PhD, University of Wales, UK) is Associate Professor and Chair of Worship Arts and Media at Life Pacific University, San Dimas, California.

[1] The actual words of the song are, 'cause His love's the power (power) His love's the glory (glory), Forever (ever and ever)'.

[2] Melissa Archer, 'Worship in the Book of Revelation', in Lee Roy Martin (ed.), *Toward a Pentecostal Theology of Worship* (Cleveland, TN: CPT Press, 2nd edn, 2020), p. 170.

This recollection should not confuse the reader who may think from the title of this volume, *More than a Song: The Public Witness of Pentecostal Worship*, that the role of music and song in worship is being disputed; on the contrary, we the editors, are convinced about the place of song and music in worship. What can be more of a soul-shaping force than song? Even when tired and depressed, old songs well up from within and dance on whistling lips.[3] There are some elderly people who may not remember what they ate for dinner, but they have an uncanny ability to sing songs learned in their youth word for word. Music has the ability to seep into our spiritual bones. Similar to organic food, such 'soul food' can sculpt identity, Witvliet suggests, providing 'resources to build spiritual muscles and ward off diseases'.[4] Whilst acknowledging that other factors including parents, friends, school, and social media contribute to soul formation, music is among the most potent. Music as soul food provides a picture of something ingested, which soon becomes indistinguishable from who we are. Aristotle and others have claimed that music has formative power, it will either corrupt, inoculate or to use a Pauline phrase, build up.[5] This is especially true of the music sung in church, for this music is offered in the name of God.[6] Witvliet states 'when it comes to matters of spirituality and faith, we are what we sing'.[7]

In Pentecostal services, the song set of the worship service, aids in ushering the adherents into an experience or encounter of God, such as the example from the choir practice above. Such an encounter is considered the very 'heartbeat' of Pentecostal spirituality, characterized as a personal, experiential encounter of the Spirit of God' and is a central aspect of the tradition.[8] Worship, expressed in music and song, for many Pentecostals and Western Christians alike, is popularly understood as occurring during the first twenty to thirty minute

---

[3] John D. Witvliet, *Worship Seeking Understanding: Windows into Christian Practice* (Grand Rapids: Baker Academic, 2003), p. 231.

[4] Witvliet, *Worship Seeking Understanding*, p. 231.

[5] Witvliet, *Worship Seeking Understanding*, p. 231. As in 1 Thess. 5.11.

[6] Witvliet, *Worship Seeking Understanding*, p. 232.

[7] Witvliet, *Worship Seeking Understanding*, p. 231.

[8] Keith Warrington, *Pentecostal Theology: A Theology of Encounter* (London: T&T Clark, 2008), p. 20, https://doi.org/10.5040/9780567705105. See also Juan Sepulveda, 'Reflections on the Pentecostal Contributions to the Mission of the Church in Latin America', *Journal of Pentecostal Theology* 1 (1992), and S.A. Ellington, 'Pentecostalism and the Authority of Scripture', *Journal of Pentecostal Theology* 9 (1996), p. 17.

of the Sunday service, in the designated 'worship' timeslot. In contrast, for many non-Western churches, worship is typically a synonym for songs or the singing of particular songs, a concept not necessarily limited to a time slot. At the very least the two are conjoined in terms of terminology, content, and practice. In both cases, while song can remain central to the church 'order of service' we the editors and many of contributors in this volume contend that worship can be more than a time slot and more than a song; the force in which, can extend beyond both the service and the sanctuary.

Critically, discussions that tend to privilege the church building and church service as the primary place of encounter, fail to account for worship that takes place outside of its walls. It does not register the worship of men and women who were enslaved or living during American reconstruction who either were unwelcome or tolerated in segregated sections in sanctuaries. Rather, God was encountered in the brush arbors and makeshift structures adorned with sawdust flooring and furnished with wooden benches. In the United States context, black and brown people, who are overrepresented in low paying domestic and unskilled roles, cannot always make the 'worship slot'. Theirs is a personal encounter with God that may be experienced while cleaning floors, looking after children or harvesting produce. Similarly, migrant churches, for a few hours, transform community centers, hotels, and homes into places of encounter.

This still brings up the question of what purpose would heaven have for contacting earth – we take the view that it is for more than a song. Worship has a redemptive and prophetic quality which Pentecostals should explore. As Jerome Boone states,

> God works redemptively through worship to transform God's people and the world in the direction of the consummation of the coming Kingdom. The resulting reality is the parallel existence of the Kingdom of God alongside of and in tension with many socially constructed cultures. [9]

It was while in Spirit-inspired worship that John the Revelator receives revelation for himself and for the seven churches.[10] Melissa Archer draws our attention to the fact that revelation is a call to

---

[9] Jerome Boone, 'Worship and the Torah', in Lee Roy Martin (ed.), *Toward a Pentecostal Theology of Worship* (Cleveland, TN: CPT Press, 2nd edn, 2020), p. 17.

[10] Archer, 'Worship in the Book of Revelation', p. 170.

discernment, to discern the church's own condition as evidenced in Jesus' words of correction in the prophetic messages, but it is also a call to discern the culture of *Babylon* around them.[11]

The Heart Behind This Project

This book consists of papers that were presented at or inspired by the Society for Pentecostal Studies' Annual Meeting which convened 13-15 March 2025 at Northwest University, Kirkland, WA. As the then Vice President of the Society and Program Chair, I (Marcia) was tasked with choosing the theme of the conference. In the previous year, I had been challenged by a paper on 'Pentecostal Worship' presented by Dr. Jacqueline Grey of Alphacrucis University College, in Australia. The paper, given at the Catholic Pentecostal International Dialogue, of which Jacqui and I were members, attempted to articulate the praxis and theology of Pentecostal worship for our Roman Catholic friends. Pentecostal worship was presented in terms of corporate worship and a lived response to God.

We the editors believe that 'true worship' is an acknowledgement, response, and submission to the Divine who is graciously revealed in Jesus through the Spirit (Jn 4.23).[12] Worshipers seek to align their actions with God's will. Yet, at its core, worship isn't confined to religious ceremonies but is woven into the fabric of our existence. However, traditionally the idea that worship only takes place in a building has been perpetuated and as such almost everything else is not classified as 'true worship'. Yet, Scripture admonishes that everything that is done should be done thankfully, having God's glory as the focus (Col. 3.17; 1 Cor. 10.31). In other words, everything we do, from the mundane to the extraordinary, expresses what we hold most valuable. This inherent human impulse to worship something, even if it's not God, is captured by Harold Best's definition. He describes 'Worship is the continuous outpouring of all that I am, all that I do and all that I can ever become in light of a chosen or choosing god'.

---

[11] Archer, 'Worship in the Book of Revelation', p. 175.
[12] Daniel Isaac Block, *For the Glory of God: Recovering a Biblical Theology of Worship* (Grand Rapids, MI: Baker Academic, Paperback edn, 2016), p. 23.

[13] Hence the academic can and should present the process and culmination of her work as an offering of worship.

It is in this sense that this volume is offered. This project suggests that Pentecostal worship should not focus on being merely personal encounter. While it may begin as such, it can lead to action which includes engagement with socio-political and economic issues. Further the project acknowledges the forward-facing role of worship leaders who attend most to the worship slot. Ten worship leaders were invited to attend the SPS conference made possible through a Vital Worship, Vital Preaching Grant from the Calvin Institute of Christian Worship, Grand Rapids, Michigan, with funds provided by Lilly Endowment Inc. This was an important interaction of worship practice and Pentecostal theological thought.[14]

Overview of the Book

This volume, featuring contributions from scholars across the U.S., the UK, Australia, Scandinavia, Latin America, Asia, and Africa, considers worship as both locally contextual and globally interconnected. Because several of these contributors also serve as pastors or worship practitioners, their contributions address both the theoretical and practical dimensions of Pentecostal worship worldwide. As a collaboration between the church and the academy, this book has two primary aims: to aid practitioners in guiding their congregations toward a robust, holistic understanding of worship of the triune God, and to present an academic discourse on contemporary public issues, as informed by Pentecostal spirituality. To facilitate this, the book is divided into two parts that deal with witness in the church and in the public, respectively.

Part 1: Witness in the Church is comprised of seven chapters that explore modern challenges related to Pentecostal worship and the church. The first chapter, titled 'Power and Praise: The Need for Critical Reflection in Worship and Leadership', is written by practical theologian Truls Åkerlund. Drawing on the work of Michel Foucault,

---

[13] Harold M. Best, *Unceasing Worship: Biblical Perspectives on Worship and the Arts* (Downers Grove, IL: InterVarsity Press, 2009), p. 18.

[14] The project team also included Dara Delgado, University of North Carolina, Wilmington; Mario Hood, Church on the Living Edge; Leah Payne, Portland Seminary; and Joshua Samuel, Christian Life Centre.

Åkerlund argues that churches are often unconsciously shaped by prevailing cultural 'discourses', or frameworks of thought that dictate what is perceived to be natural, true, or good. When the church uncritically embraces these discourses, its genuine discipleship can be compromised by secular influences such as individualism or market-oriented reasoning. Pentecostal worship might also adopt these discourses, potentially leading to an influence from celebrity culture or consumerism. In response we must learn to see past these cultural lenses and recover worship and leadership shaped by Scripture and the Spirit.

Biblical scholar Jacqueline Grey's chapter, 'Miriam's Worship as Prophetic Action', argues that worship in the biblical narrative is not merely praise but a prophetic response to God's self-revelation. This is evidenced clearly by Miriam, who in Exod. 15.20–21 functions both as a prophetess and worship leader. Uniquely, Miriam's prophetic identity is revealed through embodied worship rather than speech. Through drumming, dancing, and singing, Miriam's worship dramatizes the liberation of Israel from Pharaoh's power, revealing worship itself as an act of prophetic proclamation and social transformation. Through embodied action, the Israelites were able to process their liberation spiritually, emotionally, and bodily, as they prepared to form a new covenant identity. Pentecostal worship today can draw from Miriam's example to become spaces of prophetic testimony, healing, and communal transformation.

Chapter 3, 'A Eucharist That's Truly Eucharistic: Emphasizing Corporate Praising as a Way to Elevate the Place of the Lord's Supper in Pentecostal Congregations' is written by worship historian Lester Ruth. Ruth argues that the Lord's Supper is not only a sacrament of divine grace but also as an essential moment for the Church's corporate prayer, thanksgiving, and praise. As a sympathetic chronicler of contemporary Pentecostal worship, Ruth recognizes that the focus on praise and thanksgiving within Pentecostalism allows the Eucharist to resonate seamlessly with Pentecostal spirituality. He advocates for transforming the Eucharist into a 'truly eucharistic' experience by integrating it into the rhythm of Pentecostal praise and worship rather than treating it as a mere ritual. By merging Pentecostal ecstatic praise with Eucharistic prayer, congregations can recover the sacrament's full richness that experiences unity, divine presence, and Spirit-filled joy. Ruth envisions a Eucharist that 'groans under the weight of

God's grace' as Spirit-filled worshipers learn to feel that grace through corporate worship.

Chapter 4, titled, 'More Than a Vehicle Into God's Presence: Expanding John Wimber's Liturgical Theology of Spirit & Song', was written by worship scholar Jeremy Perigo. In this chapter, Perigo considers John Wimber's impact on contemporary worship through the Vineyard movement. In particular, Perigo highlights Wimber's pneumatological emphasis on worship that sees worship as a vehicle for experiencing the presence of the Spirit. Perigo highlights some of the formal ways this emphasis is infused into the worship, including its focus on intimacy and simplicity in lyrics, calls for spiritual warfare. Yet, Perigo cautions against equating all of worship with music, arguing that true worship is a living, Spirit-empowered response to God's revelation in Christ. Worship thus happens not only through music, but also in prayer, mission, and our everyday acts of faith.

Practical theologian Mark J. Cartledge wrote chapter 5, titled 'Pentecostal Digital Doxology: Exploring Hybridity, Liminality, and Ecclesiology'. In this chapter, Cartledge explores how Pentecostal worship in the digital era has created a new hybrid ecclesial space where believers encounter God through online participation. This worship experience, while liminal, is a legitimate expression of an ecclesial life because worshipers still are able to encounter the Spirit but in ways (i.e. by livestream or Zoom) that transcend physical boundaries. We can view this 'digital doxology' as an eschatological foretaste of what is to come, and as a missional tool that extends access to worship and community beyond physical walls.

Theologian H. Leng Toh's chapter, 'Anthem of Grace: A Theological Exploration of Divine Grace in Contemporary Congregational Songs Written by New Creation Church, Singapore', argues that charismatic worship, particularly that of New Creation Church, embodies a Spirit-formed lived theology. Worship songwriting, in this context, views songs as 'anthems of grace' – a collaborative act of grace where both composer and congregation participate in articulating divine truth through melody, lyric, and embodied expression. When the songs are sung by the congregation, the gathering is transformed into a theological space where grace is experienced and proclaimed.

Finally, theologian and spiritual director Alaine Thomson Buchanan rounds Part 1 out with a chapter titled, 'A Divine Invitation of Worship: The Intersection Among Spiritual Direction, Trauma, and Hope'. Buchanan frames spiritual direction as an act of worship where both the director and the directee come before God and listen to the Spirit in their present realities of life. Ultimately, the directee is encouraged to respond to God with faith, trust, and hope. After outlining the components of spiritual direction, Buchanan highlights that healing from trauma encompasses both spiritual and physical aspects. Through practices such as lament, grounding, breathwork, and imaginative prayer, directors assist directees in reconnecting with their bodies and emotions as channels for divine encounter and healing. This process can be viewed as an act of worship, as both the director and the directee are engaging in a response to God.

In Part 1, contributors highlight the importance of critically discerning cultural influences in the church's worship, and advocating for a worship experience rooted in Scripture, community, and the Spirit. Throughout these chapters, worship is depicted as prophetic, transformative, and holistic – incorporating sacrament, song, digital innovation, and healing. Through various forms such as embodied dance, Eucharistic praise, or even online engagement, worship serves as a venue where believers encounter divine grace, declare freedom, and feel the renewing presence of the Spirit in all aspects of life. This encapsulates the work and testimony of worship within the church.

Part 2: Witness in the Public is also comprised of seven chapters, but these consider worship's role both as a public voice and response to culture. Part 2 begins with Sanna Urvas' chapter titled, 'Insights to the Nature of Worship and How to Avoid Worshipping Nature: At the Crossroads of Ecotheology and Theology of Worship'. She argues that while Pentecostals are known for vibrant, embodied, and participatory worship, they can tend to neglect ecological responsibilities. A reliance on dispensational eschatology has created in Pentecostalism a dualistic worldview that pits heaven against the earth – if one's focus is on heaven, then environmental concerns can take a back seat. Yet, Urvas maintains, there are resources in Pentecostal scholarship that critique this eschatological detachment, namely the work of Jeffrey Lamp, A.J. Swoboda, and Peter Althouse. Influenced by Moltmann, Urvas states we can adopt a transformational eschatology that unites pneumatology and creation. Here worship would be seen as a sacramental act that anticipates the renewal of all creation. Thus, any true worship of the Creator would lead naturally to the love and protection of God's creation.

Chapter 9 is titled, 'Gloria a Dios! Pentecostal Seminarians Reading the Bible to Glorify God' and is written by NT scholar Laura Jean Torgerson. Drawing from her time teaching Pentecostal seminary students in Nicaragua, Torgerson examines how her students navigated the tensions between devotional and academic approaches to Scripture. Using an ethnography-of-literacy framework, Torgerson sees Bible reading as a culturally embedded practice, rejecting models that see the academic study of Scripture as superior. She shows that Pentecostals read Scripture devotionally for worship, prayer, and encounter with God, not for mere academic aims. Yet, Torgerson argues, a critical study of Scripture should not be viewed as a threat to devotion but can be viewed as deepening worship when one reads the Bible as an act that glorifies God through ethical reflection, communal discernment, and the pursuit of justice.

In philosopher Christian Teachout's chapter, 'Worship as Discovery: Martin Heidegger's Dasein and the Pursuit of Knowledge', the author carries on the theme that an intellectual pursuit of God could be seen as worship. For Teachout, worship involves discovering God's truth through relationship, which reflects the original communion of Eden where discovery itself was an act of worship. Just as believers sing together in worship, they also share discoveries of truth and glorify God by contributing to one another's understanding. Drawing on Heidegger's concept of *Dasein* ('being-in-time'), Teachout argues that human existence and understanding are bound to time, space, and community, and thus discovery happens within a relational web of past, present, and future learners, forming an ongoing dialogue of revealed truth.

Chapter 11 was written by Bishop Johnathan Alvarado and is titled, 'A Song in the Night: African American Pentecostal Worship as Reclamation and Resistance'. Alvarado argues that African American Pentecostal worship, has historically functioned as both a reclaiming of Black personhood and a resistance to the systemic dehumanization imposed by white supremacy. Alvarado builds on Jon Michael Spencer's framework of 'Protest and Praise' and shows that Black Pentecostal worship unites lament and celebration. It's not escapism, but a public theology of survival and hope that confronts oppression while affirming divine presence and dignity. Alvarado also believes that when African Americans reclaim the Bible as an African text and the body as a vessel of Spirit-filled power, worship becomes a declaration of faith, liberation, and endurance in the face of oppression – a 'song in the night'.

Chapter 12, written by Jonathan Bentall, is titled, '"Searching the Scriptures": David S. Ingraham's Theological Hermeneutics'. In this chapter, Bentall highlights how 19th century abolitionist missionary David S. Ingraham wove worship, theology, and social justice into a single, inseparable vocation. For Ingraham, theological reflection naturally flowed into doxology and activism as faith expressed itself through both praise and the pursuit of liberation. Bentall points out that Ingraham's repeated biblical imagery of wakefulness forms a theology of moral vigilance. The author then connects this to our contemporary 'woke' discourse, showing that Ingraham's call for the church to 'awake' to racial injustice was grounded in Scripture, not in any modern ideology. Because Ingraham's hermeneutic is rooted in Scripture, holiness, and liberation, it calls today's church to awaken from complacency, confront injustice, and read the Bible not as static text but as a living summons to worship through action.

In 'Unchained Hallelujah: Decolonizing Black Pentecostal Worship', theologian Clifton Clarke calls for a radical decolonization of Black Pentecostal worship, urging a return to its African spiritual and cultural foundations. He traces how colonialism imposed Eurocentric norms that muted the freedom, rhythm, and prophetic power of early Black worship traditions. Rejecting commercialization and respectability politics, Clarke advocates for worship that celebrates Black identity, dismantles patriarchy, and embraces the Spirit's presence in all cultural forms. Ultimately, Clarke's vision is for a worship that affirms divine encounter through Blackness itself and empowers global Pentecostalism toward greater authenticity and liberation.

Finally, ecotheologian Emmanuel Awudi wrote a chapter titled, 'Echoes of Ecology: Unpacking the Ecological Themes in Selected Akan Pentecostal Hymnology', which argues that Akan Pentecostal worship songs contain a rich ecological theology that reveals deep insights about God's relationship with creation and humanity's responsibility to care for the earth. Analyzing six hymns from some of Ghana's major Pentecostal churches, Awudi demonstrates how these songs affirm God as creator and sustainer, reveal divine attributes through nature, and celebrate creation's intrinsic goodness.

Grounded in both Scripture and Akan cosmology, the hymns challenge believers to view creation as sacred and to practice stewardship as worship.

The chapters in Part 2 collectively frame Pentecostal worship as a public act of theological and ethical engagement, not confined to the church, but speaking to matters of creation, culture, and justice. In particular, Part 2's contributors reimagined worship as a form of ecological care, intellectual devotion, and prophetic resistance. As a running theme, these essays argue that worship fundamentally glorifies God through its transformative engagement with the world, where creation care, discovery, liberation, and justice all become acts of Spirit-filled worship.

The book wraps up with a concluding chapter by theologian Philip Struyk titled 'Worship that Moves Upward, Inward, and Onward'. As both a theologian and a Pentecostal worship practitioner, Struyk was invited to attend and take part of the 2025 Society for Pentecostal Studies Annual Meeting. Writing primarily with the church leaders in mind, Struyk reflects on his time at the conference and on a few specific presentations that he found significant. Struyk concludes that the conference theme, 'More Than a Song: Scholarship as Worship in the Church, the Academy, and the Public Square', has prompted Pentecostal scholars and church leaders to explore modes of collective worship and public testimony that are both theocentric and cognizant of our socio-ethical obligation to pray, advocate, and strive for justice, and ultimately, shalom.

PART 1

WITNESS IN THE CHURCH

1

Power and Praise: The Need for Critical Reflection in Worship and Leadership

Truls Åkerlund*

Introduction

It's an early Saturday in August and we're celebrating my in-laws' 70th birthday. The family is visiting and the living room is lively, but I must withdraw to my office upstairs. I sit down in the chair where I usually pray. I kneel on the floor and glance restlessly out the veranda door. Inside, I feel like a hunted animal, unable to find peace. I'm not just a father, husband, and son-in-law; I'm also a church leader, and now it's time to gather the troops after the summer holidays and the COVID-19 pandemic.

But I'm struggling to gather myself.

After several years as a pastor and church planter, I've fought for increased volunteer engagement and against the consequences of the pandemic lockdowns – and in the end, I was also fighting against myself. I've pushed my body and soul too far and I am on the verge of burnout. Now I must throw in the towel and step down from the pastoral ministry. It tears me apart. After all, it's the following of and service to Jesus that I've dedicated my life to, and I want to remain

---

* Truls Åkerlund (PhD, Regent University) is Professor in Leadership at the Norwegian School of Leadership and Theology.

faithful. But how do I do that when the rules of the game are changing? What will be the common thread in my life when I have to step out of the role I believe God has called me to?

I come to the conclusion that the thread is called faithfulness.

If I had just craned my neck and not listened to the signals from my body and soul, I would have risked losing that very thread; that my relationship with Jesus would break down because I had to deliver results. That I would keep pushing when I should have hit the brakes. That's a price I'm not willing to pay. Commitment is important, but following Jesus must not be linked too closely with the maintenance of Christian activities or organizations. After all, the most important thing is not *what* I do, but *who* I do it for.[1]

I begin this chapter with my personal story since it is an example of how I entered a role that didn't fit my gifts and personality. I became a church planter shaped by discursive and paradigmatic models in the Norwegian Pentecostal movement through a journey where external ideals became internalized and self-disciplinary, a topic that will be addressed throughout this chapter. My emphasis will primarily be on the influence of cultures and contexts in Christian organizations, which easily become 'the operating theatre in terms of their relationship with the discourses of Christianity in its various shapes and forms'.[2] The goal is to argue for reflexivity and beneficial critical discernments that can help individual Christians and the corporate church to partake faithfully in the biblical story rather than the dominant discourses that influence our surroundings. We all enter an overarching narrative – like jumping on a moving train[3] – and we need to reflect on *what* train we have entered. And this is where academia can help us. Holistic spirituality involves a lived experience with a unique way of perceiving our conditions,[4] and academic work can hence contribute to worship as 'a way of seeing the world in the

---

[1] The introduction is translated and cited from my newest book, *Tråden Heter Trofasthet* [The Thread Is Called Faithfulness] (Oslo, Norway: Verbum, 2024), p. 10.

[2] Martin D. Stringer, *A Sociological History of Christian Worship* (Cambridge: Cambridge University Press, 2005), p. 15.

[3] Stanley Hauerwas and William H. Willimon, *Resident Aliens: Life in the Christian Colony* (Nashville, TN: Abingdon Press, 1989), p. 52.

[4] Glen G Scorgie, 'Overview of Christian Spirituality', in Glen G Scorgie et al., (eds.), *Zondervan Dictionary of Christian Spirituality* (Grand Rapids, MI: Zondervan, 2011), pp. 27–28.

light of God'.[5] This implies that worship is more than a song and that scholarship can partake in and preserve loyalty to God and his plan through analytical insight and engagement, a topic I will address in the following sections.

Discursive Power

As illustrated in the introductory narrative, we are often shaped by dominating paradigms and discourses. The lens we see and understand ourselves and the world through, is regularly polished by contextual and discursive hands. 'A project can always be kidnapped, so to speak, or exploited for different political and cultural purposes',[6] and this makes it crucial to articulate the models that influence our behaviors and understandings. To reflect critically is hence necessary and a strength of academia in Pentecostal settings: We might see our *real* selves and structures in the prism of criticizers' and disbelievers' reflections – not because they are completely correct, but because critical voices can work as a revolt against ego-centric religious perspectives. Detractors do not necessarily set the tone for the song we should sing, but they can help us to retune our praise and hinder it from being shaped by the power of dominating discourses in the culture we live.

This is why I in the following mostly will draw on Michel Foucault's conceptualization of discursive power and influence. This is obviously not because Foucault corresponded with Christian thinking and theology; in many ways he was an opponent and criticizer of it.[7] Foucault was an atheist and suspicious to religion, for instance by presenting a dual critique of Christianity by incorporating the body and sexuality into religious practice and investigating a political spirituality

---

⁵Abraham Joshua Heschel, *I Asked for Wonder: A Spiritual Anthology* (New York: Crossroad Publishing Company, 1983), p. 41.

⁶ Christopher Norris, *Derrida* (Cambridge, MA: Harvard University Press, 1987), p. 195.

⁷ Foucault was skeptical of Christianity, yet his theories can help us elucidate the dynamics of ecclesial authority and models, cf. Steven G. Ogden, *The Church, Authority, and Foucault: Imagining the Church as an Open Space of Freedom* (London: Routledge, 2017), pp. 28–29.

of the self,[8] but these points are not what I will emphasize or embrace. There are several modes of objectification of the subject in Foucault's analyses,[9] and what I will highlight is how we are shaped by discourses and therefore should develop an evaluative distance that can assist us in reflecting and relearning practices in ecclesial settings:

> It is often only the voice of outsiders that can set us right. If we have not taken the time to cultivate the skills, habits and dispositions that allow us to hear the voices of outsiders, we will fall into a situation of interpretive arrogance. That is, we will deceive ourselves into thinking that our words are God's word. The exercise of power and coercion will characterize our communities. Conformity rather than faithfulness will be the standard used to judge our lives.[10]

The perspectives of critical strangers can be taken as an incentive to self-examination rather than merely being neglected as errors,[11] which I will focus on in the subsequent parts.

Dominating Discourses

Discourse is a complex concept, mainly because there are so many inconsistent and overlapping definitions based on different disciplinary and theoretical viewpoints.[12] The term stems originally from the Latin verb *discurrere* ('to run around'), and the participle *discursus*

---

[8] E.g. Jeremy R. Carrette (ed.), 'Prologue to the Confession of the Flesh', in Michel Foucault, *Religion and Culture* (Manchester, UK: Manchester University Press, 1999), pp. 1–3. There is a clear departure from the historical context and understanding of religion in Foucault's work, which does not uphold a traditional theological worldview, cf. Jeremy R. Carrette, *Foucault and Religion: Spiritual Corporality and Political Spirituality* (London: Routledge, 2000), pp. xi–xii.

[9] Paul Rabinow, 'Introduction', in Paul Rabinow (ed.), *The Foucault Reader* (New York: Pantheon Books, 1984), pp. 3–29.

[10] Stephen E. Fowl and L. Gregory Jones, *Reading in Communion: Scripture and Ethics in Christian Life* (Eugene, OR: Wipf & Stock, Reprinted edn, 1998), p. 110.

[11] Merold Westphal, *Suspicion and Faith: The Religious Uses of Modern Atheism* (New York: Fordham University Press, 1998), pp. xiv, 29.

[12] E.g. Simo K. Määttä and Marika K. Hall, 'Introduction', in Simo K. Määttä and Marika K. Hall (eds.), *Mapping Ideology in Discourse Studies* (Contributions to the Sociology of Language 118; Berlin: De Gruyter, 2022), pp. 1–20; Teun A. van Dijk (ed.), *Discourse Studies: A Multidisciplinary Introduction* (Thousand Oaks, CA: Sage Publications, 2nd edn, 2011); Mats Alvesson and Dan Karreman, 'Varieties of Discourse: On the Study of Organizations through Discourse Analysis', *Human Relations* 53.9 (2000), pp. 1125-49.

contained the meaning of 'talk', 'speech', and 'conversation' in Late Latin. The word was included in French academia from the late 17th century as an arrangement of words intended to articulate one's thoughts,[13] and there has been a significant development in humanities and social sciences since the 1960s.[14] In this chapter, discourses function as a 'vehicle for thought, communication and action'[15] and can be spelled with a capital 'D' to emphasize the shaping of social reality beyond language: 'Big D' Discourses are always language *plus* 'other stuff'.[16] For Foucault, language arranges and establishes the social world and informs social practices, forming subjectivity in which human subjects are shaped and managed, regarded as self-evident and rational.[17] As such, language cannot alone mirror social reality, and it is therefore 'helpful to think of 'little d' discourse as focusing on language-in-use in social interaction, while 'big D' Discourse signals a more Foucauldian view of discourse as a system of thought anchored in time socio-historically'.[18] Discourse is thus *more* than language and is connected to existence and 'discursive formation',[19] and Foucault's theory is dominantly non-linguistic and centers on social and external conditions that form and transform discourses,[20] a system which includes both language *and* practice.[21] His

---

[13] Simo K. Määttä, 'Discourse and Ideology in French Thought until Foucault and Pêcheux', in Simo K. Määttä and Marika K. Hall (eds.), *Mapping Ideology in Discourse Studies* (Contributions to the Sociology of Language 118; Berlin: De Gruyter, 2022), p. 26.

[14] Teun A. van Dijk, 'Introduction: The Study of Discourse', in Teun A. van Dijk (ed.), *Discourse Studies: A Multidisciplinary Introduction* (Thousand Oaks, CA: Sage Publications, 2nd edn, 2011), pp. 1–7.

[15] Trevor Purvis and Alan Hunt, 'Discourse, Ideology, Discourse, Ideology, Discourse, Ideology', *The British Journal of Sociology* 44.3 (1993), p. 485.

[16] James Paul Gee, *An Introduction to Discourse Analysis* (New York: Routledge, 2nd edn, 2005), p. 26, cf. pp. 5-9.

[17] Alvesson and Karreman, 'Varieties of Discourse', pp. 1127-28.

[18] Gail T. Fairhurst and Mary Uhl-Bien, 'Organizational Discourse Analysis (ODA): Examining Leadership as a Relational Process', *The Leadership Quarterly* 23.6 (2012), p. 1046.

[19] Michel Foucault, *The Archaeology of Knowledge and the Discourse on Language* (New York: Pantheon Books, 1972), pp. 38, 49, 107-17.

[20] Purvis and Hunt, 'Discourse, Ideology, Discourse, Ideology, Discourse, Ideology', pp. 489-90.

[21] Stuart Hall, 'Foucault: Power, Knowledge and Discourse', in Margaret Wetherell, Stephanie Taylor, and Simeon J. Yates (eds.), *Discourse Theory and Practice: A Reader* (Thousand Oaks, CA: SAGE Publications Ltd, 2001), pp. 72-81; Vivien Burr, *Social Constructionism* (New York, NY: Routledge, 3rd edn, 2015), chap. 4.

objective has been to show that 'in our culture, human beings are made subjects',[22] shaped by a complex web of statements and contexts.[23] Subjectivity hence develops as a historical artefact of socio-cultural forces implanted within a specific context, connected to Discourses which become a base for the subject's self-understanding.[24] The knowledge in Discourses hence signify a form of power in everyday life that

> categorizes the individual, marks him by his own individuality, attaches him to his own identity, imposes a law of truth on him which he must recognize and which others have to recognize in him. It is a form of power which makes individuals subjects.[25]

In sum, the Foucauldian understanding of a Discourse is the social, historical, and cultural conditions that make it possible for an action or an utterance to be perceived as natural or acceptable.[26] Discourses are hence socially constitutive, contributing to the formation of concepts, subjects, and objects – 'a practice not just of representing the world, but of signifying the world, constituting and constructing the world in meaning'.[27] These constructive effects include social identities or types of the self, social relationships between people, and the influence on systems of knowledge and belief. In the following, I will therefore briefly show how discourses and contextual patterns shape leadership and worship, and in the subsequent section argue for the need of critical reflection to comprehend what impacts us and avoid being merely constructed by surrounding prototypes.

Discursive Leadership and Religious Organizations

Our understandings of leadership is typically constructed over time through interaction with others: 'Leadership becomes a reality when one or more individuals in a social system succeed in framing and defining how the demands of the group will be taken up and who

[22] Michel Foucault, 'The Subject and Power', *Critical Inquiry* 8.4 (1982), p. 777.

[23] Foucault, *The Archaeology of Knowledge and the Discourse on Language*, pp. 97–99; Määttä, 'Discourse and Ideology in French Thought until Foucault and Pêcheux', pp. 32-33.

[24] Fairhurst, *Discursive Leadership*, pp. 11, 80.

[25] Foucault, 'The Subject and Power', p. 781.

[26] Jan Grue, 'Diskursanalyse', in *Store norske leksikon*, June 25, 2024, https://snl.no/diskursanalyse.

[27] Norman Fairclough, *Discourse and Social Change* (Cambridge: Polity Press, 1992), p. 64.

will address the need for direction in collective action'.[28] As such, different eras with shared values and history profoundly shape individual leaders,[29] and dominant models of leadership easily become dominating due to leading paradigms in various contexts and cultures.[30] Leadership is obviously not a song, but metaphorically it impacts Christian organizations as *more* than a song. Our language and understanding of leadership is constitutive for our performance, and *discursive regimes* (i.e. specific ways of ordering human activity) often set the standard for leadership ideals that are contingent constructions in order to match current values and concerns.[31] Consequently, there is often a normative pressure to practice and embrace leadership in specific, yet ambiguous and hegemonic ways, due to a variety of discourses in organizational settings[32] – which makes discursive approaches relevant for organizational studies.[33]

Psychological perspectives on leadership have usually been leader-centric with emphasis on the selves who are separable from society and context. In contrast, a discursive and Foucauldian approach holds that individuals and society are inseparable and that leaders are subjects, passive receptors, and managers of meaning, hence opening for 'the study of *leadership* discourse, not solely *leader* discourse, [that] creates the kind of window in which to study the reflexive agency of its actors'.[34] Paradigms are produced and reproduced in discursive

---

[28] Sonia Ospina and Georgia J. Sorenson, 'A Constructionist Lens on Leadership: Charting New Territory', in George R. Goethals and Georgia J. Sorenson (eds.), *A Quest for a General Theory of Leadership* (Cheltenham, UK: Edward Elgar Publishing Limited, 2006), p. 190.

[29] Warren G. Bennis and Robert J. Thomas, *Geeks & Geezers: How Era, Values, and Defining Moments Shape Leaders* (Boston, MA: Harvard Business School Press, 2002), pp. 10–14.

[30] E.g. Truls Åkerlund and Åse-Miriam Smidsrød, 'When Dominant Models Become Dominating: A Narrative Identity Approach to Female Leadership in Pentecostal Organizations', *Journal of Pentecostal and Charismatic Christianity*, 2024, pp. 1-21.

[31] Suze Wilson, *Thinking Differently about Leadership: A Critical History of Leadership Studies* (Northampton, MA: Edward Elgar Publishing, 2016), pp. 8-11.

[32] Mats Alvesson and Stefan Sveningsson, 'Good Visions, Bad Micro-Management and Ugly Ambiguity: Contradictions of (Non-)Leadership in a Knowledge-Intensive Organization', *Organization Studies* 24.6 (2003), pp. 961–88; Martin Blom and Mats Alvesson, 'All-Inclusive and All Good: The Hegemonic Ambiguity of Leadership', *Scandinavian Journal of Management* 31.4 (2015), pp. 480–92.

[33] E.g. Sverre Raffnsøe, Andrea Mennicken, and Peter Miller, 'The Foucault Effect in Organization Studies', *Organization Studies* 40.2 (2019), pp. 155–82.

[34] Fairhurst, *Discursive Leadership*, p. 14, cf. pp. 9–11, 76.

practices, implying that specific discourses, when liberated from their claims of universality or finality, could contribute significantly to the broader dialogue about organizational life.[35] Since our concept of leadership habitually is shaped by the lens we look through, we must therefore step back and 'look where we have not looked before'.[36] According to Mark Learmonth and Kevin Morrell, discourses construct the social world and practices are shared by the communities in certain times and places, creating assumptions about what is sacred or taboo. Our understanding of being a leader hence echoes prevalent customs, habits, and conventions of a community, and create local versions of 'the truth' about leadership.[37] Discourses both illuminate and conceal different aspects of leadership, and 'if a particular discourse becomes habitually inculcated, it tends to become canonized'.[38] This often entails that a leader takes responsibility, including the making of a leadership identity, that is coherent with the organization's expectations.[39]

From a religious angle, the discursive approach can also be used to probe activities and developments in Christian congregations and denominations. Religion is a social practice that intertwines with other features of everyday life, and the study of religious discourses can thus bring the impact of language and social forces to the surface.[40] From a leadership perspective, the style and semantics of religious leaders may generate that 'Church-people … borrow, customize, and reproduce the … speech of their preachers and other leaders in their daily lives'. From a more sociological perspective, it is evident that there has been continuing change and transformation in the Western religious setting since the mid-20th century, a development

---

[35] Stanley Deetz, 'Crossroads – Describing Differences in Approaches to Organization Science: Rethinking Burrell and Morgan and Their Legacy', *Organization Science* 7.2 (1996), p. 193.

[36] Kathleen Allen, 'Diverse Voices of Leadership: Different Rhythms and Emerging Harmonies' (EdD Dissertation, University of San Diego, 1990), p. 8, https://digital.sandiego.edu/dissertations/535.

[37] Mark Learmonth and Kevin Morrell, *Critical Perspectives on Leadership: The Language of Corporate Power* (New York, NY: Routledge, 2019), pp. 76-77.

[38] Amanda Sinclair, *Leadership for the Disillusioned: Moving Beyond Myths and Heroes to Leading That Liberates* (Crows Nest, NSW: Allen & Unwin, 2007), p. 26.

[39] Sinclair, *Leadership for the Disillusioned*, pp. 132–33.

[40] Robert J. Wuthnow, 'Taking Talk Seriously: Religious Discourse as Social Practice', *Journal for the Scientific Study of Religion* 50.1 (2011), p. 15.

that can be considered as a partly discourse-driven process.[41] There is a dialectic relationship between structures and practices where 'discourse has effects upon social structures, as well as being determined by them, and so contributes to social continuity and social change'.[42] By focusing on discursive formations, then, one can emphasize how religious organizations shape their self-understandings in relation to the dominant discursive currents in broader society, including phenomena such *New Public Management*, *marketization*, and *individualization*. Marcus Moberg shows that the phenomenon of individualism needs to be considered as a fundamentally discursive process that has created the concept of autonomy and self-determination, even to the point that religious communities have become increasingly understood as collections of atomized individuals.[43] This subjective turn escalates individualized spirituality over established religions, leading to a development where 'subjective-life spirituality attract more people than do "congregational" activities having to do with life-as religion'.[44]

The terminology of management has also colonized public organizations and institutions,[45] a process Moberg describes as an 'amalgamation' where several aspects of ecclesial activities are connected to market-associated discourses.[46] The responses of the churches, which were deeply ideational and discursive in nature, hence led to significant and lasting shifts in their discursive frameworks, including how they perceived themselves, as well as their roles and positions within society.

> Many more newly established religious organizations – ranging from neo-evangelical and Pentecostal congregations to organizations in the fields of alternative spiritualities and new religious movements – have both purposely and successfully merged their

---

[41] Marcus Moberg, 'Studying Change in Religious Organizations: A Discourse-Centered Framework', *Method & Theory in the Study of Religion* 32.2 (2020), pp. 89-114; Marcus Moberg, *Religion, Discourse, and Society: Towards a Discursive Sociology of Religion* (London: Routledge, 2022).

[42] Norman Fairclough, *Language and Power* (London: Longman, 1989), p. 17.

[43] Moberg, *Religion, Discourse, and Society*, chap. 5.

[44] Paul Heelas and Linda Woodhead, *The Spiritual Revolution: Why Religion Is Giving Way to Spirituality* (Oxford, UK: Blackwell Publishing, 2005), p. 7.

[45] Norman Fairclough, *Critical Discourse Analysis: The Critical Study of Language* (London: Routledge, 2nd edn, 2010), p. 283.

[46] Moberg, *Religion, Discourse, and Society*, chap. 6.

own teachings with broader culturally prevalent discourses on personal development, successful living, and the 'entrepreneurial self'.[47]

Such practices are forms of *re-contextualization*,[48] where patterns from other settings are integrated as part of the organization's order, for example how churches increasingly incorporate and adapt discourses from the managerial and private business sectors within their own official strategic frameworks.[49]

Worship as Shaper and Shaped

The influence of discourses is also related to worship. On the one hand, worship is a *shaper*.[50] 'What makes Christians Christian is our worship of God',[51] meaning that congregational gatherings are important for the establishing of a community capable of praising and living out the image of God. As *homo adorans*, our worship of God involves entering a story already in motion, attuning ourselves to the fundamental tone of the universe, and discovering our identity in One who is greater than ourselves.[52] We express our allegiance through liturgical practices, and worship molds our shared identity as a faithful, mission-driven community devoted solely to God.[53] This is especially central to Pentecostal settings as 'the engine of Pentecostalism is its worship',[54] indicating that worship also is the core of the church's life and the foundation upon which Christian identity is

---

[47] Moberg, 'Studying Change in Religious Organizations', p. 99.

[48] Fairclough, *Critical Discourse Analysis*, p. 181.

[49] See examples in Moberg, 'Studying Change in Religious Organizations', p. 103-10.

[50] E.g. James K.A. Smith, *Desiring the Kingdom: Worship, Worldview, and Cultural Formation* (Grand Rapids, MI: Baker Academic, 2009); James K.A. Smith, *Imagining the Kingdom: How Worship Works* (Grand Rapids: Baker Academic, 2013); Laura Benjamins, 'Musicking as Liturgical Speech Acts: An Examination of Contemporary Worship Music Practices', *Studia Liturgica* 51.2 (2021), pp. 148–51.

[51] Stanley Hauerwas, 'The Liturgical Shape of the Christian Life: Teaching Christian Ethics as Worship', in Stanley Hauerwas, *In Good Company: The Church as Polis* (Notre Dame, IN: University of Notre Dame Press, 1995), pp. 153-54.

[52] Truls Åkerlund, *Men vi var ikke hjemme [But we were not at home]* (Oslo: Verbum, 2021), p. 125.

[53] Dean Flemming, *Recovering the Full Mission of God: A Biblical Perspective on Being, Doing and Telling* (Downers Grove, IL: InterVarsity Press, 2013), p. 250.

[54] Donald E. Miller and Tetsunao Yamamori, *Global Pentecostalism: The New Face of Christian Social Engagement* (Berkeley, CA: University of California Press, 2007), p. 23.

built.[55] Worship hence calibrates our thinking, longing, and love, and 'it does so by inviting us into the biblical story and implanting that story in our bones'.[56] According to Steven Félix-Jäger, worship is shaping Pentecostal stories and form a guiding narrative in Pentecostal settings which enables believers to align with God's will and respond to God's self-revelation by turning their hearts toward him.[57] Worship shapes doctrine and engages every sensory aspect of our human nature, and the comprehensive story of redemption becomes personalized through spontaneous worship and intercession. People can obviously idolize musical worship where 'anything put forward in front of God becomes a tribal deity',[58] still the unison found in worship might embrace variety and promote diversity as a differentiated unity. The Pentecostal expansion around the world takes part of the 'musical localization' in a diversity of places,[59] but the renewal worship contributes to the Pentecostal revitalization throughout the world by advancing a charismatic and global community that is united by the Spirit.[60] In sum, 'the truth of God is known in genuine worship of God',[61] indicating that worship and liturgies shape Christian individuals and congregations through their emphasis on and faithfulness to God.

On the other hand, however, worship is also *shaped* by culture and context since 'singing is a discursive practice, in that hymns have semantically meaningful contents'.[62] Pete Ward shows that celebrity worship can be understood as an interactive and vibrant discourse of

---

[55] Frank D. Macchia, 'Signs of Grace: Towards a Charismatic Theology of Worship', in Lee Roy Martin (ed.), *Toward a Pentecostal Theology of Worship* (Cleveland, TN: CPT Press, 2016), pp. 153-54.

[56] James K.A. Smith, *You Are What You Love: The Spiritual Power of Habit* (Grand Rapids, MI: Brazos Press, 2016), p. 85.

[57] Steven Félix-Jäger, *Renewal Worship: A Theology of Pentecostal Doxology* (Downers Grove, IL: IVP Academic, 2022), chap. 3.

[58] Félix-Jäger, *Renewal Worship*, p. 191.

[59] Monique M. Ingalls, Muriel Swijghuisen Reigersberg, and Zoe C. Sherinian, 'Music as Local and Global Positioning: How Congregational Music-Making Produces the Local in Christian Communities Worldwide', in Monique M. Ingalls, Muriel Swijghuisen Reigersberg, and Zoe C. Sherinian (eds.), *Making Congregational Music Local in Christian Communities Worldwide* (New York: Routledge, 2018), pp. 1–31.

[60] Félix-Jäger, *Renewal Worship*, p. 207.

[61] Richard Bauckham, *The Theology of the Book of Revelation* (Cambridge: Cambridge University Press, 1993), p. 162.

[62] Martin Lindhardt, *Power in Powerlessness: A Study of Pentecostal Life Worlds in Urban Chile* (Religion in the Americas Series; Leiden: Brill, 2012), p. 131.

the sacred self in contemporary societies,[63] and that a charismatic discourse can shape identity connected to popular culture.[64] As stated by Paul Brownback, 'the greatest peril of self-love is that it is worship of self. It is idolatry with self as the idol, the antithesis of the legitimate blessedness that comes from being poor in the spirit'.[65] Individualism and self-worship might thus lead to narcissism, nihilism, or amoral selfishness – and God, who deserves our worship, is reduced to a tool for our use, while creation, meant for our rightful use and blessing, becomes the focus of our worship.[66] Individuals can engage in Pentecostal worship without needing a formal, intellectual theology where music manages the self and adapts according to the specific environments one immerse oneself in.[67] Religious subjectivation can thus critically be seen as 'active and free work of the self on the self' in some Pentecostal surroundings,[68] and local praise and worship can shape and convey theological knowledge in various settings.[69]

From a broader perspective, Martin D. Stringer explores the practice of Christian worship across two thousand years and traces the play of Christian discourses through the centuries.[70] An overarching conclusion is that discourses change, constrict, and restrict what can be said or done, and that forms and patterns of worship are embedded in the church's social and political situation at each specific time and place. From an analytical viewpoint, then, we should examine what we gather for or around, as worship often is molded by cultural

---

[63] Pete Ward, *Celebrity Worship* (London: Routledge, 2020).

[64] Pete Ward, 'Affective Alliance or Circuits of Power: The Production and Consumption of Contemporary Charismatic Worship in Britain', *International Journal of Practical Theology* 9.1 (2005), p. 33.

[65] Paul Brownback, *The Danger of Self-Love* (Chicago: Moody Press, 1982), p. 130.

[66] Christopher J.H. Wright, *'Here Are Your Gods': Faithful Discipleship in Idolatrous Times* (Downers Grove; IL: IVP Academic, 2020), p. 34.

[67] Gerardo Martí, 'Maranatha (O Lord, Come): The Power–Surrender Dynamic of Pentecostal Worship', *Liturgy* 33.3 (2018), pp. 24-26.

[68] Naomi Richman, 'Machine Gun Prayer: The Politics of Embodied Desire in Pentecostal Worship', *Journal of Contemporary Religion* 35.3 (2020), pp. 469–83; Ruth Marshall, *Political Spiritualities: The Pentecostal Revolution in Nigeria* (Chicago, IL: The University of Chicago Press, 2009), p. 46.

[69] Martina Prosén, 'Pentecostal Praise and Worship as a Mode of Theology', in Karen Lauterbach and Mika Vähäkangas (eds.), *Faith in African Lived Christianity: Bridging Anthropological and Theological Perspectives* (Leiden: Brill, 2020), pp. 156-79.

[70] Stringer, *A Sociological History of Christian Worship*.

circumstances. 'Liturgy lives in cultural modes of communication'[71] and worship might be influenced by cultural and dominating discourses.[72] Music can be an object of adoration instead of God,[73] and even in Pentecostal settings 'musical worship too can be made into an idol'.[74] The places and cultures in which people gather as churches often influence rites and liturgies, and it seems impossible to define a stringent nature of Christian worship if one looks at the changes across denominations and throughout church history.[75] As noted by Don E. Saliers, 'Christian liturgy speaks within its particular culture, always using a range of the available cultural languages. But the truth-claims made by and explored therein are not founded upon the culture.'[76] Still, Pentecostalism's capacity to contextualize and adapt to various locations, expressed for instance in liturgies and worship, are energetic and energizing.[77] Pentecostal worship often incorporates a 'free-wheeling, Spirit-filled style',[78] which is flexible and allows cultures to contribute to the meaning of rites and rituals. Yet, the influence of prosperity gospel and megachurches may lead to 'arena rock worship' where liturgies are shaped by success, performance, and a turn to the therapeutic religion and feel-good messages: 'Churches could move from abstraction to context, from a template to a market-research-driven custom experience where the worship music was

---

[71] Don E. Saliers, *Worship as Theology: Foretaste of Glory Divine* (Nashville, TN: Abingdon Press, 1994), p. 154.

[72] E.g. R. Khari Brown, Angela Kaiser, and James S. Jackson, 'Worship Discourse and White Race-Based Policy Attitudes', *Review of Religious Research* 56.2 (2014), pp. 291-312; Vitalii Hura, 'Comparative Discourse Analysis of The Practices of Church Worship of Ukrainian and American Pentecostals', *Skhid* 1.2 (2021), pp. 38-42.

[73] Harold M. Best, *Unceasing Worship: Biblical Perspectives on Worship and the Arts* (Downers Grove, IL: IVP, 2003), chap. 11.

[74] Félix-Jäger, *Renewal Worship*, p. 96.

[75] Geoffrey Wainwright and Karen B. Westerfield Tucker, 'Retrospect and Prospect', in Geoffrey Wainwright and Karen B. Westerfield Tucker (eds.), *The Oxford History of Christian Worship*, (Oxford: Oxford University Press, 2006), pp. 858-65; Stringer, *A Sociological History of Christian Worship*.

[76] Saliers, *Worship as Theology*, p. 204.

[77] Allan Heaton Anderson, *Spirit-Filled World: Religious Dis/Continuity in African Pentecostalism* (New York: Palgrave Macmillan, 2018), p. 256.

[78] Harvey Cox, *Fire from Heaven: The Rise of Pentecostal Spirituality and the Reshaping of Religion in the 21st Century* (Cambridge, MA: Da Capo Press, 1995), p. 249.

geared toward church growth and target audiences'.[79] To sum up the argument so far, we hence need to create reflexive spaces to disclose and discuss discourses that dominate worship and our ecclesial settings, which is addressed in the following section.

Critical Reflection

From a theoretical and theological perspective, the belief in God as a creator, shaper, and sustainer of life could undermine the idea that everything that sets direction for our lives is formed by social power and paradigms – still our *understanding* and *participation* in God's mission is often molded by the context we live in. Even theologies are regularly contextual in the sense that they are shaped by surroundings,[80] implying that we need careful exegesis of our settings as well as Scripture.[81] Human reflexivity thus opens the door for people to 'recapture their experience, think about it, mull it over and evaluate it',[82] which increases learning and broadens the perspective without turning our backs to the congregational activities we should partake in.

As Merold Westphal argues, the suspicion of critics and atheists may give vital contribution to our Christian self-understanding: 'The illusory god we create in our own image to conform to our knowledge and our values provides us with confidence and security; but as we are secretly the masters of this god, it turns out to be "No-God" at all'.[83] This accentuates the importance of listening to critical scholars also in Christian settings – without claiming that discursive analyses or Foucault's perspectives are always correct:

There are still serious 'sins' associated with Foucauldian work ... [and] we may need to further doubt the Foucauldian 'truth effect',

---

[79] Kate Bowler and Wen Reagan, 'Bigger, Better, Louder: The Prosperity Gospel's Impact on Contemporary Christian Worship', *Religion and American Culture* 24.2 (2014), p. 202.

[80] Stephen B. Bevans, *Models of Contextual Theology* (Maryknoll, NY: Orbis Books, 2002), p. 2.

[81] Paul G. Hiebert, *Anthropological Insights for Missionaries* (Grand Rapids, MI: Baker Academic, 1985), pp. 197-204.

[82] David Boud, Rosemary Keogh, and David Walker, 'Promoting Reflection in Learning: A Model', in *Reflection: Turning Experience into Learning* (ed. David Boud, Rosemary Keogh, and David Walker; London: Routledge, 1985), p. 19.

[83] Westphal, *Suspicion and Faith*, p. 5.

if only to pay greater consideration to other theoretical perspectives which might inform our understanding of power and subjectivity.[84]

As such, we must avoid 'authoritarianism' where scholars celebrate and strictly follow major authors in critical studies and avoid being critical to central authors as Foucault,[85] still we should seek to reformulate rather than abandon these analytical perspectives.[86]

All Foucault's conclusions are seldom right from a Christian perspective, but the processes of discursive analyses can allow us to analytically explore dominating powers and paradigms that shape Christians' understandings and practices. It is thus important for believers to use *Christianity* as a resource for critiquing their own mistakes in a way that our time and context cannot alone provide, implying that what Foucault has done for thought in general, theologians should do for theology.[87] Since any discourse is linked to specific contexts, scholars have an adequate position to reflect critically on the discourses that dominate ecclesial milieus and 'take a step outside our everyday theoretical repertoire and start questioning our assumptions and favoured vocabulary'.[88] As Stephen Sykes points out, 'to understand the gospel as real power implies having to face the danger of the dominative use of the gospel, a gospel misappropriated and misused sometimes through a form of wilful self-deception'.[89] Discourses can function as a frame of reference, and it thus makes sense that Sykes argues for Foucault's studies as a kaleidoscope that gives critique and insights into the nature of power, revealing what binds

---

[84] Tim Newton, 'Theorizing Subjectivity in Organizations: The Failure of Foucauldian Studies?' *Organization Studies* 19.3 (1998), pp. 441-42.

[85] André Spicer and Mats Alvesson, 'Critical Management Studies: A Critical Review', *Journal of Management Studies* (2024), p. 23.

[86] Jean-Michel Landry, 'Foucault on Christianity: The Impasse of Subjectivation', *Political Theology* 22.1 (2021), p. 58; Talal Asad, *Genealogies of Religion* (Baltimore, MD: Johns Hopkins University Press, 1993). Asad draws a lot on Foucault but also provides different conceptions, for instance, on how Christians not only were conceptualized as pre-existing selves but also constructed themselves as obedient subjects (pp. 140-41).

[87] John McSweeney, 'Foucault and Theology', *Foucault Studies* 2 (2005), p. 121.

[88] Blom and Alvesson, 'All-Inclusive and All Good', p. 488.

[89] Stephen Sykes, *Power and Christian Theology* (London: Continuum, 2006), pp. 110-11.

people in imprisoning networks where they are both victims and agents without knowing it.[90]

A critical distance to the place in which one is rooted can therefore facilitate a 'free thought from what it silently thinks, and so enable it to think differently'[91] – which includes consideration of ruling ideas and assumptions, analysis of one's own position, and attempts to understand the interplay between society and individuals by shifting perspectives.[92] Reflexivity can reveal the processes of social construction and help Christian leaders and worshipers to comprehend what they *are* formed by and what they *should* form – also with followers in Pentecostal organizations.[93] This involves not only an activity against power and organizations *out there*; 'it involves *living* with these complexities'[94] which have consequences for how we understand ourselves and how we lead and engage with other people. Critical reflection can therefore help us avoid being overly influenced by thinking traps and confirmation bias.[95] In sum, taking a step back and critically analyzing what shapes our lives and perspectives may create the space for reflection, revealing, and resisting dominant discourses by 'questioning what we, and others, might be taking for granted – what is being said and not said – and examining the impact this has or might have'.[96] We should not restrict these practices to what we *do* but also include who we should *be*, hence being reflexive to organizational

---

[90] Sykes, *Power and Christian Theology*, p. 101.

[91] Michel Foucault, *The History of Sexuality, Vol. 2: The Use of Pleasure* (trans. Robert Hurley; New York: Vintage Books, Reissue edn, 1990), p. 9.

[92] Blom and Alvesson, 'All-Inclusive and All Good', p. 487.

[93] Truls Åkerlund and Karl Inge Tangen, 'Charismatic Cultures: Another Shadow Side Confessed', *Pneuma* 40.1-2 (2018), pp. 109–29. If this reflexive space is not open in Pentecostal settings, the opportunity for active agency may be restricted for church members, cf. Hans Eskil Vigdel, Marianne Rodriguez Nygaard, and Tormod Kleiven, 'Cultures Shaped by Elements of Ideological Totalism – Experiences of Misuse of Power in Some Pentecostal Christian Fellowships', *Diaconia* 13.1 (2022), pp. 70–94.

[94] Leah Tomkins and Eda Ulus, 'Is Narcissism Undermining Critical Reflection in Our Business Schools?' *Academy of Management Learning & Education* 14.4 (2015), p. 601.

[95] Susann Gjerde, *Ledere og Ledelsesutvikling: Refleksjoner for Problemløsning, Innsikt og Nytenkning* [*Leaders and Leadership Development: Reflections for Problem Solving, Insight, and Innovation*] (Bergen: Fagbokforlaget, 2022), pp. 53-54.

[96] Ann L. Cunliffe, 'On Becoming a Critically Reflexive Practitioner. Redux: What Does It Mean to Be Reflexive?', *Journal of Management Education* 40.6 (2016), p. 741.

structures and practices but also being *self-reflexive* about our own values, beliefs, and relationships with others.[97]

On a more individual level, critical reflection can help people evaluate how their lives are influenced by culturally created standards and norms. Modern power may form individuals as self-monitoring subjects through active involvement in both formation and assessment of their lives, relationships, and identity, and reflexive practices may hence create a critical distance to the narratives and discourses that shape them as persons.[98] In my own experience, this was exactly what helped me to realize that I had stepped into congregational roles that mismatched my personal gifts and capacities. There was no hierarchical powers that forced me to take on the role of an entrepreneurial church planter; it was more a dominant paradigm in the Norwegian Pentecostal movement that I implemented and induced – an example of modern power that became self-disciplinary by 'recruiting people into the disciplining of their own and each other's lives according to socially constructed norms'.[99] Consequently, we should promote reflectivity with the purpose of seeing ourselves and our settings from multiple perspectives. This is especially important in Pentecostal congregations as high levels of enthusiasm can obstruct reflective spaces and thereby hinder a person's integrity.[100]

Beyond the individual, we need to see our own culture and context from biblical perspectives, like for instance Revelation's critique of the Roman Empire.[101] This does mean that there is only *one* way of how we should live out the Theo-drama. The Bible does present an overarching narrative that includes its various contents, but the story is not a restrictive framework that forces everything into a rigidly defined uniformity. 'The biblical story refuses to be summed up in a finally adequate interpretation that would never need to be revised or

---

[97] Cunliffe, 'On Becoming a Critically Reflexive Practitioner', pp. 741–43.

[98] Michala Schnoor and Gitte Haslebo, 'Lederen Som Coach - Forskellige Vinkler på Magt og Etik' ['The Leader as Coach – Different Perspectives on Power and Ethics'] *Erhvervspsykologi* 5.2 (2007), pp. 22-43.

[99] Michael White, 'Addressing Personal Failure', *International Journal of Narrative Therapy and Community Work* 3 (2002), p. 67.

[100] Karl Inge Tangen, *Ecclesial Identification beyond Late Modern Individualism?: A Case Study of Life Strategies in Growing Late Modern Churches* (Leiden: Brill Academic, 2012), pp. 325-28.

[101] E.g. David A. deSilva, *Seeing Things John's Way: The Rhetoric of the Book of Revelation* (Louisville, KY: Westminster John Knox Press, 2009).

replaced',[102] which underscores the necessity of discernment to understand both Scripture, settings, and selves. Stringer argues that discourses shape Christian worship within its many and assorted social contexts, implying that there can never be a pure form of Christian discourse due to the social, cultural, and other religious traditions. The practice and pattern of worship are formed by the church's social and political context at each specific time and place, and the present moment is unique and should not be replicated. At the end of his book, Stringer concludes that variety should be celebrated, and from it, we should once again learn to be creative in our own time and place:

> There must come a point when any form of Christian worship verges on the edge of a truly Christian discourse and even appears to topple over. It is, I would suggest, the core of that discourse that must always be our guide for the future, whatever forms the worship of the church actually takes.[103]

As such, there is not one model of worship and we must therefore show diversity and variety in Christian practices, still the overarching biblical narrative should shape us and build a critical distance to the dominating discourses in our temporal culture.

Conclusion

As Christian scholars, leaders, and worshipers, our research and practices should always be determined by allegiance to God and his will. For this to take place, however, we must create a critical distance to our contextual understandings shaped by dominant discourses and cultures. Not because critical perspectives provide answers in themselves; 'we should be suspect to our suspicion, knowing of their danger'.[104] Still, we must create a reflexive space to expose and eliminate self-deceptions and misperceptions in reflecting on what impacts and distorts our thinking and practice. Westphal suggests that suspicion may be a kind of spirituality,[105] a claim corresponding with Walter

---

[102] Richard Bauckham, *Bible and Mission: Christian Witness in a Postmodern World* (Grand Rapids, MI: Baker Academic, 2003), p. 93.

[103] Stringer, *A Sociological History of Christian Worship*, p. 239.

[104] Westphal, *Suspicion and Faith*, p. 284.

[105] Westphal, *Suspicion and Faith*, p. 288.

Hollenweger's opinion that self-critical reflection is a mark of spirituality.[106] Since we are not *of* the world but *in* the world (Jn 17.15-18), social engagement is necessary for the church to make Christ present and to fulfill its purpose:

> The church is a chameleon. It finds colors that fit it into various environments. It continues, yet changes; this is the value of its social nature. Yet it stands always under the order and judgment of God to whom it professes loyalty and in whom it beliefs. It is a human community, with a particular vocation, purpose, and power.[107]

For the ecclesial chameleon not to adapt smoothly to major discourses and cultural trends, however, critical consideration is obviously necessary.

Since Pentecostal worship traditionally has prioritized spontaneity and freedom over structured liturgy and uniformity, there is a need for deeper dialogue that goes beyond mere discussions of worship style.[108] The Spirit renews and relates, but discernment and reflexivity is important to avoid that dominating discourses shape both individuals and communities, since 'people interpret events through their own interpretive lenses, and their lenses are shaped by those very experiences'.[109] Worship must thus be opened to reflection,[110] and the same is the case for congregational leadership. To expose the discursive lens may explicate the interaction between the being of organizational and congregational members and make it possible to see 'into' the things we tend to look 'at'.[111] Or as Lesslie Newbigin claims, 'the Christian story provides us with such a set of lenses, not something for us to look *at*, but for us to look *through*'.[112] This can create

---

[106] Neil Hudson, 'Pentecostalism, Past, Present and Future: An Interview with Walter Hollenweger', *Journal of the European Pentecostal Theological Association* 21.1 (2001), p. 41.

[107] James M. Gustafson, *Treasure in Earthen Vessels: The Church as Human Community* (Louisville, KY: Westminster John Knox Press, 1961, 2009), p. 112.

[108] Lee Roy Martin, 'Introduction to Pentecostal Worship', in Lee Roy Martin (ed.), *Toward a Pentecostal Theology of Worship* (Cleveland, TN: CPT Press, Kindle edn, 2016), pp. 1-4.

[109] Félix-Jäger, *Renewal Worship*, p. 101.

[110] Saliers, *Worship as Theology*, chap. 9.

[111] Stephen G. Green in Fairhurst, *Discursive Leadership*, pp. 175-78.

[112] Lesslie Newbigin, *The Gospel in a Pluralist Society* (Grand Rapids: Eerdmans, 1989), p. 38.

an analytical distance to cultural and discursive impact that shapes our understandings of God, worship, leadership, and ourselves – and help us participate in the mission of God through more than a song.

2

MIRIAM'S WORSHIP AS PROPHETIC ACTION

JACQUELINE N. GREY*

Introduction

Worship is our heartfelt response to God. It is God who initiates relationship with us by revealing himself and rescuing us.[1] Steven Félix-Jäger defines worship 'as turning our hearts toward God as a response to God's self-revelation'.[2] Following the crossing of the Red Sea, Moses and Miriam lead the people in celebratory worship (Exodus 15). Here we are introduced to Miriam, the 'prophetess'. Miriam is a worship leader and prophet. A prophet in the OT can be understood as one who communicates on behalf of God his perspective and passion for the purpose of faithful living. So, in what way is Miriam considered a prophet? And what does she do that is so prophetic? This chapter explores Miriam's role in the Exodus event, focusing on her actions in leading the people in worship. As recorded in Exod. 15.20-21, Miriam worships God with singing, dancing, and playing the hand-drum. These worship activities are considered prophetic because Miriam's prophetic performance of liberation functions in the narrative to dismantle Pharaoh's power and prepare the

---

* Jacqueline Grey (PhD, Charles Sturt University) is Professor of Biblical Studies at Alphacrucis University College, Australia.
[1] Jacqueline Grey, 'Worship: A Pentecostal Perspective', *Australasian Pentecostal Studies* 24.1 (2023), p. 53.

[2] Steven Félix-Jäger, *Renewal Worship: A Theology of Pentecostal Doxology* (Downers Grove: IVP Academic, 2022), p. 33.

way for a new community based on God's freedom. Miriam models for readers today the need for prophetic expression in worship that communicates God's freedom and liberation.

A key component in the worship service of many Pentecostal traditions is the ritual of testimony. Through testimony, believers share their story of God's intervention and self-revelation. Félix-Jäger describes testimony as 'the subjective recounting of the gospel message as it applies to the life of a believer'.[3] In the worship service, the testimony both gives thanks to God but also inspires faith in other believers that they can similarly experience the saving grace of God in their own lives. Miriam's story in the biblical text can serve as a type of testimony inspiring believers today to consider how prophetic worship can function in our contemporary contexts.

Miriam's Testimony

The book of Exodus opens with the flourishing fertility of the people of God (Exod. 1.7) as they shift from being a large family to a burgeoning nation. However, this population growth causes the current Pharaoh to be concerned for Egyptian sovereignty. To control the Israelites, Pharaoh oppresses them through a program of enforced labor (1.10). Pharaoh's fears subsequently give rise to his policy of infanticide (Exod. 1.16). However, the brave and shrewd midwives (who are named: Shiphrah and Puah) subvert Pharaoh's instructions to ensure the survival of the Hebrew male children. Therefore, the Israelites multiplied; according to God's blessing of, and intention for, humanity outlined in the creation narrative (Gen. 1.28). It is in this context that the first possible reference to Miriam in the biblical text is given.

Exodus 2 begins with the birth story of Moses. Initially, the baby Moses is hidden by his mother. However, after three months he can no longer be concealed. Moses is placed into a papyrus basket (literally an 'ark' as in a miniature form of what Noah built)[4] and is left exposed on the edge of the Nile riverbank. Moses' sister watches over him from a distance to see what comes of him. According to

---

[3] Félix-Jäger, *Renewal Worship*, p. 82.

[4] Christopher J.H. Wright, *Exodus* (The Story of God Bible Commentary; Grand Rapids: Zondervan, 2021), p. 72.

tradition, Miriam is this older sister of Moses (1 Chron. 6.3).[5] However, the baby Moses, vulnerable and exposed on the Nile River, is rescued by Pharaoh's daughter. The sister (assumed to be Miriam) then steps in and cleverly offers to locate a local wetnurse to care for the baby. The speech of this Hebrew girl addressing Pharaoh's daughter is important enough to be recorded (2.7). Miriam then recruits Moses' (and her) mother to act as a paid carer for baby Moses (2.8). Miriam has a key role as an agent in this story as she negotiates the arrangements and ensures the survival of Moses.[6] Pharaoh's daughter later adopts Moses as her son. Note the pattern of women who have functioned as rescuers of Moses: the midwives, his mother, Miriam, and Pharaoh's daughter.[7] Rescue is a central theme in the book of Exodus modelled by these women. Carmen Imes notes the importance of Miriam's role in the literary structure of Exodus as she appears strategically at the two rescue events, the rescue of Moses and the rescue of the Israelites.[8] Imes also notes how Miriam's encounter with Pharaoh's daughter (Exod. 2.7-8) anticipates the encounter of Moses with the Pharaoh as both seek royal permission 'to go' (Exod. 8.20-5).[9]

As an adult, Moses is called by God to lead the Israelites from Egypt to worship God. This requires Moses to confront the Pharaoh with these words from God: 'Let my people go, so that they may worship me in the wilderness' (7.16). The liberation of Israel from Egypt was for the purpose of worshipping God. While the people were under the servitude of the Pharaoh (who had a god-like status) they were not free to worship their covenant God alone.

Following the disastrous plagues, Pharaoh relents and gives permission for the people to go to the wilderness to worship God. The people defiantly march out from Egypt (14.8). They are led by God via a longer but peaceful route, requiring them to cross the Red Sea. However, Pharaoh changed his mind and pursued the Israelites with his army in chariots. The refugees were seemingly trapped between

---

[5] The Midrashic literature identifies Miriam as the eldest child of Jochebed and Amram.

[6] Brevard S. Childs, *The Book of Exodus: A Critical, Theological Commentary* (Louisville, KY: Westminster John Knox Press, 2004), p. 18.

[7] Wright, *Exodus*, p. 283.

[8] Carmen Joy Imes, 'Can I Get a Witness? Miriam's Song in the Literary Design of Exodus', *Bulletin for Biblical Research* 33.4 (2023), p. 427.

[9] Imes, 'Can I Get a Witness?', p. 433.

the desert and the sea (14.5). Upon seeing Pharaoh and his army, the Israelites were terrified and cried out to God (14.10). Following God's instructions, Moses stretched out his arms over the sea, which parted to allow the people to cross on dry land into the desert and their freedom (14.21-22). Miraculously, the people were saved by God while Pharaoh and his armies drown in the sea (14.28). God rescued them.

The first explicit reference to Miriam is following the crossing of the Red Sea (15.20-21). Exodus 15 describes Moses leading the people in a victory song to celebrate their liberation from Egypt and deliverance from Pharaoh's army. Standing in the wilderness, on the other side of the Red Sea (or Sea of Reeds), they sing in response to God's intervention and salvation. The Song of Moses and Miriam (Exod. 15.1-21) uses cosmic language to give praise and glory to God for rescuing them. This song is considered some of the oldest poetry in the Bible.[10] However, later in the chapter we discover that Moses is not the only worship leader.

The Exodus narrative describes Miriam also leading the people in song (Exod. 15.20-21). Miriam sings to (or answers) 'them', both men and women (15.21). She also commands both men and women to 'sing',[11] and join her in joyful celebration of God their deliverer. In fact, Carmen Imes highlights the narrative structure of Exodus in which Miriam stands on the shore of the Nile to rescue Moses and now stands on the shore of the Sea of Reeds to celebrate God's rescue of the Israelites. The Egyptians, who threw the baby boys to be drowned in the water, are now drowned themselves.[12] However, by examining the repetition of the poetic couplet in 15.1 and 15.21, J. Gerald Janzen suggests that the Exodus text uses the literary technique of *analepsis* (like a flashback) in the narrative, so that 15.19 should follow chronologically the summary of events in 14.26-8. He argues that it is actually Miriam who initiates the singing, and that Moses sings in response to her imperative to 'sing!'[13] This argument

---

[10] Terence E. Fretheim, *Exodus* (Interpretation; Louisville, KY: Westminster John Knox Press, 2010), p. 161.

[11] The word 'them' in 15.21 is masculine plural, as is the imperative 'sing'.

[12] Imes, 'Can I Get a Witness?', p. 436.

[13] J. Gerald Janzen, 'Song of Moses, Song of Miriam: Who Is Seconding Whom?' in Athalya Brenner (ed.), *A Feminist Companion to Exodus to Deuteronomy* (Sheffield, UK: Sheffield Academic Press, 2001), p. 196.

intensifies the role of Miriam as worship leader and interpreter of the Exodus deliverance and delays her introduction.

In Exodus 15, according to the final form of the text, we are explicitly introduced to Miriam and given her name for the first time.

> Then Miriam the prophet, Aaron's sister, took a timbrel in her hand, and all the women followed her, with timbrels and dancing. [21] Miriam sang to them.
> 'Sing to the LORD,
>   for he is highly exalted.
> Both horse and driver
>   he has hurled into the sea'. (Exod. 15.20-21)

The meaning of Miriam's name is contested but is most likely derived from the Egyptian word meaning 'Beloved'.[14] Importantly, she is identified first as prophet (literally *nevi'āh*, 'prophetess'), then second by her familial role, a sister. In fact, Miriam is the first woman in the Bible to be explicitly called a 'prophet' (15.20a) – even Moses is not given this title as yet in the narrative (see Deuteronomy 18).[15]

Interestingly, Miriam is identified in Exodus 15 as the sister of Aaron (and not Moses). The genealogical record noted in Exodus 6.20 identifies Aaron as the older brother of Moses (6.20). This makes Miriam the sister of both Aaron and Moses. This is confirmed in the genealogies of Num. 26.59 and 1 Chron. 5.29 in which Miriam is listed as the sister of Moses and Aaron. Why, then, is Miriam noted in Exod. 15.20 as Aaron's sister and not Moses's? Victor Hamilton suggests this connection to Aaron might hint at Miriam having some kind of priestly role in the Israelite community prior to the Sinai covenant.[16] Previously in the Exodus narrative, some priestly functions (such as circumcision) seem to have been performed by either gender. We see Moses' wife Zipporah performing the circumcision of their son in Exod. 4.24-26. The male-only priesthood was established

---

[14] Rita J. Burns, p. 10. However there are other theories as to the etymology of her name, such as Judith Dowling who notes that in the *midrashic* tradition her name is connected to the experience in Egypt (*marah* meaning 'bitterness') and to the location (*meri* meaning 'rebellion' and *yam* 'sea'). See Judith Dowling, 'Lost Voices of the Feminine', *Jung Journal: Culture & Psyche* 12.2 (2018), p. 57.

[15] Abraham is the only person previously named as a prophet (Gen. 20.7).

[16] Victor P. Hamilton, *Exodus: An Exegetical Commentary* (Grand Rapids: Baker Academic, 2011), p. 400.

later in the narrative as part of the conditions of the Law (Exod. 28.1). Yet, the Exodus tradition, reflected in Mic. 6.4, reinforces that the three siblings worked together in leading the people out of Egypt despite their later conflicts and failures.[17]

Miriam's Prophetic Performance

When someone is given the title of a prophet, we should expect some kind of prophetic activity to follow.[18] The focus of this section is to examine what Miriam does following her introduction as a prophet in Exod. 15.20-21 to justify or explain her designated title. What does Miriam do after she is first called a prophet? Miriam takes up a hand-drum and leads the women in drumming and dancing, then calls the whole community (men and women) to join her in singing a victory song (Exod. 15.20-21). Miriam is a prophet and expresses this function through leading prophetic worship. However, this is not an everyday worship event. This is a prophetic re-enactment of the victory of God and the rescue of the Israelites from slavery expressed through drumming, dancing, and song. Miriam presents a prophetic performance of liberation.

We see prophetic performances all through the Bible: Isaiah walked around naked to symbolize the shame of defeat to Assyria (Isaiah 20); Jeremiah broke a pot to represent the impending destruction of Jerusalem (Jer. 19.1-13); Ezekiel had to lie on his side to signify the sins of the people (Ezek. 4.4-8); and many more. David Stacey suggests there are over forty such examples of prophetic dramatic actions in the OT.[19] This reminds us that communication of a prophetic message is not always spoken (oral) but is sometimes presented through physical actions.

While prophetic performance can refer to the speech of a prophet as a dramatic presentation, it can also refer to the actions and objects used by a prophet. It includes the use of symbolic activity presented to communicate a message from God. A prophetic performance (or

---

[17] Wright, *Exodus*, p. 282.

[18] Wilda C. Gafney. *Daughters of Miriam: Women Prophets in Ancient Israel* (Minneapolis, MN: Fortress Press, 2008), p. 6.

[19] David Stacey, *Prophetic Drama in the Old Testament* (Eugene, OR: Wipf & Stock, 1990), p. 3.

prophetic drama[20]) is not just odd, eccentric behavior associated with prophets.[21] The actions or objects used in prophetic communication are deliberate and meaningful beyond their regular, everyday usage (such as breaking pottery or announcing a pregnancy).[22] Jeanette Mathews refers to such prophets as 'embodied communicators';[23] using their physical bodies and objects to convey their message. She links it to the idea of street theater or performance art. In prophetic action, the prophet provides a visual experience and a creative message from God.[24] The action is intended to arouse the feelings of the observers and provoke a response from the audience;[25] it is not mere cognitive information being relayed but a holistic message that addresses the whole person.

Interpreting the meaning of prophetic actions is complex but not elusive. That is, we are not necessarily told what a prophet intended their actions to communicate. If a prophetic text provides an explanation or commentary for their actions (such as Isaiah 20), then the task of interpretation is considerably easier. Yet, even if an explanation is not provided, the study of the literary context can provide an interpretive key to understand the actions performed by a prophet. Of course, no interpretation is *the* definitive answer. There are always new understandings and new insights that can be gleaned. But, through careful analysis, we can discern and interpret the message of the prophets. In the case of Miriam, we are not told what her actions of dancing, drumming, and singing signified, but by reading her story in its context of the liberation from Egypt we can glean some key insights.

However, it is also important not to impose contemporary meanings onto prophetic actions described in the Bible. For example, to walk around naked in some contemporary Western cultures might supposedly symbolize freedom from social and sexual constraints. It would be a mistake to impose this meaning onto a prophetic action described in the Bible. The prophetic performance of Isaiah is a case in point (Isaiah 20). Isaiah's nakedness does not represent freedom

---

[20] Stacey, *Prophetic Drama in the Old Testament,* p. 22.
[21] Stacey, *Prophetic Drama in the Old Testament,* p. 11.
[22] Jeanette Mathews, *Prophets as Performers: Biblical Performance Criticism and Israel's Prophets* (Eugene, OR: Cascade, 2020), p. 8.
[23] Mathews, *Prophets as Performers,* p. 74.
[24] Mathews, *Prophets as Performers,* p. 89.
[25] Stacey, *Prophetic Drama in the Old Testament,* p. 20.

but symbolizes shame and humiliation. The actions of the prophets in the Bible must be understood according to their history and culture. They are descriptions of events performed in a time and place. As Mathews writes, 'Rather than just words on a page, embodied performance means that real bodies in real time will act out the truths of the tradition'.[26] So, in the light of this concept of prophetic performance, what might Miriam's actions of playing the hand-drum, dance, and song represent in this prophetic drama of Exod. 15.20-21?

Prophetic Worship: Drumming, Dancing, and Singing

Through her worship and actions, Miriam interprets the events of the Exodus as a liberation from the bondage of Pharaoh and his army. This is the first record of God intervening in Israel's history as an agent of liberation. Miriam reveals God's intention for their freedom and rescue from Egypt; to worship God in the wilderness (Exod. 7.16). They were not rescued merely because God opposes slavery. While the Israelites were in the service of Pharaoh, who was considered divine, they were not free to worship God. Their loyalties were divided between their covenant God and the god Pharaoh, and their worldview shaped by Egyptian thinking. Therefore, the Israelites were liberated for the purpose of worship; to know God, to be renewed in their mind into his image, and to reflect his character to those around them.

Worship is 'our human expression of reverence and devotion directed towards God'.[27] Worship is our response to God for his saving acts. As Terence Fretheim notes, their worship is 'the product of a new experience, an experience of both God and people as liberator and liberated'.[28] Their worship is a response to their new, and deeply felt experience of freedom, provided by God.[29] Miriam prophetically shapes this worship act as she drums, dances, and sings. That is, Miriam's embodied performance communicates the prophetic importance of the Exodus event. God is greater than Pharaoh. In fact,

---

[26] Mathews, *Prophets as Performers*, p. 90.
[27] Jacqueline N. Grey, 'Worship: A Pentecostal Perspective', *Australasian Pentecostal Studies* 24 (2023), p. 53.
[28] Fretheim, *Exodus*, p. 163.
[29] Fretheim, *Exodus*, p. 163.

God is greater that all future Pharaohs and dominating forces that seek to undermine God's life-giving plan for creation.

Miriam's worship interprets the Exodus event as it provides and reminds the Israelites of the purpose for their rescue: to worship God. They are rescued from Egypt so that they may worship God in the wilderness (7.16). Therefore, the location of Miriam's prophetic worship is important. They are celebrating the victory of God in the wilderness. They are no longer in Egypt and slaves to Pharaoh. The wilderness is their current location, the place where they are now free to worship God. The wilderness is a liminal space; a place where they must rely on God for survival. It is a place where their previous mind-set and Egyptian thinking will be deconstructed, and their worldview re-made based on God's ways and laws.[30] Miriam has the last word because she interprets the defeat of their enslavers from God's perspective. In a prophetic sense, her song also brings a sense of closure to the experience of slavery so that the Israelites can begin anew in the desert as a transformed community.

Miriam's prophetic activity is expressed in three key creative forms. We will now consider each of these activities in turn to see how they function as prophetic performances.

Hand-Drumming

The first of Miriam's prophetic actions is that she takes up and plays the hand-drum. The narrative tells us that all the women followed her, also playing the hand-drum (15.20). Usually translated as a 'timbrel', which can wrongly suggest to the modern reader a tambourine style instrument with cymbals. The hand-drum was a small disk covered with animal skin. Carol Meyers highlights numerous examples of ancient pottery unearthed by archaeologists that depict women playing such instruments.[31] Other sources suggest that this activity of drumming by women was well-known in the ancient Near East before this event. Laban's reference to the use of music and hand-drums in Gen. 31.27 testifies to its use in the broader culture before

---

[30] Narelle J. Coetzee, *Wilderness Theophanies in Exodus: The Wonder and Wildness of Yahweh's Appearance in the Wilderness* (Bern: Peter Lang, 2024), p. xx.

[31] Carol Meyers, 'Miriam the Musician', in A. Brenner (ed.), *A Feminist Companion to Exodus to Deuteronomy* (Sheffield, UK: Sheffield Academic Press, 2001), pp. 210-13.

the Exodus event.[32] Then, after Exodus 15, there are numerous examples in the Bible of women playing the hand-drum, dancing, and singing victory songs in celebration of Israel's success in battle (see, for example, Judg. 11.34; 1 Sam. 18.6). According to Susan Ackerman, Israelite women were responsible for 'singing victory songs after an Israelite triumph in holy war and appear to have assumed a principal position as ritual musicians upon occasions of lament'.[33] Descriptions of bands of prophets include the use of hand-drums in their ecstatic worship (1 Sam. 10.5).[34] However, Miriam taking up the hand-drum seems to be the first occasion for the Israelites to incorporate such an instrument in their worship.[35] Drumming, dancing, and worship cannot be captured in words but must be acted out and experienced. Miriam's worship communicates their new freedom in God through this embodied activity.

Dancing

Miriam is then described as leading the women in dancing. In the OT, dancing is primarily connected to the Temple worship and the sacrificial system but also to the prophetic tradition. Miriam is the model *par excellence* for the combining of these two traditions as she performs a prophetic dance. Dancing is, as Stacey asserts, 'an act of celebration'.[36] In fact, Stacey notes all kinds of dancing connected to worship: processional dances (2 Sam. 6.5), dancing at sacrifices (Exod. 32.6, 19), dancing in state of prophetic trance (1 Sam. 10.5), festival dances (Judg. 21.16-24), and victory dances (Exod. 15.20).[37] Prophetic dance uses the movement of the body to communicate a message physically.

While we have no record of how Miriam danced, or her dance steps, the meaning of her dance is directly connected to the worship refrain celebrating the defeat of Pharaoh. Using prophetic

---

[32] Though it is noted that historically the poetry of Exodus 15 is most likely older than the narrative of Genesis 31.

[33] Susan Ackerman, 'Why is Miriam also among the Prophets? (And is Zipporah among the Priests?)', *Journal of Biblical Literature* 121.1 (2002), p. 48.

[34] Hamilton, *Exodus*, p. 397.

[35] Craig A. Evans, 'Celebrating Victory from the Sea of Reeds to the Eschatological Battle Field: Miriam's Timbrels and Dances in Exodus 15 and Beyond', *Biblical Theology Bulletin* 51.4 (2021)', p. 206.

[36] Stacey, *Prophetic Drama in the Old Testament,* p. 30.

[37] Stacey, *Prophetic Drama in the Old Testament,* p. 31.

performance, Miriam interprets the Exodus event. They are free. The freedom of release from the shackles and fear of Pharaoh is expressed through free bodily movement. Imagine Miriam and the dancers shaking off the slavery. Imagine them using their bodies in new ways that resist the containment of Egypt. Together, as they dance, their whole beings are free to love God and worship God – all their mind, strength, body, and emotions.

The recent interest among biblical scholars in utilizing trauma as a lens through which to interpret biblical texts also contributes to this analysis. Trauma is usually focused on 'the range of responses evoked by an experience perceived to pose an extreme threat and that overwhelms an individual's ordinary means of coping'.[38] The ongoing threat of slavery and the immediate threat of pursuit by Pharaoh's armies while crossing the Red Sea is arguably a traumatic experience. Worship and dance provide a physical release of the stress of trauma,[39] but also help through non-verbal mechanisms to interpret and process the impact of traumatic experiences. Through the expression of dance, unprocessed trauma can be released. This is crucial in the Israelite's journey to Sinai to establish a new community in covenant with God. While they still have the hard work of formation, they can leave behind at the seashore some of their old fears and walk towards freedom in God. They have gotten out of Egypt and danced off the shackles of slavery and injustice. Their freedom dance prepares them for the next stage in their journey of getting Egypt out of their thinking and patterns of behavior by embracing a new life, new law, and new community founded on God's justice in the Mosaic covenant at Sinai.

Singing

Finally, the narrative of Exodus 15 describes Miriam leading all the Israelites in song. Miriam commands both men and women, to 'sing' (15.21), leading all the people in celebration of the victory of God.

---

[38] Christopher G. Frechette and Elizabeth Boase, 'Defining 'Trauma' as a Useful Lens for Biblical Interpretation', in E. Boase & C. Frechette (eds.), *Bible Through the Lens of Trauma* (Atlanta, GA: SBL Press, 2016), p. 4.

[39] Jo Ann B. Higginbotham, 'Dance and Pentecostal Worship' (Paper Presented at the Twenty Sixth Annual Meeting of the Society for Pentecostal Studies, 13-15 March 1997, Oakland, CA), p. 4.

Miriam's song announces God's victory; the lyrics focus on exalting God who has defeated Pharaoh's army. The repetition of her song aids the Israelites to process this new reality that their oppressor is no more. The power and bondage of Pharaoh have been broken by God's liberative work. The expression of this new reality in prophetic performance – through voice, body, movement, and song – allows them to comprehend holistically (and not just cognitively) God's victory and its implications for their community. It is Yahweh who has delivered them from Egypt. This victory of God over Pharaoh has significance beyond its own time and place. As Pharaoh is a symbol of oppression, Miriam's song can be re-used by later generations to celebrate God's justice and defeat of all Pharaohs. [40]

We will now turn to consider how the concept of prophetic worship, particularly using dance, has been adapted in some contemporary settings. These examples provide a sample of possibilities for communities seeking to integrate prophetic practices into their worship.

What Can Miriam Teach Us Today?

Exuberant singing and dance are often highlighted as distinct features of Pentecostal worship. The exuberance of early Pentecostal worship – lifting hands, clapping, dancing – resulted in much criticism in many contexts. Yet, the example of Miriam was utilized by early Pentecostals as biblical support for the practice of dancing in the Spirit to counter such criticism. [41] Yet, the passionate expressions of worship and dance of the early Pentecostals (and still utilized today in many congregations across the world), were arguably most influenced by the African-American forms of worship originating from the informal gatherings of African plantation slaves of the eighteenth century. [42]

The experience of the oppression and suffering of slavery by significant segments of the African-American community continued

---

[40] Walter Brueggemann, *The Prophetic Imagination* (Minneapolis: Fortress Press, rev. edn, 2001), p. 3.

[41] Isaiah C. Padgett, 'Murmurs and Miracles: A Pentecostal Reception History of Miriam the Prophetess', *Pneuma* 45 (2023), pp. 252, 257.

[42] Wayne C. Solomon and Franco Crosby, 'Liberation in Black Urban Pentecostal Worship' (Paper Presented at the 45th Annual Meeting of the Society for Pentecostal Studies Meeting, 10-12 March 2016, San Dimas, CA), p. 6.

following the Proclamation of Emancipation. Craig Scandrett-Leatherman notes that from the Civil War to the 1930s, 'the most common form of violence was lynching'.[43] During this Jim Crowe era, new (or renewed) rituals of liberation emerged within the Church of God in Christ (COGIC)[44] in response to this oppression and attempt to dehumanize African American men.[45] In particular, dance in Afro-Pentecostal worship became a form of expressing non-violent resistance. Dance developed as an important ritual for Afro-Pentecostal men during this time as it provided a counter-response to the systemic ritual of lynching by their white oppressors. Dance and spirituality within the ecclesial spaces emerged as an act of resistance by providing agency to men. Afro-Pentecostals could move in a way that involved black style of dance, song, and worship; a 'celebration of black ritual aesthetics'.[46] Dance provided counter-cultural bodily expressions of freedom and victory not experienced in social contexts but found in Christ's death and resurrection. As Scandrett-Leatherman writes, 'Afro-Pentecostals gave men the right to speak freely without uttering a word, and the right to move freely without serving a white master – the sweet rights of dancing in joy and victory'.[47] The expression of dance at this time by Afro-Pentecostals can be considered a prophetic activity as it communicated a message of freedom and justice to give hope for the future of the African-American community.

Dance as therapy has also been utilized in contemporary contexts by African-American women who have experienced trauma. Kahlia Williams describes the use of liturgical dance in a congregational setting as a mechanism for women to experience freedom through their physical movements that helped them to process and release the trauma carried in their bodies. As the worship engaged the participants in both their imaginative and physical senses, they expressed

---

[43] Craig Scandrett-Leatherman, 'Rites of Lynching and Rights of Dance: Historic, Anthropological, and Afro-Pentecostal Perspectives on Black Manhood after 1895', in Amos Yong & Estrelda Alexander (eds.), *Afro-Pentecostalism: Black Pentecostal and Charismatic Christianity in History and Culture* (New York: New York University Press, 2011), p. 95.

[44] COGIC is the largest Pentecostal denomination in the USA and has a predominantly African-American membership.

[45] Scandrett-Leatherman, 'Rites of Lynching and Rights of Dance', p. 95.

[46] Scandrett-Leatherman, 'Rites of Lynching and Rights of Dance', p. 109.

[47] Scandrett-Leatherman, 'Rites of Lynching and Rights of Dance', p. 108.

feelings of receiving God's love and grace. The impact, while not consistent, did alter the self (and community's) perceptions of many participants to address their intrinsic worth, particularly of their bodies. Dance as a therapeutic activity provided a way to express their pain of marginalization and (mostly) subsequent experience of inclusion in congregational life.[48] Therefore, Miriam's use of dance as a prophetic act and expression of freedom can provide a model for other communities and individuals seeking liberation from trauma.

Miriam models for us today the use of dance, singing, and drumming as prophetic expressions of worship. In their worship, the Israelites celebrated God's victory in the unique event of the Exodus deliverance. Yet, the Exodus story has been reappropriated time and again as a symbol of liberation for marginalized communities.[49] Moreover, Egypt was not Miriam's future, nor should it be ours. In the Christian tradition, crossing the Red Sea is represented in the ordinance (or sacrament) of baptism. Believers leave the slavery of sin, are 'buried' in the waters of the sea and rise again to a new life and new identity in Christ. To dance prophetically, as Miriam danced, is to express bodily the liberation found in Jesus Christ. Miriam interpreted the events of the Exodus revealing God's intention for the freedom and liberation of his covenant community. In the same way, worship in the contemporary church may use dance or other physical forms of expression to communicate prophetically God's truth, justice, and freedom for God's people.

---

[48] K.J. Williams, 'Love Your Flesh: The Power and Protest of Embodied Worship', *Liturgy* 35.1 (2020), pp. 3-9.

[49] For example, the contemporary use of the exodus as symbol of liberation in Black Theology in James H. Cone, *Black Theology of Liberation* (Maryknoll, NY: Orbis, 20th Anniversary edn, 1990).

3

A Eucharist That's Truly Eucharistic: Emphasizing Corporate Praising as a Way to Elevate the Place of the Lord's Supper in Pentecostal Congregations

Lester Ruth*

Introduction

So rich and abundant are the mercies from God to be found at the Lord's Supper that it is easy to forget that its administration is a (perhaps *the*) critical opportunity for corporate praying to God. Indeed, in Justin Martyr's famous, second century description of a eucharistic service – perhaps the earliest that exists – one of the few details he highlights is the prayer said at the table. But over the centuries it has been easy to be mesmerized by the abundance of sacramental graces in theological discussions of sacramental efficacy, divine presence, and other technical matters.

But at the core of its essence is that gathering around the table is also about God's people praying, especially the lifting up of thanks and praise to God. If at the table, the Almighty offers grace (*charis* in Greek) to us, then also the altar is our opportunity to offer praise and thanks (*eu-charisteo*) to that same God.

---

* Lester Ruth (PhD, University of Notre Dame) is Research Professor of Christian Worship at Duke Divinity School, Durham, NC.

Since Pentecostal worship – especially in its widespread Praise & Worship form – usually emphasizes praise and thanksgiving, it would seem that the Eucharist could be a natural and important part of Pentecostal Praise & Worship services. Indeed, with that conviction in mind, I have been exploring and experimenting with ways to pray eucharistically in a fashion fitting to the liturgical ethos of Contemporary Praise & Worship. In so doing, I have found myself in harmony with a growing number of Pentecostal theologians who have increasingly highlighted Communion and advocated for it to have a more prominent role in Pentecostal services. With this Chapter I hope, as a non-Pentecostal but sympathetic liturgical historian, to contribute what amounts to an *amicus curiae* brief – a friend-of-the-courts argument – to those advocating a great importance for the Eucharist in Pentecostal worship. More specifically, I hope to advocate how emphasizing the element of corporate praising, i.e. letting a Pentecostal Eucharist be truly eucharistic in a Pentecostal way, is key to having this ordinance[1] be a more prominent and more regular part of congregational worship by Pentecostals.

After briefly reviewing the eucharistic discussions from several of the most prominent, recent theologian advocates, I will then also succinctly review the history of sacramentally-related praising, both its waxing and waning, as well as the historical emphasis of praising within the rise of Contemporary Praise & Worship. To suggest the inherent fittingness of Eucharist-based praising within Pentecostal worship, I will highlight the connection made between praising and Spirit-infilling in the Luke-Acts biblical materials. Finally, I will describe my experiments of integrating more ecstatic and music-driven practices of corporate praising of God within administrations of the Lord's Supper. My goal is – as the title of this chapter suggests – to have the Eucharist be truly eucharistic.

Recent Pentecostal Advocacy for a More Central Eucharist

In recent years several prominent academic Pentecostal theologians have reconsidered the marginal role that the Lord's Supper usually

---

[1] Note that for the purposes of this chapter, I will use as synonyms the terms 'ordinance' and 'sacrament' as they refer to the Lord's Supper.

has in Pentecostal congregations and have begun to call for it to have a more important place in the worship of those congregations. Generally, these authors are distressed by that marginal position and have appropriated ecumenical lines of thought on this ordinance's rightful role in Christian worship to advocate for that role in Pentecostal worship. Among these theologians would be persons with both national and international recognition like Simon Chan, Chris E.W. Green, Christopher A. Stephenson, and Frank D. Macchia.[2] While their specific arguments differ in details – as do the specifics on how to incorporate Communion more fully into Pentecostal worship – they share a common vision to see Pentecostal worship be more eucharistic. Let us consider each theologian's advocacy with respect to the basis upon which they advocate for the Supper and their ideas for how to more fully and actually incorporate it into Pentecostal worship.[3] In other words, let us briefly consider the 'why?' and 'how?' for each.[4]

Singaporean Simon Chan argues for a vibrant place for the Eucharist as part of a desire to recover a stronger eschatological and Trinitarian ecclesiology. As Philip Struyk has noted, for Chan the worship of the church, normalized in the liturgy, is what makes the church the church.[5] Chan's understanding of this normative liturgy is strongly influenced by the work of Dom Gregory Dix.[6] Following that mid-twentieth century Anglican liturgical scholar, Chan argues for a 'basic shape or *ordo*' of Word and sacrament underlying the variety in worship across Christianity,[7] whether descriptively for the

---

[2] Similarly, one could add Daniel Tomberlin's pastoral apologetic as contributing to the same goal. See Daniel Tomberlin, *Pentecostal Sacraments: Encountering God at the Altar* (Cleveland, TN: Center for Pentecostal Leadership and Care, 2010), p. especially pp. 184-90.

[3] I am indebted to Fuller doctoral student, Philip Struyk, whose recently completed dissertation, 'Moved by the Spirit: Toward a Method of Pentecostal Liturgical Theology' (PhD diss., Fuller Theological Seminary, 2025), first made me aware of this development among Pentecostal theologians.

[4] Note that I will be attempting neither an exhaustive review of any particular theologian's writings on the subject nor a comprehensive search for all Pentecostals who might be writing in this vein. For a more extensive review of Pentecostal theologizing on the Eucharist, see Chapter 2 in Chris E.W. Green, *Toward a Pentecostal Theology of the Lord's Supper: Foretasting the Kingdom* (Cleveland, TN: CPT Press, 2012), pp. 5-73.

[5] Struyk, 'Moved by the Spirit', p. 133.

[6] See the role of Dix in Chapter 3, 'The Shape of the Liturgy', in Simon Chan's *Liturgical Theology: The Church as Worshiping Community* (Downers Grove, IL: IVP Academic, 2006), pp. 62-84.

[7] Chan, *Liturgical Theology*, p. 62.

text- and sacrament-based liturgical traditions that Chan admires or prescriptively for evangelical worship, including his own Pentecostal tradition. This shape or *ordo* as portrayed by Chan is a particular sequencing of elements within a service, first the Bible-oriented acts of worship and then the sacramental, within which 'the Eucharist holds a special place as the "sacrament of sacraments"'.[8] But it is not ultimately a desire for historical fidelity that motivates Chan's eucharistic advocacy. For him the table is where Christians realize themselves as the ecclesial Body of Christ even as they receive the sacramental body of Christ.[9] It is the liturgical moment pregnant with utter graciousness as Christ gives himself to us in the Supper.[10]

In terms of envisioning how Communion might take a more prominent role in Pentecostal worship, Chan is most comfortable talking about this *ordo* as normative and suggesting that charismatic elements like 'spontaneous praise and worship' be placed at 'appropriate points of the liturgy' so that 'the charismatic dimension of joyful worship might enliven the liturgy'.[11] (Chan envisions this approach as Pentecostal worship dying 'to itself' and being 'reborn as the dynamic element within the liturgical structure so that the liturgy becomes charismatic'.)[12] While some of these 'appropriate points' involve the eucharistic liturgy (i.e. 'joyful thanksgiving' at the conclusion of the eucharistic consecratory prayer), Chan's disdain for Contemporary Worship Music and its normal modes of use keep him from suggesting any musical dimension.[13]

Theologian Chris E.W. Green shares some of the same basic commitments as does Simon Chan, namely, firm beliefs that the sacrament is an occasion in worship for real encounter with the Risen Christ and his abundance of grace and that there is merit in using the

---

[8] Chan, *Liturgical Theology*, p. 63.

[9] Chan, *Liturgical Theology*, p. 68.

[10] Chan, *Liturgical Theology*, p. 70.

[11] Simon Chan, 'The Mutual Challenges of Pentecostal-charismatic and Liturgical Worship', in Peter Hocken et al. (eds.), *Pentecostal Theology and Ecumenical Theology: Interpretations and Intersections* (Leiden: Brill, 2019), p. 271. For a detailed outlining of the content of the Word and sacrament *ordo*, see Chan, *Liturgical Theology*, p. 129.

[12] Chan, 'Mutual Challenges', pp. 261, 279.

[13] Chan, 'Mutual Challenges', p. 271. For Chan's contempt, see 'Mutual Challenges', p. 279, and *Liturgical Theology*, pp. 153, 157. His abhorrence of Contemporary Worship Music and its use in extended times of congregational singing as he knows them seems to make considering its use anathema.

classic form of the 'liturgy' with its sense of a normative *ordo*.[14] Green sees multiple benefits from 'liturgical worship', namely that it 'stories us into the history of God's life with us', 'deepens and purifies our affections', and 'disciplines our imaginations and spiritual ambitions to love'.[15] Since, according to Green, 'the Eucharist embodies in its own way every other act of worship',[16] it would seem that whatever good can be found in 'the liturgy' generally should be found in a heightened way in the sacrament. Overall, Green affirms the distinctiveness of the Lord's Supper (it belongs at 'the heart of the Christian life' and should be recognized as 'the hub of the worship service')[17] and the vividness of Christ's presence in its administration and reception.

In recovering a more central role for the Eucharist, Green does not envision a simple, wholesale adoption of a liturgy borrowed from another tradition even as he also affirms a useful liturgical approach residing in the so-called 'great tradition' and speaks appreciatively of 'pre-determined rites and practices' and 'mandated ritual words and actions'.[18] Even then, however, Green consistently argues that, however the Supper is celebrated, it must be done in a way that stays true to Pentecostal spirituality and practices that characterize and sustain that spirituality like the altar call, 'tarrying', prayer for healing, testimonies, foot washing, 'inspired spontaneity', and 'skilled improvisation'.[19] Indeed, Green advocates careful attentiveness to the Holy Spirit's leading in each celebration of Communion. Unlike Chan, Green seems not to discuss the role of congregational music with

---

[14] See Chris E.W. Green, 'Saving Liturgy: (Re)imagining Pentecostal Liturgical Theology and Practice', Chapter 7 in Mark J. Cartledge and A.J. Swoboda (eds.), *Scripting Pentecost: A Study of Pentecostals, Worship and Liturgy* (London: Routledge, 2017), p. 115, for a description of the Word and sacrament order adapted for Pentecostalism.

[15] Green, 'Saving Liturgy', p. 111.

[16] Green, *Toward a Pentecostal Theology*, p. 316, n. 356. For a similar argument, although not one presented for a distinctly Pentecostal advocacy for the Eucharist, see James K.A. Smith, *Desiring the Kingdom: Worship, Worldview, and Cultural Formation* (Grand Rapids, MI: Baker Academic, 2009), pp. 197-203. Smith's summary (p. 197) is that the Lord's Supper is 'a compacted microcosm of the whole of worship'.

[17] Green, *Toward a Pentecostal Theology*, p. 316.

[18] Green, 'Saving Liturgy', p. 114; Green, *Toward a Pentecostal Theology*, p. 252. He likewise affirms the critical position that praise and thanksgiving play in classic liturgies without plunging fully or deeply into specific practices associated with those.

[19] Green, *Toward a Pentecostal Theology*, pp. 317, 320; Green, 'Saving Liturgy', pp. 108, 114-15.

respect to the administration of the Eucharist, either to provide a point of negative contrast (as does Chan) or to explore possibilities for its use in joyful, S/spirited eucharistic liturgy (as I will do so below).[20]

Other Pentecostal theologians follow parallels paths of affirming the Eucharist's criticalness even if the theologians do not strictly walk in each other's footsteps. For example, Christopher Stephenson highlights the Lord's Supper as an exercise to demonstrate the theological method (*regula spiritualitatis, regular doctrina*) he advocates. In so doing, he ends up affirming several strong affirmations for the Supper, including that it is more than mere cognitive remembrance, that there is a divine presence at the Supper (although he stresses the Spirit's presence more than Christ's), and that it's celebration is 'a catalyst that enlivens eschatological passions'.[21] In his brief discussion of how Pentecostals might consider celebrating it more frequently and make it more central to corporate worship, Stephenson notes that there should be opportunity to pause in the Holy Spirit's presence, that there ought to be robust preaching on the sacrament, and that Pentecostals ought to consider doing it more in small group settings.[22] Likewise, Frank Macchia speaks eloquently about the Eucharist and its graces and thus implies a greater prominence for it in Pentecostal worship. For Macchia, in the Lord's Supper 'the very substance of our life together in communion, in the embrace of the Triune God, is presented with clarity'.[23] It is an especially true

---

[20] However, elsewhere Green does discuss music in worship appreciatively, even to the point of quoting another theologian about music's 'sacramental potency': 'Dwelling at music's heart is a sacramental potency, awaiting only appropriate times and places for its actualization, for manifesting the holy and for expressing our experience of the holy'. See Chris E.W. Green, 'Thus Sings the Lord: The Spirit, the Body, and the Sacramental Nature of Singing', Chapter 1 in Chris E.W. Green and Steven Félix-Jäger (eds.), *The Spirit and the Song: Pneumatological Reflections on Popular Music* (Lanham: Fortress Academic, 2024), p. 15.

[21] Christopher A. Stephenson, *Types of Pentecostal Theology: Method, System, Spirit* (New York: Oxford University Press, 2013), pp. 115, 120-24.

[22] Stephenson, *Types of Pentecostal Theology*, pp. 127-29.

[23] Frank D. Macchia, *The Spirit-Baptized Church: A Dogmatic Inquiry* (London: T&T Clark, 2020), p. 198. Macchia seems especially to like the notions of communion and divine embrace with respect to the effects of the sacrament. See Frank D. Macchia, *Justified in the Spirit: Creation, Redemption, and the Triune God* (Grand Rapids, MI: Eerdmans, 2010), p. 289, and Frank D. Macchia, 'Signs of Grace: Towards a Charismatic Theology of Worship', Chapter 9 in Lee Roy Martin (ed.), *Toward a Pentecostal Theology of Worship* (Cleveland, TN: CPT Press, 2nd edn, 2020), p. 211.

opportunity for a 'congregational mediation' (of grace) as Christians 'commune together in unity at the table of the Lord, receiving one another as Christ receives us'.[24]

As mentioned previously, these authors generally not only provide theological rationales for why the Eucharist should have a more central role in Pentecostal worship but also ideas for how that might or should be achieved. However, in reviewing these theologians, I think more could be done by highlighting and dreaming about the Eucharist as a premier opportunity for corporate praying of praise and thanksgiving, especially in ways harmonious with the musical practices of Contemporary Praise & Worship. Some of these authors might tickle these notions, but none embrace it to the degree that I believe would generate ideas for enticing rank-and-file Pentecostals to desire the Supper more strongly. To that possibility let us now turn, first referencing historical and biblical materials to do so.

How the Eucharist Was Eucharistic – and Then Wasn't As Much

'How truly it is fitting and right, proper and obligatory, to praise you …'[25] This sentiment – or one like it – is the classic beginning of the central prayer prayed at the Lord's Supper in the patristic period. In other words, the prayer not only honored God in praise and thanksgiving but the eventually commonplace form of these prayers made a point of acknowledging the utter appropriateness of doing so. Whatever else an ancient eucharistic prayer did, it was going to praise and thank God, but not just in any way. These prayers honor God by a commemorative recitation of God's mighty acts of salvation, especially as manifested in Jesus Christ, and, usually, with a nod to how this activity of exaltation engaged the entirety of heaven and earth. For example, to reinforce the propriety of this type of corporate, heaven-linked praising, the ancient Liturgy of Basil piled on the honorific verbs: '… it is truly fitting and right and befitting the magnificence of your holiness to praise you, to hymn you, to bless you, to

---

[24] Macchia, *The Spirit-Baptized Church*, p. 199.
[25] From the anaphora of St. James. See Lester Ruth et al., *Walking Where Jesus Walked: Worship in Fourth-Century Jerusalem* (Grand Rapids, MI: Eerdmans, 2010), p. 86.

worship you, to give you thanks, (and) to glorify you, the only truly existing God …'[26]

This emphasis upon commemoration-based praising reflected ancient Jewish sensibilities, easily seen in multiple biblical examples from both the Old and New Testaments.[27] Indeed, in the Luke-Acts corpus, bursting forth in praise by commemorating God's activity is a common occurrence when one is moved by or filled with the Holy Spirit. Examples include Zechariah, Mary, Cornelius, and his household, and, perhaps, even the disciples on the day of Pentecost.[28] And so, not surprisingly, commemoration-based praise and thanksgiving to honor the God who raised Jesus Christ became a centerpiece of the meal through which Christians continued to fellowship with this same Christ Jesus. As Justin in the second century described it, a worship service's presider offered up prayers and thanksgiving according to the best of his ability to which all the congregation assented by saying 'Amen'.[29]

However, from the late patristic period onward through the Reformation, a variety of dynamics contributed to obscure the centrality of the Eucharist as a pre-eminent place for congregationally-affirmed praise and thanksgiving to God. Increasingly, presiders at the table began to say the praise in a quieter voice that could not have been heard. Even if the people could have heard what was said, hearing became less and less important as archaic forms of language – and not the people's current vernacular – became more and more common. Architecture and orientation also often worked against the Eucharist as occasion for congregational praising as altars were moved farther from the people, screens separating chancel from nave continued to grow in height, and presiders began to face away from the people, not toward them. Of course, in the late medieval period, the development of widespread private masses (like Chantry masses) meant that no people were present whatsoever to hear anything said

---

[26] Walter D. Ray, *Tasting Heaven on Earth: Worship in Sixth-Century Constantinople* (Grand Rapids, MI: Eerdmans, 2012), p. 94.

[27] For an example from the OT, see Solomon's prayers in 1 Kings 8. For the NT, consider Paul's opening of the letter to the Ephesians.

[28] See Lk. 1.67-79; 1.46-55; Acts 10.46, and 2.11. My attribution of this phenomenon to the day of Pentecost is based on the bystanders saying that those filled with the Spirit were speaking about God's mighty acts, i.e. God's *megaleia*.

[29] See Denis Minns and Paul Parvis (eds.), *Justin, Philosopher and Martyr: Apologies* (New York: Oxford University Press, 2009), pp. 258-61.

or done in worship. Moreover, by the late Middle Ages, there was a fixation on the Words of Institution – the so-called *Verba* – as the critical part of the prayer even as a more penitential piety before the mystery of Christ's eucharistic presence captured the hearts of laity and clergy alike. The Protestant Reformation was not a total reversal of these trends – not to mention that Protestants generally were highly suspicious of the Roman Catholic Church's eucharistic prayer – and so, not surprisingly, the sacramental forms of worship developed by Protestants showed variance in how strongly Communion was approached as an opportunity for robust praise and thanksgiving.[30] This Reformation legacy lingers in many Protestant liturgical circles, especially those belonging to the Free Church world.

How a Pentecostal Eucharist Might Get Its Praise Groove Back

But, I want to suggest, it need not be that way, especially within Pentecostalism. The Eucharist can be/should be truly eucharistic even in (perhaps, better, especially in) Pentecostalism. It is possible and desirable to emphasize Spirit-led and music-driven corporate praising within eucharistic celebrations as a viable possibility for achieving the elevation of the ordinance in Pentecostal services. On the one hand, having commemoration-based praising of God would seem to fit the ethos of Pentecostalism generally since it is associated with the infilling of the Holy Spirit in Luke-Acts and praise has often been a mainstay of classic forms of Pentecostal Worship. Simply put, praising God does seem to be one of the things the coming of the Spirit brings about. On the other hand, highlighting corporate thanksgiving and praising as the centerpiece of eucharistic celebration would fit the ethos of Pentecostal Praise & Worship specifically, which has become a dominant form of Pentecostal worship worldwide. This form has emphasized the priority of corporate praise as the occasion for

---

[30] The variety among early Protestants on this issue can be seen in the various liturgies found in Bard Thompson (ed.), *Liturgies of the Western Church* (Philadelphia: Fortress Press, 1961), pp. 134, 154, 178, 202-203, 205-208, 222-23, 249-56, 304, 337, 369-730, 393-401, and Robert E. Webber (ed.), *Twenty Centuries of Christian Worship* (*The Complete Library of Christian Worship* 2; Nashville, TN: StarSong Publishing Group, 1994), pp. 222-24.

experiencing the Manifest Presence of God.[31] Utilizing Psalm 22.3b (i.e. the notion that God inhabits or is enthroned upon the praises of his people) as a foundational text, Praise & Worship as a distinct form of Pentecostal worship has showcased corporate praise, especially sung praise, as absolutely foundational liturgical activity.

To fit the ethos of Praise & Worship – and to utilize its practices – is critical if one hopes to have success in moving the needle on rank-and-file devotion to the Supper. In this regard, my suggestion runs parallel to those of Chris Green who once noted that 'it is crucial that the Eucharist-event be framed and undergirded by characteristic Pentecostal practices'.[32] I only want to add to Green's list by making central some music-related practices associated with Praise & Worship.

Before describing several possible practices with which I have been doing some limited liturgical experimentation, it is useful to discuss the ethos that characterizes Contemporary Praise & Worship so that my assumptions for the subsequent suggested practices might be known. Eight aspects of this ethos are particularly relevant. The first is the most obvious to anyone familiar with this way of worship: the service is largely organized by music, especially by extended periods of congregational singing (as compared to the occasional insertion of a piece of music into the service order). Praise & Worship services typically use some popular form of music making, including songs whose structure reflects the structure of pop songs (i.e. with verses, chorus, bridge, etc. as compared to multi-verse strophic hymns). This pop structure, along with how time generally is managed, leads to the third common dynamic: time is experienced as circular and cyclical (rather than sequential and linear). In other words, the liturgical activity and content will revisit points and material revisited earlier in the service. Moreover, there is a desire for good flow as the service moves along with items blending seamlessly into the next. This desire is closely linked to the next dimension since having good flow contributes greatly to this dimension: the service should be affectively intense and physically expressive. Worshipers should feel things deeply and should have the freedom to express themselves physically

---

[31] For a review of this history, see Lester Ruth and Lim Swee Hong, *A History of Contemporary Praise & Worship: Understanding the Ideas that Reshaped the Protestant Church* (Grand Rapids, MI: Baker Academic, 2021), pp. 7-161.

[32] Green, *Toward a Pentecostal Theology*, p. 317.

as they feel led. Indeed, a picture of hands upraised by worshipers caught in the exuberance of the liturgical moment has become a universal image for this way of worship. Also attributing to the affective intensity is the propensity for layering multiple liturgical actions simultaneously (rather than a strict one-thing-at-a-time sequencing), especially as it involves a musical underlay for other activity done 'over the top'. The seventh aspect of the ethos is a predilection for extemporaneity (or, at least, its appearance) rather than a comfort with liturgical texts, the singing of pre-written song lyrics being the obvious exception to this predilection. Finally, the manner of leadership is relaxed and informal as contrasted with liturgical leadership that is more measured and formal. This informality informs how presiders handle their bodies (including their clothing) as well as their speech.

Experiments in a Praise & Worship-Located Eucharist

With this portrayal of Praise & Worship in mind, let us consider some possibilities for the Lord's Supper. The examples below, with one exception, have all been tried and have worked. They have all centered on incorporating additional dynamics into a significant prayer of praise and thanksgiving so that this praying felt at home within the Pentecostal ethos of Praise & Worship.

The first has involved fusing commemorative prayer of praise with congregational singing. This experiment has been done with two different songs: Sinach's 'Way Maker' and Judith McAllister's 'O Give Thanks Unto the Lord'.[33] The first was chosen because of its strong affirmation of divine activity, all offered in anticipation of God's continued activity; the second was chosen because the two root sentiments in its simple lyrics (an exhortation to give thanks because God

---

[33] What songs lend themselves easily to Eucharistic use in this fashion? These two examples suggest several useful criteria: 1) familiarity by the congregation; 2) ease of singing, including simple, repetitive lyrics; 3) a joyful tone appropriate for thanksgiving and praise; 4) reinforcement of the main liturgical activity taking place (thanksgiving and praise especially); and 5) strong commemorative content that likewise is in harmony with the various dimensions of prayer constructed using the trio of triads (E.g. 'Way Maker's recurring confession that the Lord is here and is moving harmonizes well with the eucharistic prayer's emphasis on God's activity and even the implicit sense that the Supper is an opportunity to benefit from Christ's presence in the Supper. Even the mystery of the Supper is heightened by the song's bridge that confesses how God is always active even when we do not see or feel it).

is worthy) are intrinsic in classic eucharistic prayers. In this first approach, a worship leader begins to lead the congregation in singing the song. After a few minutes, when the congregation is fully engaged in the song, the presider starts to pray extemporaneously over the top of the song, shifting and shaping the content of the prayer to interact simultaneously with the song's content and affect.

To shape the spoken prayer further, the presider relies upon an internalization of a trio of triads often found in eucharistic prayers, ancient and modern: the first is Trinitarian (God the Father, Jesus Christ, and the Holy Spirit); the second deals with types of prayer (thanksgiving and praise, offering, and petitioning); and the third is temporal (past, present, and future). Each triad provides guidance and direction to the prayer. For example, the Trinitarian triad helps the presider to remember to direct the prayer to God the Father, remembering God's mighty acts first in creation and with Israel and then culminating in the life and ministry of Jesus Christ, especially as manifested in his death and resurrection and as evidenced in his institution at the Last Supper. After this commemoration, then prayer will move on to reference the Holy Spirit.

This Trinitarian triad is not totally independent from the second triad dealing with types of prayer. Following the general flow of classic and modern eucharistic prayers, the presider begins by offering up thanksgiving and praise, especially as directed to God the Father. Commemoration of Jesus Christ then leads to a prayer of offering in which the presider utters a statement of the congregation's willingness to offer a sacrifice of praise and thanksgiving as well as themselves as living sacrifices. After that, the presider then petitions God for a fresh outpouring of the Holy Spirit.

The third triad is likewise related to the other two in that the initial praise and thanksgiving tends to be oriented toward remembering God's past mighty acts; the prayer of offering is linked to Christ's present priestly ministry as well as to that congregation's willingness to offer themselves to God; and the petitioning for the Holy Spirit naturally flows into contemplation of our future with God, especially as it relates to the return of Christ, the consummation of God's redeeming purposes, and the propriety of an unending doxology before God.

In my experiments with this fusion of song and prayer, the experience has been most powerful if the presider and worship leader can be attentive to each other as well as the possible move of the Spirit in the moment. In that way, the presider can pick up on phrases and words from the song lyrics to be integrated into the content of the prayer as well as shift the affective dynamics and rhythm of the prayer to match what is happening in the song at that moment. Similarly, the attentive worship leader can choose to circle back to parts of the song that reinforce what is being prayed by the presider as well as adjust volume and intensity of the song or, sometimes, choose to back off entirely on singing, allowing only the instruments to continue.

To be able to do this type of Eucharistic president, the formation of the presider is critical in terms of a deep internalization of the trio of triads – perhaps best achieved by long private devotional use of written eucharistic prayers, ancient and modern, as well as commemoration-based prayers from the Bible. The presider's familiarity with the specific song as well as the normal manner of leading by that worship leader is also useful. Similarly, it is very helpful if the worship leader has some familiarity with the models of Eucharistic prayers that have shaped the presider as well as having a clear ability to recognize progress through the trio of triads. This team's formation and preparation is what facilitates a good dynamic and flow in this approach.

There is a variation of this approach that I would love to explore but have not yet had the chance to do so. It would be to work with a songwriter who could craft a song specifically to serve as the musical underlay for eucharistic praying. Specifically, I envision a song whose verses provide the commemoration-based praising that is foundational to eucharistic prayers, whose chorus achieves the offering function of classic prayers, and whose bridge petitions God for a fresh outpouring of the Holy Spirit. Perhaps a creative songwriter could adjust the content of the verses across the year so that the commemoration is season-specific (e.g. the prayer used around Easter would highlight God's work in the resurrection of Christ) in a way that is similar to how the proper prefaces in written eucharistic prayers tease out time-appropriate aspects to remember why we are praising God on this occasion.

Another experiment has been less dependent upon the music of Praise & Worship and more reliant upon the Pentecostal propensity for simultaneous group praying by all members of the worshiping assembly. Drawing specific inspiration from the Korean practice of *tongsung kido* (simultaneous, out-loud congregational praying), I have prepared worshiping congregations ahead of time by asking them to spend a few days considering every reason they could think of to praise God from the OT and likewise for every reason they could think of as it relates to the life and ministry of Jesus Christ. If the assembly is not familiar with simultaneous out loud praying, I have first rehearsed them in doing so until they become more comfortable with how this manner of prayer will sound and feel. In the actual administration of the ordinance, the presider asks the congregation to listen for a predetermined phrase (e.g. something like 'as we lift our voices in one accord') that will trigger their own simultaneous, out loud praising in the middle of my overarching Communion prayer.[34] The first of these triggers the presider utilizes at the point where written eucharistic prayers have the formula that would introduce the Sanctus (i.e. Holy, Holy, Holy Lord, etc.). The congregation have been instructed to lift up all their OT-based praises at this point. Similarly, later in the prayer at the point where written versions would have a formula to set up the Acclamation of Faith (e.g. Christ has died, Christ is risen, Christ will come again), the presider uses the same phrase to trigger the congregation's Jesus-related praises. In both instances, presiders can join in this simultaneous praying as they feel led. Presiders should allow this congregational praising to proceed until it naturally fades before resuming with the overarching prayer. An attentive presider will be listening to the congregational praising in order to draw content once the simultaneous praying has faded, especially in finding appropriate words to transition out of the time of simultaneous praying.

This attentiveness to the praises of the assembly is the seedbed for my third experiment in Praise and Worship-related eucharistic praying. This third approach is the least intense of the three models. It involves listening to the congregation in order to hear how the goodness and activity of God is stirring their hearts. This listening occurs prior to praying at the Lord's Table. This listening can be very intentional, i.e. asking worshipers why it is that God ought to be thanked and praised, perhaps with reference both to the OT and to Jesus Christ, or it can be very subtly done by overhearing content early in a worship service, whether in song lyrics, spoken prayers,

---

[34] I use the same trio of triads to pray extemporaneously an eucharistic prayer.

testimonies, etc. This attentiveness to the congregation's voice provides the raw content that the presider can draw from in order to praise – whether extemporaneously or by writing notes ahead of time – at the Table. If the gathering of material has been done intentionally by having queried worshipers, I have found it raises congregational investment in the eucharistic prayer if worshipers have been informed that the presider will use information they themselves have provided. That would be especially crucial where the presider has chosen to write out the prayer or use written notes during the administration (given the propensity away from written liturgical texts in Pentecostal Praise & Worship).

Conclusion

The classic approach toward the sacrament requires a sort of playful imagination in order to perceive rightly the wonders of God's grace to be found in the simplest of foods shared among the simplest of people. Indeed, Augustine once used this tension itself to provide a definition for a sacrament, saying, 'These things are called sacraments because in them one thing is seen while another is perceived'.[35]

Thankfully, contemporary forms of Pentecostal worship are able to achieve such degrees of serious playfulness of perception. Consider the recent description, for instance, of one sociologist's appraisal of the heightened capacities of worshipers in the services he observed:

> It is possible to discern both a horizontal and vertical dimension … Individuals engage in peak experiences of self-transcendence, which has the effect of lifting them into ecstasy, literally a 'standing outside oneself'. Historically this has been linked with the spiritual realm … At the same time, people experience less self-consciousness and inhibition while engaging with the peak experience. Participants experience a more profound sense of unity where social boundaries regarding touching and personal space are lowered, becoming fuzzy and indistinct. In the same movement, participants are lifted up from within their own experience

---

[35] Augustine, Sermon 272. See J.P. Migne, *Patrologia Latina*, 38.1247: '… ideo dicuntur sacramenta, quia in eis aliud videtur, aliud intelligitur'.

of self and joined to others present. This joining with other people represents the horizontal dimension of the realm.[36]

These sorts of heightened, playful spiritual perceptions – both in discerning God's presence and activity and in a strengthened sense of unity as the Body of Christ – are what many Pentecostal theologians are hoping for as they advocate for a more central role for the Eucharist in their worship.[37] However, this sociologist was not speaking about bread and wine shared in Christian community but about the effects of contemporary worship music.[38] God's presence, divine activity, and a strong sense of unity among worshipers, these are what decades of participating in Praise & Worship have formed Pentecostal worshipers to perceive in congregational worship.

And so, why not find ways to utilize the common, ecstatic, and often music-driven practices of Pentecostal Praise & Worship to bring the Eucharist into a more central place in Pentecostal worship? My goal in this chapter has been merely to describe how my liturgical experiments, limited though they might be, suggest that praising in ways that worshipers are used to praising creates a natural liturgical home in which these worshipers can perceive the rich and abundant mercies from God that are to be found at the Lord's Supper. The Lord's Table groans under the weight of God's grace. Let us do what we can to enable worshipers to feel that weight.

---

[36] Mark Jennings, *Exaltation: Ecstatic Experience in Pentecostalism and Popular Music* (Bern: Peter Lang, 2014), p. 206.

[37] See, for example, Chan, *Liturgical Theology*, pp. 68, 70; Green, *Toward a Pentecostal Theology*, pp. 35, 317 n. 362; Stephenson, *Types of Pentecostal Theology*, p. 122; Macchia, *The Spirit-Baptized Church*, p. 198.

[38] Compare the similar affirmations of Pentecostal liturgical theologians Chris E.W. Green and Steven Félix-Jäger. For Green, see 'Thus Sings the Lord', esp. pp. 10-12, 15-16. For Félix-Jäger, see 'We Feel Fire When It's Hot: Affect and Manipulation in Worship', Chapter 3 in Chris E.W. Green and Steven Félix-Jäger (eds.), *The Spirit and the Song: Pneumatological Reflections on Popular Music* (Lanham: Lexington Books/Fortress Academic, 2024), esp. pp. 43-44, and *Renewal Worship: A Theology of Pentecostal Doxology* (Downers Grove, IL: IVP Academic, 2022). For a more thorough study, see Emily Snider Andrews, 'Exploring Evangelical Sacramentality: Modern Worship Music and the Possibility of Divine-Human Encounter' (PhD diss, Fuller Theological Seminary, 2019).

4

MORE THAN A VEHICLE INTO GOD'S PRESENCE: EXPANDING JOHN WIMBER'S LITURGICAL THEOLOGY OF SPIRIT & SONG

JEREMY PERIGO*

Introduction

Worship is more than a song. It includes preaching, prayer, silence, artistic expression, and Soli Deo Gloria, a whole life response to God, the ultimate source of all good gifts. Worship is also a theological field of study. Liturgical theology, the traditional name for the study of Christian worship, seeks to understand Christians' beliefs and unique worship practices as they encounter God and express their faith. Liturgical theology is novel within the Renewal tradition.[1]

---

* Jeremy Perigo (Doctor of Worship Studies, Robert E. Webber Institute for Worship Studies) is Co-director of Children's Worship Initiative and Professor of Theology and Worship Arts at Dordt University, Sioux Center, Iowa.
[1] There are several recent works on Pentecostal and Charismatic liturgical theology contributing to studies in Renewal theology. See Monte Lee Rice, *Pentecostal Liturgical Theology: On the Altar, Willed to Pentecost* (New York: Bloomsbury, 2025); Steven Félix-Jäger, *Renewal Worship: A Theology of Pentecostal Doxology* (Downers Grove: IVP Academic, 2022); and Simon Chan, *Liturgical Theology: The Church as Worshiping Community* (Downers Grove: IVP, 2006). Numerous scholars outside of the Renewal tradition have assessed their worship theology and practices. See, for example, John Witvliet, 'At Play in the House of the Lord: Why Worship Matters', *Books & Culture* 4.6 (1998), pp. 20-25, and Monique M. Ingalls, 'Introduction: Interconnection, Interface, and Identification in Pentecostal-Charismatic Music and

While this stream of Christianity is gradually contributing to this critical field of study, the impact of their worship theology and practices is expansive. As churches around the globe adopt the music of Pentecostals and Charismatics, communities from diverse theological traditions are receiving more than the songs from Pentecostals. They are receiving their liturgical theologies. Brad Christerson and Richard Flory define the unique connections of robust noncentralized, non-denominational church networks as 'Independent Network Charismatic' Christianity or 'INC Christianity', which in their view 'could reshape the global religious landscape for years to come'. [2] Charismatic beliefs and practices are shared through global relational networks, online media, and conferences. Linked not by formal organization structures, 'INC Christianity is … simply a collection of strong leaders who know each other and combine and recombine for specific projects, but who are functionally independent of one another'. [3] The supporters of these movements 'define their faith more by their practices and allegiance to an individual leader than by their connection with a congregation, denomination, or tradition'. [4] Through these networks, Charismatic ecclesial practices such as experiential worship music, intercessory prayer, prophecy, healing, and deliverance are exported and experienced globally. Additionally, their theology and practice of worship are exported globally. Describing the spread of this worship music, Monique Ingalls states, 'Moving along pathways formed by mass mediation, migration, and missionization, Pentecostal music and worship evidence and spur on religious globalization, as songs from influential Pentecostal churches – and the record companies and media industry to which they are often intimately connected – make their way into churches across denominational lines'. [5] Christerson and Flory see John Wimber and the Vineyard as one of the roots of this new phenomenon. [6]

Worship', in Monique M. Ingalls and Amos Yong (eds.), *The Spirit of Praise: Music and Worship in Global Pentecostal Charismatic Christianity* (University Park: The Pennsylvania State University Press, 2015).

[2] Brad Christerson and Richard Flory, *The Rise of Network Christianity* (Oxford: Oxford Press, 2017), pp. 1-12.

[3] Christerson and Flory, *The Rise of Network Christianity*, p. 11.

[4] Christerson and Flory, *The Rise of Network Christianity*, p. 11.

[5] Ingalls, 'Introduction: Interconnection, Interface, and Identification in Pentecostal-Charismatic Music and Worship', p. 1.

[6] Christerson and Flory, *The Rise of Network Christianity*, pp. 18-26.

John Wimber and the Vineyard movement uniquely distributed their locally developed worship resources worldwide. About Wimber, Vineyard Historian Bill Jackson writes, 'in one setting he was the pastor of a large church (VCF Anaheim), in another the leader of a growing denomination (AVC), in yet another the president of a music company (VMG), and yet again spokesman for renewal around the world (VMI)'.[7] In the 1980s and 1990s, thousands of people personally experienced Wimber's teaching on worship and modeling worship practices. Through teaching videos and worship music cassettes, this ministry grew and impacted the global church, where today, even independent Bible churches in Muslim majority contexts still sing the early Vineyard worship songs.[8]

The Vineyard Music Group was one of the early distributors of Christian worship music. Along with their songs, their liturgical theology of sung worship, where worship songs are seen as vehicles to experience God's presence, was also exported. This movement's connection of worship music and the work of the Holy Spirit was not new; Lester Ruth and Lim Swee Hong trace the roots of a theology of praise and presence to the mid-twentieth century through Canadian Pentecostal Reg Layzell's use of Ps. 22.3 highlighting that God is enthroned in the praises of his people. Here, worship music becomes the key corporate act of invoking and experiencing God's presence.[9] Reflecting on the impact of this worship theology, Maranatha! Music producer, Chuck Fromm, stated, '… in the early church the presence of God was found in the Eucharist, the Reformers shifted it to the Word, and this generation finds it in music'.[10]

Though innovative, the link to God's presence and praise exists outside of the Pentecostal Charismatic movement, even the Roman Catholic Constitution on Sacred Liturgy states that Jesus is 'present

---

[7] Bill Jackson, *The Quest for the Radical Middle* (Cape Town, South Africa: Vineyard International Publishing, 1999), p. 362.

[8] See Jeremy Perigo, 'Beyond Translated vs. Indigenous: Turkish Protestant Christian Hymnody as Global and Local Identity', *Religions* 12.11 (2021), p. 905.

[9] Swee Hong Lim and Lester Ruth, *Lovin' on Jesus: A Concise History of Contemporary Worship* (Nashville: Abingdon Press, 2017), pp. 121-39.

[10] As cited in Robert Webber, 'Where are We Going?', *Worship Leader* (2002), p. 12. Wimber served as a Marantha! Board member and consultant along with pastors Calvary Chapel Yorba Linda before leading the Vineyard movement.

… when the Church prays and sing'.[11] In the fourth century, Church Fathers responding against the orgiastic pagan worship services banned instruments for their congregations, yet still highlighted the Spirit's activity in congregational song stating, 'Demons congregate where there are licentious chants, but where there are spiritual ones, there the grace of the Spirit descends'.[12] The point of this chapter is not to research the role of the Holy Spirit and worship music throughout church history; instead, our task is to assess and expand the theology of this movement.[13] Recognizing Wimber and the Vineyards' liturgical impact, we will first consider Wimber's worship theology, considering the history, theology, service structure, and song lyrics with particular analysis on their connection between worship song and the coming of the Holy Spirit. Wimber's theology of Spirit and worship song has been a foundational understanding of corporate Christian worship for many worship leaders.[14] With sympathetic nuance and discernment, this specific view of worship as a vehicle into God's presence will be assessed and expanded within a larger biblical theology of the Holy Spirit in worship. This study aims to help scholars in the Renewal tradition and theologically minded worship leaders increase their theological discernment as they adopt and adapt theologies and practices from leaders, churches, and movements around the world.

---

[11] Second Vatican Council, *Sacrosanctum Concilium: Constitution on the Sacred Liturgy*, promulgated December 4, 1963, accessed April 26, 2025, https://www.vatican.va/archive/hist_councils/ii_vatican_council/documents/vat-ii_const_19631204_sacrosanctum-concilium_en.html.

[12] Quote attributed to St. John Chrysostom as cited in Calvin Stapert, *A New Song for an Old World: Musical Though in the Early Church* (Grand Rapids: Eerdmans, 2007), p. 109.

[13] For more expansive analysis on a theology of sung worship and historical discussions on Charismatic worship, see Mark Cartledge and A.J. Swoboda (eds.), *Scripting Pentecost* (London: Routledge, 2017).

[14] Personally, I have been impacted by Wimber's desire for a 'middle way' between knowledge and experience of God. Also, I nearly served in pastoral roles in a few different Vineyard churches. My stance is a sympathetic outsider arguing for a constructive and critical approach to this influential practical theology of worship. For discussions on stance in practical theology, see Mark J. Cartledge, 'Can Theology Be "Practical"?: Part II: A Reflection on Renewal Methodology and the Practice of Research', *Journal of Contemporary Ministry* 3.29 (2017). Available online: https://www.journalofcontemporaryministry.com/index.php/jcm/article/view/98/88 (accessed on 19 November 2024).

John Wimber & the Vineyard

As a young boy, John Wimber listened to the music of African American artists played on the jazz station even though his grandpa disapproved. When he was six or seven, he wanted a saxophone, and his mother saved her money to buy it for him and have private lessons.[15] Wimber learned to play over twenty different instruments. In 1953, he won first prize at the Lighthouse International Jazz Festival. By 1962, he managed and arranged music for a successful rock group, the Righteous Brothers, in Las Vegas.[16] In the early 1960's the Righteous Brothers had two top ten albums under Wimber's direction.[17] Musically, Wimber was 'a hit', but his marriage and family life were 'a flop'.[18] In a place of depression and desperation, John and his wife Carol cried out for God and supernaturally experienced his touch, and were converted to Christ.

Over the next decade, John received a degree in biblical studies from Azusa Pacific University and joined the Yorba Linda Friends Church staff as co-pastor with an emphasis on evangelism.[19] The Friends Church, a branch of the Quaker tradition, rooted Wimber in contemplative liturgical spirituality that emphasized individuals waiting on the promptings of the Holy Spirit in the lives of worshipers. Amid quiet contemplation, Quakers believed that the Spirit would move in the hearts and minds of individual worshippers to help prompt the overall flow of worship and inspire particular acts of worship. Even today, some Quaker services, usually called meetings, have near spontaneous corporate worship that begins in silent waiting for divine promptings that lead to specific public acts of worship such as a prayer, song, testimony, or short sermon.

In 1974, based on the invitation of C. Peter Wagner, Wimber joined the Charles E. Fuller Institute of Evangelism and Church Growth. While consulting for Fuller, Wimber came into contact with

---

[15] Carol Wimber, *John Wimber: The Way it Was* (London: Hodder & Stoughton, 1999), p. 16.

[16] Bill Jackson, *The Quest for the Radical Middle* (Cape Town, South Africa: Vineyard International Publishing, 1999), p. 45.

[17] Wimber, John Wimber, p. 16, and Jackson, *The Quest for the Radical Middle*, p. 45.

[18] Wimber, *John Wimber*, p. 16.

[19] John Wimber, *Power Healing* (San Francisco: Harper San Francisco, 1991), p. 23.

Charles Kraft, Russell Spittler, and many foreign missionaries, who all helped John to become more sympathetic with the idea of the Holy Spirit and the possibility of the miraculous. In addition, while working with Fuller, Wimber's pneumatology and theology of healing were influenced by George Ladd. Bill Jackson states, 'Ladd's understanding of the kingdom of God gave Wimber the theological ground he needed to explain the combination of evangelism and the miraculous that he was hearing from the missionaries at Fuller'.[20] Relying heavily on Ladd, Wimber adhered to a confrontation model of healing where the kingdom of God directly challenges the kingdom of Satan.[21] Wimber believed that Jesus inaugurated the rule of God by destroying the devil's work through signs and wonders. This same power was given to the disciples through the outpouring of the Holy Spirit at Pentecost and, according to Wimber, is available to all Christians who desire it. With this power from on high, believers can wage war against Satan, proclaiming the kingdom of God through signs and wonders or *power encounters*.[22] The theology of the kingdom of God, combined with Wimber's background as a musician and producer, paved the way for him to influence global Christian worship music, marrying the work of the Holy Spirit with musical worship.[23]

In 1978, Wimber received a vision from the Lord about a fresh wave of worship coming to the world. Jackson writes, 'In the vision John saw many garage bands made up of amateur musicians. God would sovereignly use rock 'n roll, John was told, and he was going to raise up garage band musicians to touch the heart of the generation that had cut its teeth on rock music'.[24] After two successful pastoral positions, Wimber began to lead a small fellowship of churches called the Vineyard.[25] As the leader of this network, John's mission to the rock 'n roll culture that he had been immersed in all of his life

---

[20] Jackson, *The Quest for the Radical Middle*, p. 54.

[21] Ronald A.N. Kydd, 'Healing in the Christian Church', in Stanley M. Burgess and Eduard M. Van Der Maas (eds.), *The New International Dictionary of Pentecostal and Charismatic Movements* (Grand Rapids, MI: Zondervan, 2002), p. 699.

[22] Wimber defines *power encounters* as 'the clashing of the kingdom of God with the kingdom of Satan'. John Wimber, *Power Evangelism* (San Francisco: Harper & Row, 1986), p. 16.

[23] Jackson states, 'Besides healing, worship has been the biggest contribution the Vineyard has made to the church'. Jackson, *The Quest for the Radical Middle*, p. 131.

[24] Jackson, *The Quest for the Radical Middle*, pp. 131-32.

[25] Jackson, *The Quest for the Radical Middle*, pp. 86-87.

began solidifying. He desired to create worship services that were contextualized to the emerging culture. Wimber began leading music-driven worship services that were, as Jackson describes, a 'casual, non-hyped, non-religious atmosphere'.[26]

In the 1980's emerging from Wimber's vision and his experience in popular music, a new style of worship with laid back, free-flowing, Spirit-led, soft rock music began to be distributed globally through the Vineyard Music Group, a non-profit arm of Vineyard Ministries International.[27] New worship songs emerging from the growing Association of Vineyard Churches were published on Mercy Publications. These worship songs were accessible for rock musicians of all levels to play, with lyrics focused on intimacy with God experienced in anthropomorphic terms (i.e. feeling, seeing, hearing, touching, holding, and kissing God).[28] Wimber and the Vineyard were contextual to their surrounding culture, both in the lyrical content and musical style of congregational song. Robb Redman states, 'Because of his (Wimber's) musicianship, contemporary worship music was a leading feature of the new church, and before long the church attracted several songwriters and many musicians'.[29] The Vineyard continues to write and distribute worship songs across the globe.

Liturgical Theology of Wimber & the Early Vineyard

As we will see, Wimber and the Vineyard shared more than their songs with other churches around the globe. Through their teachings, free-flowing structure of musical worship, and intimate, individualistic, experiential songs, this movement contributed a liturgical theology emphasizing a personal experience of the Holy Spirit in corporate worship through music and congregational singing.[30] Describing the liturgical theology, Mark Stibbe writes, 'The key feature of

---

[26] Jackson, *The Quest for the Radical Middle*, p. 107.

[27] Robb Redman, *The Great Worship Awakening: Sing a New Song in the Postmodern Church* (San Francisco: Jossey-Bass, 2002), p. 56.

[28] Redman, *The Great Worship Awakening*, p. 35, and Wimber, *John Wimber*, p. 33.

[29] Redman, *The Great Worship Awakening*, p. 56.

[30] Though the term 'worship' as a vehicle into God's presence exists elsewhere, Jordan Stone uses it to characterize Vineyard's unique link between Spirit, worship, and song. See Jordan Stone, *Lots of Love with a Little Cross: The Spirituality of Vineyard Music* (Research Chapter, The Southern Baptist Theological Seminary, 2015), p. 13.

Vineyard worship music is the notion of intimacy with a God of love'.[31] Throughout his ministry, Wimber continually attempted to define worship by preaching and teaching continuously. Rather than summarizing Wimber's view, we will prioritize his own words as a key source for exploring his theology of worship. Often, Wimber highlighted the relational dynamic in worship, stating, 'That's what worship is, loving God'.[32] In a conference in 1984, he worked to expand worship beyond a song to highlight the link between Word and the Spirit and the idea of whole-life worship, teaching,

> Worshipping God is our highest value. It is an end, not a means. We want to give God that which is due to him as we are led by the Word and the Spirit. We want to worship with our whole beings through the culture-current music God has given us. We also worship him by sacrificing our time, energy, and resources.[33]

In Wimber's words, the role of Scripture and the Spirit is vital, but the way or the vehicle for worship is primarily musical. When Wimber works to define worship in a teaching titled 'Why do we worship?' he states,

> … I make no apologies in the Vineyard … that our number one priority is worship. And by that I do not mean just the activity of singing the lovely songs that God has given us to sing, which do express our heart and are an index of our commitment to Christ, but starts with the expression of love to God in worship.[34]

What initially seems to be a distinction between worship as larger expression of love to God is clarified as he begins to share with visitors about the initial thirty minutes of singing in Vineyard service stating, 'What we're doing is, by the songs that we sing, trying to express in contemporary idioms and in intimate language, the love that we feel for God. And we believe that, as we do so, that God is touched by that, and that he will respond and confer on us his presence because of that love-making that goes on with the expressing

[31] John Gustone (ed.), *Meeting John Wimber* (Crowborough: Monarch, 1996), p. 97.

[32] John Wimber's sermon 'Why do we worship?', as cited in Andy Park, Lester Ruth, and Cindy Rethmeier, *Worshipping with the Anaheim Vineyard: The Emergence of Contemporary Worship* (Grand Rapids, MI: Eerdmans: 2017), p. 91.

[33] As cited in Jackson, *The Quest for the Radical Middle*, p. 105.

[34] Wimber, 'Why do we worship?', p. 104.

of our intimate care for God'.[35] Corporate worship provokes an intimate encounter with God, where God's presence responds to expressive congregational singing. Aware of the need for a whole-life response of worship, Wimber continues:

> … what we do in that half hour oughta characterize our whole week. We should constantly be singing these songs, constantly reviewing our care and our love for God. And in every transaction, and in every exchange, whether it is the water cooler or finding a parking spot, we need to learn how to honor our God in the way we defer to and care for people. You got it? And that's Christianity.[36]

Wimber stressed that worship cannot be reduced simply to singing in church. Still, these comments do not mean he is highlighting other liturgical actions or arguing for a whole-life, Soli Deo Gloria view of worship. Instead, he often enhances his musical theology to emphasize the relational aspects of singing between an individual worshiper and the Triune God. In another teaching entitled 'The Essence of Worship', Wimber preaches, 'So when we worship, we're not just singing songs. We're entering into the Holy of Holies and ministering unto the Lord and he unto us. So we worship God on the grounds of that shed blood of Jesus.'[37] The grounds of worship are Christological, but the vehicle for accessing the divine is clearly musical worship. When Wimber often stresses that worship is about a lifestyle or a relational dynamic, his illustrations turn toward musical worship. Though constantly trying to balance the trajectory, Vineyard worship became synonymous with music, and one of the preeminent ways to experience God's presence is via musical worship. A reductionist view of this theology is that worship equals music, which produces an encounter with the Holy Spirit.

---

[35] Wimber, 'Why do we worship?', p. 104.

[36] Wimber, 'Why do we worship?', p. 104.

[37] John Wimber's sermon 'Essence of Worship', as cited in Andy Park, Lester Ruth, and Cindy Rethmeier, *Worshipping with the Anaheim Vineyard: The Emergence of Contemporary Worship* (Grand Rapid, MI: Eerdmans: 2017), pp. 107-108. In the editors' summary analysis of this sermon, they state, 'The word "worship" is so strongly connected to singing that the words are almost synonyms'.

Liturgical Shape

Though Charismatics and Pentecostals seldom emphasize the theological implications of the specific order of worship, what other traditions call the liturgical shape or ordo, Wimber and the early Vineyard worship leaders taught and wrote extensively on creating a biblical structure of worship. In many Pentecostal congregations, this liturgical shape is often called the song list, service order, or even this Sunday's 'flow'. Vineyard songwriter and worship leader Eddie Espinosa and Wimber utilized Psalm 95 to undergird biblical support for creating five phases of worship for their church. The entire musical set is designed to lead the congregation into an intimate experience with God's presence in this liturgical structure. This process is broken down into the following phases of worship connected with particular verses of Ps. 95: (1) invitation (v. 1), (2) engagement (v. 2), (3) exaltation (vv.3-5), (4) adoration (v. 6), and (5) intimacy (v. 7).[38] Though the entire worship service would also include preaching and ministry time where attendees could receive prayer for healing or make a profession of faith, their discussion on liturgical shape or flow of worship centered on the musical set list. When reflecting on the meaning of this structure, Jackson writes, 'Expression moves to a zenith where God begins to respond to us, to our prayers and to our worship. His visitation is a by-product of worship.'[39] The Holy Spirit comes as they worship through music within a particular liturgical flow. Though continually reminding one another that worship is more than music and worship is a lifestyle, at its core, the Vineyard's liturgical structure reveals a theology that the coming of the Spirit is primarily a response to the intimate, heartfelt worship music. Drawing from the Quaker tradition of a congregation waiting in silence for God to move on an individual, Wimber utilizes intimate worship songs to create space for a congregation to share their love and praise to God as a vehicle to enter into his presence. As they worship, almost exclusively through singing, they expect God to respond. While discussing the characteristics of 'what makes a good worship experience', Wimber

---

[38] Barry Leisch, *The New Worship* (Grand Rapids, MI: Baker Books, 2002), p. 55. These terms had a level of fluidity between Vineyard worship leader, though there are lots of thematic overlap. For example, Bill Jackson utilizes slightly different terms for these phases: 1) call to worship, 2) engagement, 3) expression, 4) visitation, and 5) giving. See Jackson, *The Quest for the Radical Middle*, p. 133.

[39] Jackson, *The Quest for the Radical Middle*, p. 133.

emphasizes that worshippers are 'waiting on God's response', which he defines as 'a move of the Spirit'. [40] In the Vineyard context, this could include a testimony, an exhortation from Scripture, or possibly tongues or prophecy. Waiting on the Spirit and the moves of the Spirit would often be accompanied musically.

In the Vineyard and the churches influenced by their teachings, an encounter with the Spirit where revival manifestations occur and/or the charismatic gifts are unleashed is typical. Most often, these dialogical encounters happened during the first portion of the worship service, usually twenty to forty minutes of musical worship, and after the sermon during a time of additional musical worship that accompanied individual prayer ministry. When describing worship at the Toronto Airport Vineyard Church, Sociologist Margaret Paloma states, '… music facilitates a personal altered state of consciousness that brings many into a heightened sense of mystical unity with God and with other worshipers'.[41] During these extended times of sung worship, the musical sounds, percussive rhythms, and song lyrics catalyze a sense of encounter with the Spirit, and divine presence is believed to be made manifest to the worshipers.[42] The liturgical shape of the movement displays a relational, active God who responds to his people's singing of songs filled with intimate language with God's visitation as a 'by-product' of their worship.

Lyrical Theology

One of the most considerable contributions of the Vineyard is their songs. Churches of all denominations have waved palm branches on Palm Sunday, singing 'Hosanna to the King', and artists as diverse as gospel artist Bishop Marvin Winans and Reformed-leaning worship duo Shane and Shane have recorded arrangements of Vineyard songs like 'Draw Me Close'.[43] Globally, Vineyard music produced translated

---

[40] John Wimber, 'The Theology of Worship', Worship: Program #1-13, Overhead Notes, n.d., Box 2, John Wimber Collection, Special Collections, Regent University, Virginia Beach, VA.

[41] Margaret Poloma, *Main Street Mystics* (Walnut Creek: AltaMira Press, 2003), p. 38.

[42] Poloma, *Main Street Mystics*, pp. 38-41.

[43] Vineyard Music, 'Hosanna to the King', YouTube Video, 3.10, Posted by Vineyard Worship Feb 7, 2025. Https//youtu.be/jcgZPEZrXSQ?si=c8mtwYS

versions of their songs and even entire albums, such as the French *Viens* and the Turkish album, *Sonsuzluklar Boyunca*.[44] These resources fueled the use of Vineyard songs in churches worldwide.

Early Vineyard worship songs are known for their simple yet intimate, vertical lyrics that focus on expressing personal love to God.[45] Carol Wimber, John's wife, stated, 'He wanted simple love songs that were direct to Jesus'.[46] While traditional Protestant hymns typically declare corporate shared theological beliefs about God's character and cosmic salvation, and many Evangelical gospel songs testify of God's goodness to one another, the Vineyard songs are nearly exclusively vertical, singing directly to God. If you have ever been in a worship service where someone from the platform states, 'It's not about you; it's all about Him', there is a good chance the phrase has links to the Vineyard. About Vineyard music, John Leach states, 'The lyrics were unashamedly intimate and loving, and songs were sung to Jesus, and hardly ever simply *about* him. The style of the songs was deliberately simple so that worship in small groups during the week could use the same material without the resources of the full band used on Sundays'.[47]

Utilizing biblical and extra-biblical romantic, anthropomorphic language, many songs emphasize hearing, touch, kissing, and being held by God. For example, drawing from the poetry in the Song of Solomon, Vineyard worship leader and pastor, David Ruis' 'True Love' starts with 'Jesus, I need to know true love', so 'take me into the King's chambers/Cause my love to mature'.[48] The song

---

lOJrZ74ze; Shane & Shane, 'Draw Me Close', YouTube Video, 5.54, Posted by Shane and Shane July 9, 2020, https://youtu.be/dkj4ET3XNyE?si=X5Yj 5K9rUmsGTXkU; and Marvin Winans, 'Draw Me Close/Thy Will Be Done', YouTube Video, 6.26, Posted by Marvin Winans – Topic October 18, 2024, https://youtu.be/dDuKb77Vwgc?si=YvXJrR37djXd0eof.

[44] Vineyard Music, *Viens* (Spotify, 2002), https://open.spotify.com/album/1HsAQDs6HGxefxGAz1Qdge and Vinyeard Music, *Sonsuzluklar boyunca (Canlı)* (Spotify, 2001), https://open.spotify.com/album/6PqfOWdSAntkjr83st2 BDg.

[45] A full lyrical analysis of Vineyard songs is beyond the scope of this project.

[46] Wimber, *John Wimber*, p. 32.

[47] In Gustone (ed.), *Meeting John Wimber*, pp. 152-52.

[48] Vineyard Music Group, '08 True Love', YouTube Video 10.45, Posted by JP January 21, 2015. Carol Wimber states that within the early Vineyard movement there was discussion and critique about lyrical theology mainly emphasizing a personal experience of God. At one point, she shares that John Wimber gave

continues, 'Let me know the kisses of Your mouth/Let me feel your embrace'. Though theologians such John Calvin describe relationship with God through Christ as a 'pledge of … sacred union' and Bernard of Clairvaux discusses a divine kiss within the life of the Triune God,[49] Vineyard worship leaders uniquely utilized soft rock popular music containing expressive and relational lyrics within a liturgical structure that focused on leading to a personal, intimate encounter with God. This combination of music and metaphor within a specific worship space created a transcendent atmosphere that induced an expectation of encounter with divine presence.

Music & the Spirit(s)

In addition to linking music with the Holy Spirit, Wimber often highlighted the link between music and exorcisms from evil spirits (1 Sam. 16.14-23), especially evident in his sermon on 2 Chron. 20.20-26 titled, 'Worship Breaks Down Satanic Strongholds'. In his opening remarks about the story of Jehoshaphat and musical worship, he states, '… it's a very important illustration of this whole business of worship as the first line of offence against Satan'.[50] In his exegesis of the text, Wimber states, 'Worship elicits power from the throne of God. When we worship God, God interacts with us and releases things …'[51] The message climaxes as Wimber applies this principle of worship as warfare to sexual strongholds and other demonic strongholds.[52] He closed the service with the call, 'Do you understand that

---

songwriters Martyn Lloyd-Jones's *The Cross*, so they could study the cross. He asked them to study it and write songs on Jesus and the Cross. Out of this came 'Holy and Anointed One', 'It's Your Blood that Cleanses Me', 'You Gave Your Body', 'At the Cross', 'The Blood of Jesus', and many others. Wimber, p. 171.

[49] John Calvin, *Commentaries on the Prophet Jeremiah and the Lamentations,* vol. 1, (trans. John Owen; Edinburgh: Calvin Translation Society, 1850), p. 160. St. Bernard of Clairvaux states, 'If, as is properly understood, the Father is he who kisses, the Son he who is kissed, then it cannot be wrong to see in the kiss the Holy Spirit, for he is the imperturbable peace of the Father and the Son, their unshakable bond, their undivided love, their indivisible unity. Bernard of Clairvaux, *Sermons on the Song of Songs* (trans. Irene Edmonds; Kalamazoo, MI: Cistercian Publications, 1980), p. 77.

[50] John Wimber, 'Spiritual Warfare Series #11: Worship Breaks Down Satanic Strongholds', Sermon transcript on II Chronicles 20.20-26, 28 March, Box 8, John Wimber Collection, Special Collections, Regent University, Virginia Beach, VA.

[51] Wimber, 'Spiritual Warfare Series #11'.

[52] Wimber, 'Spiritual Warfare Series #11'.

God has told you to worship? Has called you to worship? Has commanded you to worship? Worship is to be the center of your very existence. The center of your very being. And in that context you'll see the blessing of God and you'll see the mighty hand of God as he moves.'[53] In this teaching, Wimber combines the theology of the kingdom with worship music by emphasizing the use of worship music as a strategy for pushing back the enemy and a release of God's mighty hand. Worship through music is a strategy to push back evil spirits and a vehicle to experience the Holy Spirit.

In addition to the teaching, order of worship, and songs, the experience of the Spirit through music was also promoted in the early 1990s through the Vineyard music albums. In album promotional materials, Vineyard stated, 'The songs of praise are certain to bring you closer to God's presence. From dynamic live worship albums to high-quality devotional and inspirational recordings, encounter the glory of God through the beauty of music.'[54] Even the Vineyard album advertisements reflected a theology where the Holy Spirit comes and empowers his people as a response to worship music. This view parallels several biblical accounts of OT prophets of YHWH 10.5-12; 1 Kgs 3.15; 1 Chron. 25.1; 2 Chron. 20.14-18) passages, which are often discussed in Charismatic settings.

Wimber provides a unique contribution, integrating music, worship, and the dynamic work of the Holy Spirit. Wimber expands the role of church music and congregational singing to, at times, become synonymous with worship and synonymous with an encounter with the Holy Spirit. In a Vineyard-influenced Anglican church outside of London, worship leader Matt Redman and his team felt led to 'strip it all back' to the heart of worship without sound systems, mics, worship leaders, or musicians.[55] They testified to coming back to the heart of worship. As they reflected on the season of bringing more than a song, they wrote a song that was exported around the world. Those

---

[53] Wimber, 'Spiritual Warfare Series #11'.

[54] Vineyard Music Group, 'CDs and Tapes' in accompanying booklet, *The River is Here: Touching the Father's Heart Vol. 20* performed by VCF Anaheim, California and VCF Fulton, Washington, Vineyard Music Group VMD 9184, 1995, compact disc.

[55] The story behind Matt Redman's 'The Heart of Worship' has been shared in numerous books, articles, and videos. See BBC Radio 2, 'Matt Redman talks about writing The Heart of Worship', YouTube Video 5.41, Posted by BBC Radio 2, September 19, 2013, https.//www.youtube.com/watch?v=m83TSHhg-jU.

influenced by Wimber often stress that a song is insufficient and a whole-life, heartfelt response is needed; yet 'when the music fades', the theology and practice of their worship are ultimately known through a song.

Songs, their structure within the service, and the teachings surrounding their meanings are vital in understanding a liturgical theology, particularly in a non-liturgical or 'free church' traditions like Vineyard. Though many Pentecostals and Charismatics rarely utilize the term liturgical theology, it is helpful to begin to understand their unique theological contributions in areas of belief and practices in corporate worship. For Wimber and the Vineyard, the dialogical use of worship music is central to their liturgical theology. God's people sing heartfelt songs directly to God, and he responds by sending his presence. This movement hoped to 'bring more than a song' but instead identified musical worship as a central aspect of corporate ecclesial life and personal encounter with God as a vehicle into his presence.

Expanding Wimber's Liturgical Theology of Song & Spirit

The goal of the above has not been to offer a full liturgical theology or pneumatology but to provide an introductory analysis of Wimber and the Vineyard's unique contribution, uniting song and Spirit for our theological evaluation. In their view, musical worship is a primary vehicle into God's presence and encounter with the dynamic work of the Holy Spirit. The theology and practices associated with this view have been exported via network Christianity across the globe. Given these unique contributions and their global impact, let's turn to place them in broader discussions on worship and the Holy Spirit.

Wimber's theology was not novel. Throughout history, there has been a connection between music and the spirit world. Johannes Quasten states, '… all antiquity was convinced that music had the power of epiclesis'.[56] The combination of melody, harmony, and rhythm in worship rituals has always created an environment that fosters ecstasy and a sense of epiclesis. Even the unique covenantal faith of Israel contains a sense that God comes in a special way through

---

[56] As cited in Stapert, *A New Song for an Old World*, p. 18.

sung praises (Ps. 22.3). In addition to the epiclesis in music, there has been a consistent belief that music is a vehicle to transport the human spirit toward the divine, bringing spiritual and physical relief. In religious rituals, music is often used to invoke divine presence, carry the human spirit towards the divine, and fight off evil spirits.[57]

In the OT, the prophets of YHWH, who often were musicians, were known to 1) receive the Spirit and sing forth divine prophecy (1 Chron. 25.1; 2 Chron. 20.14-18), 2), to play prophetic music invoking the Spirit of YHWH to possess others (1 Sam. 10.5-12), and 3) to use music to aid in prophetic inspiration (1 Kgs 3.15). Therefore, in the OT, 1) the Spirit comes upon people as a response to music (music as invocation of the Spirit), and 2) when the Spirit comes upon musicians they respond by prophesying with song (Spirit-inspired music). In these passages, music is never seen as a way to manipulate God, as in other religious traditions. Still, the coming of the Spirit is a voluntary response to the musical invocation. Additionally, a connection between music and the supernatural is observed through using music in exorcisms from evil spirits (1 Sam. 16.14-23). Though the NT has less emphasis on music and the Spirit,[58] as the Spirit is poured out on the gathered church, inspired praise erupts (Acts 2.11), and congregations and possibly even soloists within the congregations sing *spiritual songs* and *charismatic hymns*, under the direct influence of the Holy Spirit.[59] Though Wimber's view of Spirit and song resonates with several key portions of Scripture, engaging and encountering the activity of the Spirit in worship is so much more than a song. A broader engagement with Scripture is needed to expand Wimber's theology of worship and the role of the Holy Spirit.[60]

---

[57] In Greek mythology, Orpheus is able to tame the creatures of the underworld by playing the lyre. See Andrew Wilson-Dickson, *The Story of Christian Music: From Gregorian Chant to Black Gospel* (Minneapolis, MN: Augsburg Fortress, 1992), p. 9.

[58] This is due to quite a bit of skepticism in the early church over the use of instrumentals in music due to the orgiastic, ecstatic nature of music from the Greek and Eastern religions. See Stapert, *A New Song for an Old World*, pp. 134-35.

[59] James Dunn, *Jesus and the Spirit* (Philadelphia, PA: Westminster, 1975), p. 238. See also Wilson-Dickson, *The Story of Christian Music*, p. 23, and Gordon Fee, *God's Empowering Presence* (Peabody: Hendrickson, 1994), pp. 885-86.

[60] Broader theological and historical engagement is also needed but beyond the scope of this initial research. As leaders from the Pentecostal and Charismatic movement stress Scripture as the crucial and, often, only source for determining the theology and practices of their communities, our theological engagement will prioritize biblical theology.

All Christian Worship is in the Spirit

Churches and worship leaders who mainly see that worship equals music, which brings the Holy Spirit, are myopic, needing a wider view of the Holy Spirit and worship. Instead of a reductionist view of worship that mainly emphasizes the connection between songs and God's presence, the role of the Holy Spirit in worship in the NT is a more expansive vision. In one of the most important NT passages on worship, the question of worship and divine presence is brought to Jesus by a Samaritan woman in John 4.[61] Jesus challenges the woman's question by speaking of a coming eschatological hour which through his death and resurrection initiates the new age of the kingdom of God. In this age, the worship of the Father is no longer tied to a specific place of divine presence but is 'in spirit and in truth' (Jn 4.23-24).[62] Therefore, the worship that God is seeking is centered on Jesus' redemptive truth and made possible by the power of the Spirit. The outpouring of the Spirit on the church in Jerusalem and elsewhere extends this new worship to anywhere and everywhere the Spirit is present and the redemptive truth of Christ's work is proclaimed. Therefore, worship in the New Covenant is the Spirit-empowered response of God's people to the redemptive truth of Christ. In other words, all Christian worship is in the Spirit. The worship equation is not singing songs to experience God's presence; instead, the invitation is for all Christians to respond to the revelation of God in Christ and be filled with the Holy Spirit and then sing (Eph. 5.18-20). Additionally, beyond a reductionist view of song and the Spirit,

---

[61] Barry Liesch states, 'Many Christians consider the dialogue between Jesus and the woman of Samaria to be the critical passage on worship in the New Testament'. Barry Liesch, *People in the Presence of God* (Grand Rapids, MI: Zondervan, 1988), p. 36.

[62] In this passage, the term *spirit* combined with *truth* does not denote the human soul or understanding but denotes the reality of God. Most scholars believe that the worship in spirit and truth as inaugurated by Jesus relates to the Holy Spirit and the truth revealed by and through Jesus. E.g. Raymond E. Brown, *The Gospel According to John (I-XII)* (The Anchor Bible 29; New York: Doubleday, 1966), p. 180; George Eldon Ladd, *A Theology of the New Testament* (Grand Rapids, MI: Eerdmans, 1974), p. 225. To the contrary, Leon Morris interprets *spirit* to be the human spirit and not the Holy Spirit, and furthermore states, 'The combination 'spirit and truth' points to the need for complete sincerity and complete reality in our approach to God'. Leon Morris, *The Gospel According to John* (The New International Commentary on the New Testament; Grand Rapids, MI: Eerdmans, 1995), p. 239. Morris' interpretation seems to be outside of the context of the passage where in the next verse (v. 24) God's nature is referred to as *spirit*.

worshippers respond to the gift of salvation in Christ by offering their entire life as worship (Rom. 12.1-2). Christians are welcomed to participate in the work of the Spirit within them who brings about adoption, where we cry out in prayer 'Abba, Father' (Rom. 8.15). The Spirit reminds us of that we are loved and nothing can separate us from the love of this Father that is in Christ Jesus (Rom. 8.38-39). Additionally, the Spirit inspires the church's intercession by groaning from within us. Our Spirit-led prayers yearn for the fullness of God's shalom amid the bondage, decay, and brokenness of the whole creation (Rom. 8.26-27). In this more expansive view, worship is a Spirit-led, Christ-mediated response, yes, through singing and prayer, but also in whole-life allegiance to a loving God.

The Temple of the Holy Spirit

The presence of the Holy Spirit is more than a by-product of our singing. Additionally, corporate worship cannot be reduced to God's dwelling in our praise. More than a song, it is the people of God who are filled with the Holy Spirit. The Tabernacle and Temple were the centralized places of engagement with the divine presence and remembrance of the covenant (1 Kgs 8.11; Isaiah 63). Their purpose was to be a place where God would live among his people and where they could meet with him (Exod. 25.8; 29.43). But the post-Resurrection, post-Pentecost people of God found the place of divine presence in the midst of the gathered community. Andrew Hill states, 'After Pentecost and the beginning of the church, God dwells with his people in the new covenant by means of his indwelling Holy Spirit. The Apostle Paul can then write that the believer in Christ is now the temple of God (1 Cor. 3.16-17; 6.19-20)'.[63] The prophetic promise of an eternal and internal covenant and an outpouring of the Spirit had been fulfilled. God had once again become present with his people in the new temple of the Holy Spirit – the individual believer and the unified gathering of believers (1 Cor. 3.16-17; 2 Cor. 6.16; Eph. 2.19-22; 1 Tim. 3.15-16). According to Gordon Fee, 'The church and the individual believer are the new locus of God's own presence with his people; and the Spirit is the way God is now present'.[64] As the Tabernacle and Temple showed Israel and their

---

[63] Andrew Hill, *Enter His Gates: A Biblical Theology of Worship* (Grand Rapids, MI: Baker Books, 1997), p. 162.

[64] Gordon Fee, *God's Empowering Presence* (Peabody, MA: Hendrickson, 1994), p. 874.

neighbors that God was present and active, the gathered church becomes the temple of the Spirit that reminds and reveals God's presence to his people and those outside of the community. The church is distinct from the temples of other gods because the Holy Spirit dwells within them, and since God is present, their lives and worship should be different too. They should be pure, live in unity, and leave their idolatry. Not only does the Spirit dwell in the church as a worshiping community, but God's people are empowered by his Spirit to worship. Worship is not by human rituals but 'by the Spirit' (Phil. 3.1-11). Worship by the Spirit includes the music, arts, sacred festivals, and dramatic reenactments, but also extends beyond these activities, giving the church the power to live a distinct life of worship. The Spirit is now present in the worshiping community, the Temple of the Holy Spirit (1 Cor. 3.16-17; 6.19-20). Therefore, the Holy Spirit is experienced in the worship of local churches yet also empowers and energizes the church in all areas of worship and mission.

Spirit-Directed Corporate Worship & Mission

The NT contains a diversity of worship rituals and activities, including singing, prayer, anointing with oil, foot washing, Communion, instruction, ordination, and preaching, which are all directed and orchestrated by the indwelling Spirit. Some of these acts of spiritual service are similar to other pagan rituals, but the presence of the Holy Spirit distinguishes the church from other religious assemblies. Ralph Martin writes, 'Amid the diversity of forms and practices the presence and power of the Spirit of God are the decisive factors'.[65] Fee states, '… for Paul the gathered church was first of all a worshiping community; and the key to their worship was the presence of the Holy Spirit'.[66] The Spirit is present in a real way, yes, in the singing of the church, but also by bringing both missional and liturgical direction.

In Lukan and Pauline literature, the Spirit's presence and/or filling in the gatherings of the worshipping community brings empowerment and direction for mission. As the gathered church obeys the Spirit's missional direction, the truth of Christ is proclaimed inviting outsiders into the covenant relationship and the promise of the Spirit

---

[65] Ralph Martin, *Worship in the Early Church* (Grand Rapids, MI: Eerdmans, 2001), p. 132.
[66] Fee, *God's Empowering Presence*, p. 884

is poured out on both Jews and Gentiles (Joel 2.28; Acts 2; 8.14-17; 10.44-47; 15.1-29; 1 Thess. 1.5). During worship gatherings, the missional directions come as the Holy Spirit 1) gives boldness for mission (Acts 2.1-4;4.23-31), 2) identifies those who are to be sent on mission (Acts 13.1-3), 3) singles someone out for ministry and leadership (1 Tim. 1.18; 4.14); and 4) empowers disciples with boldness for mission in the face of persecution (Acts 4.23-31). In Luke's accounts, these dramatic encounters with the presence of God send the worshipers out into the world from the place of prayer, filling them with praise and boldness to proclaim the gospel with power.

In the worshiping church, the Holy Spirit dwells and gives missional direction; additionally, he provides specific liturgical direction by manifesting himself through special gifts in his people and directing their spontaneous prayer and praise. According to Hill, 'As Christians yield to the indwelling Holy Spirit, the charismata or gifts of the Spirit are unleashed for the edification of the church, in this case gathered for worship (1 Cor. 14.26)'.[67] For the 1 Corinthians 12 list of spiritual gifts, Fee categorizes them under three headings, *service*, *miracles*, and *inspired utterance*.[68] These gifts are given for the 'common good' (1 Cor. 12.7) but can also have a missiological function to reveal to the outsider that God is present (1 Cor. 14.24-25). Particularly in the Pauline churches, the Spirit not only directs the spontaneous nature of worship through the gifts but also leads in the order and structure of the service (1 Corinthians 12–14).

The Spirit helps direct worship by inspiring prayer and praise. According to Paul, spontaneous prayer and songs can be 'in a tongue' with his spirit (1 Cor. 14.13-17). In fact, in Pauline theology, *tongues* can be Spirit-inspired speech directed to God as prayer or praise. Paul encourages his churches 'to be filled with the Spirit' and to sing as a response to that filling. All of these activities of worship are led by the Spirit but are worthless without love (1 Corinthians 13). For the Pauline churches, liturgical direction by the Spirit with much spontaneity seems normative. Still, the service is always to be done orderly as the church leadership and the gathered worshipers are led by the Spirit (1 Cor. 14.26-40). Whether praying an ancient psalm together, declaring a newly written hymn about Jesus, or singing a spontaneous

---

[67] Hill, *Enter His Gates*, p. 55.
[68] Fee, *God's Empowering Presence*, pp. 866-94.

Spirit-inspired song, all these artistic responses were seen as Spirit-filled and Spirit-led. The presence and activity of the Spirit in worship is more than a song, as the Spirit uniquely distinguishes the community from other religious communities and brings both missional and liturgical direction to the congregation and leaders.

Conclusions

Wimber and the Vineyard prompt the church on the importance of core theological themes such as the kingdom of God, the work of the Spirit in worship, and worship as expressing intimate love to a covenant-making God. Their contributions have been influential and deserve additional study. Their liturgical theology, emphasizing dialogical, embodied, presence-sensitive musical worship, reminds churches around the world of the God present in Christian worship. When Anglicans influenced by the Vineyard pray, 'The Lord is here. His Spirit is with us', they recognize that these are not simply empty words but intimate encounters.[69] For churches who embraced Wimber's theology of worship in a reductionist way, they may be limiting their beliefs and practices of worship, reducing an expansive biblical theology to primarily seeing that music is worship and is the primary vehicle to experience God's presence. For these communities, our engagement with an expanded biblical theology of the Holy Spirit and worship can pave the way towards fresh understandings of the presence and work of the Spirit in the Church.

Our discussion focused on the Spirit, worship, and song. It is important to note that these discussions need to be expanded and discerned, with additional studies on the Vineyard movement and Charismatic liturgical theologies. Related topics such as 1) discerning the dangerous potential of musical idolatry when the work of the Holy Spirit is seen as interwoven with music or 2) analyzing the emphasis on the Spirit's work in spontaneous acts of worship and de-emphasizing the Spirit work in inspiring long-term communal works of worship art (Exod. 31.3-6) are worthy of future theological reflection.

---

[69] Church of England, 'New Patterns for Worship', accessed April 26, 2025, https://www.churchofengland.org/prayer-and-worship/worship-texts-and-resources/common-worship/common-material/new-patterns-17.

Reflecting Christologically on the unique work of Jesus is also essential. In addition to the work of the Spirit, Christ mediates our worship. Wimber also preached, 'it's the blood of Jesus that makes it possible for us to worship God the way we do'.[70] Additional theological reflection is needed on the role of Christ as the true mediator. Songs are a unique way to communicate corporately, express love, proclaim our faith collectively, and be formed by the Spirit. Yet, songs are not the primary vehicle into God's presence. A 'King of endless worth' deserves more than a song. Could we even begin to bring something that was truly of worth? Is there a song or act of worship perfect enough to transport us into his presence? No, it is only through Jesus that we can enter a 'new and living way which He inaugurated for us through the veil' (Heb. 10.19-20). Based on his redemptive work of obedience and empowered by the Holy Spirit, we respond with songs and so much more. Wimber says it best:

> Worship God in everything you do and say. Worship him in all deeds, worship him in all thoughts. In the sanctuary of your inner being. Worship him through the spirit, worship him in your body … with your finances. Worship him with your relationships at home. Worship him on the freeway. Lock, stock, and barrel. No hold barred. Everything you have. All you ever hoped to be lay at his feet.[71]

---

[70] John Wimber's sermon 'Essence of Worship', as cited in Andy Park, Lester Ruth, and Cindy Rethmeier, *Worshipping with the Anaheim Vineyard: The Emergence of Contemporary Worship* (Grand Rapids, MI: Eerdmans: 2017), p. 107.

[71] John Wimber's sermon on 'Loving God', as cited in Andy Park, Lester Ruth, and Cindy Rethmeier, *Worshipping with the Anaheim Vineyard: The Emergence of Contemporary Worship* (Grand Rapids, MI: Eerdmans: 2017), p. 101.

5

PENTECOSTAL DIGITAL DOXOLOGY: EXPLORING HYBRIDITY, LIMINALITY, AND ECCLESIOLOGY

MARK J. CARTLEDGE[*]

Introduction

The development of technology arising from the emergence of the internet has meant that there is now a cultural phenomenon of many, if not most, people with access to digital media 24/7. The smart phone means that we are constantly connected to information and networks of people, including church congregations and their worshipping practices. One of these key worshipping practices is the singing of contemporary worship songs. In Pentecostalism, a three-fold rite has been identified of praise, preaching, and altar ministry. Extended times of sung worship are often regarded as essential to Pentecostal and Charismatic worship culture. Very often the material used in this sung worship is drawn from well-known music brands such as Hillsong, Bethel, Jesus Culture, and Elevation; and the popularity of specific songs can be seen across different cultural and ecclesial contexts.

In this study, I address four main areas. The first is a general description of Pentecostal worship and in particular the role that sung

---

[*] Mark J. Cartledge (PhD, University of Wales) is Principal of the London School of Theology and Professor of Practical Theology.

worship plays within the overall structure of the worship service in the context of Pentecostal spirituality. Second, I discuss the blurring of the public/private distinction in hybrid worship, whereby some people are together in a physical and concrete setting, while others are watching and participating in their own private, domestic, and ancillary space made possible by the internet. Third, I reflect on the role of this ancillary space in relation to ritual time and develop the concept using the notion of liminality. Finally, I draw these different threads together and suggest some implications of this hybrid liminality for Pentecostal ecclesiology.

To make this theological exploration more specific and concrete, let me introduce a Pentecostal digital worshipper and her liturgical practice.

Anna is a woman in her mid-forties, and she is married to Frank, who is disabled, having limited mobility. He has been required to restrict his movement outside of the home to essential activity. They are both longstanding members of their local Pentecostal church and they are well known in this community. Therefore, because of Frank's disability, they have both limited their Sunday morning attendance much more, attending in-person only occasionally. During the Covid-19 pandemic, they were both introduced to online worship services. Since the pandemic, the church has maintained its livestreaming of the main Sunday morning worship service and uses Zoom software to create a hybrid experience for worshippers in their homes. Frank finds this arrangement less satisfactory and tends not to participate, but Anna has embraced it with alacrity. It has nurtured her spiritual life and sustained her through some dark times.

Most Sundays this is how she worships, on her own, in her living room, watching the service as it is livestreamed. She logs in via the Zoom software and participates in the worship through this digital platform. Each Sunday she has a similar routine: (1) she makes the living room a worshipping space – a sacred space for her to focus on God; (2) she sets up her laptop on a small table in front of her favourite chair and adjusts the sound; (3) she clears the furniture so that there is space to move to the music, dance if she wishes, or kneel or even lie down in worship; and (4) she places her Bible and notepad on a small table beside her chair, together with elements for communion, should the pastor include it in the service.

Five minutes before the service is due to start, she crosses the digital threshold. She clicks the Zoom link and is placed within a waiting room for a minute or so. Then the host lets her in, and she sees several familiar friends from the church who now attend services via Zoom. She greets everyone with a chat message and then prepares for the service to start. The service follows a familiar liturgical pattern of welcome and notices, sung worship (usually four or five songs), followed by the sermon and then a response time or altar call. Occasionally, the pastor invites Zoom participants to contribute Scripture verses, prophetic insights, or prayers. But, as yet, the technology does not enable their faces to be seen, or their voices to be heard in the in-person, physical service space. They communicate using the chat function and someone reads out what they have written to the congregation at an appropriate point in the service.

The service closes with the offertory, any further notices, a closing song and then a final prayer or blessing. The people on Zoom can stay online after the service has finished for a social chat while making themselves a cup of coffee or tea. This set of hybrid worshipping practices has become just as much a part of Anna's spiritual life as the in-person worshipping experience was before the pandemic.

This enquiry focuses on the first main liturgical component called 'sung worship' or doxology. It is this component in the context of hybrid worship that is the central element of theological exploration. *The argument of this study is that hybrid doxology is a legitimate dimension of Pentecostal spirituality because it enables worshippers to connect with God and belong to an ecclesial community in an authentically Pentecostal manner.* It has implications for ecclesiology because it illuminates the nature of doxological participation, the boundaries of hybrid ecclesial space and the role of liminality for Pentecostalism and its approach to missiological praxis.

Doxology in Pentecostal Worship

Pentecostal Christians have drawn upon the Latter Rain tradition to express the role that praise and worship play in the life of the Church.[1] There is an emphasis on the importance of music for worship, using contemporary styles. Elsewhere, I have argued that Pentecostal and Charismatic spirituality has a search-encounter-transformation process to it.[2] It begins with a desire to meet with God, who is encountered in worship by the Holy Spirit and who changes the worshippers by his presence and power. Certainly, both the search and the encounter phases of this spirituality, if not all of them, can be located in the act of sung worship.[3] The whole service leads to moments of encounter, most obviously during the altar call. But I have also witnessed powerful times of sung worship where the sermon has been bypassed completely because the search to encounter phase has been so significant in the sung worship element. The intimacy stage of singing has elicited dramatic and powerful manifestations of the Holy Spirit's work, such that one can infer there is the beginnings of significant transformation as well.

Albrecht, in his anthropological study of Pentecostal worship, identified three main or macro rites that constitute the typical worship event.[4] He describes these as: a period of sung worship, the sermon, and the altar call or ministry time. In between these three main

---

[1] Lester Ruth and Lim Swee Hong, *A History of Contemporary Praise & Worship: Understanding the Ideas that Reshaped the Protestant Church* (Grand Rapids, MI: Baker Academic, 2021), pp. 310-13. They argue that there are two 'rivers' within twentieth century American Protestant worship. The first is 'praise and worship', which focuses on God inhabiting the praises of his people; and the second is the pragmatic use of songs to bridge the gap between church and unchurched people, associated with the seeker sensitive forms of worship.

[2] Mark J. Cartledge, *Encountering the Spirit: The Charismatic Tradition* (London: Darton, Longman & Todd, 2006), pp. 25-27; also see Florian M.P. Simatupang, *The Eucharistic Spirit: A Renewal Theology of the Lord's Supper* (Word and Spirit: Pentecostal Investigations in Theology and History; Eugene, OR: Cascade Books, 2025) for a discussion of how this SET (search-encounter-transformation) approach can be applied to eucharistic theology.

[3] See Martina Björkander, *Worship, Ritual, and Pentecostal Spirituality-as-Theology* (Leiden: Brill, 2024), p. 375, who states: 'For while worship and music are "not identical" in pentecostal understanding, music is nevertheless considered a core conduit of God's presence and a prime facilitator of the transformative and intimate relationship with the triune God that is at the heart of Pentecostal spirituality.'

[4] Daniel Albrecht, *Rites in the Spirit: A Ritual Approach to Pentecostal/Charismatic Spirituality* (JPTSup 17; Sheffield: Sheffield Academic Press, 1999), pp. 154-70.

features are micro rites that link them and provide continuity between them. Of course, worship music may be played or sung outside of this main block of songs and, indeed, music is so important to Pentecostals that it can permeate the whole service, so that it can undergird the micro rites as well as the macro rites. It is also the case that most, if not all, Pentecostal worship services end on a musical note as people are sent out to live for Christ in the world. This element is not unique to Pentecostals and can be found in most Christian traditions.

The shape of the sung worship macro rite can vary, however, and worship leader styles can also differ quite considerably, depending on cultural and contextual factors. A Black Pentecostal style is very different, for example, to a Vineyard or a Hillsong style of worship. It is also the case that younger worship leaders are developing their own musical styles and addressing different types of content in their lyrics.[5] In Pentecostal worship there is typically a block of four or five songs sung in sequence without a break. Often, the songs start with an upbeat celebratory tempo, which tends to slow down and become more meditative for the final couple of songs before the transition.[6] Therefore, celebration as a mood gives way to reflection, contemplation, and even silence. Towards the end of this time of sung worship, there is a stillness as well as a sense of intimacy with God. Often songs use phrases with first person pronouns (e.g. 'I love you, Lord') contributing to this sense of personal intimacy. The bodily posture changes from standing, clapping, the waving of arms or flags to more passive postures of sitting, kneeling, and lying down. There is an 'atmosphere' in the physical worshipping space, which contributes to the emotional connection between the worshippers and each other, and between them and God.

---

[5] See the historical sketch by Neil Hudson, 'An Ever-Renewed Renewal: Fifty Years of Charismatic Worship', in Mark J. Cartledge and A.J. Swoboda (eds.), *Scripting Pentecost: A Study of Pentecostals, Worship and Liturgy* (London: Routledge, 2017), pp. 69-83.

[6] Daniel Thornton and Mark Evans, 'YouTube: A New Mediator of Christian Community', in A.E. Nekola and T. Wagner (eds.), *Congregational Music-Making and Community in a Mediated Age* (Farnham, UK: Ashgate Publishing, 2016), pp. 146-48. Björkander, *Worship*, pp. 379-80, notes how Kenyan Pentecostals also think in terms of the temple model of approaching God through music in three phases: celebration (expressing joy) to reflection (expressing penitence) and then reception (expressing affection and gratitude), that achieve a deep spiritual experience of transformation.

Lord has identified three key theological characteristics that can be drawn from the practices of Pentecostals.[7] First, he argues that sung worship is a 'place' of God's creative presence. God the creator has given humanity the gift of creativity and the songs that are created by individuals and groups are a gift that comes from God. Second, he observes that sung worship is a 'place' of God's action. It takes time to prepare for and to allow the Spirit's action in and through this macro rite. This is important because it is not formulaic, but dynamic and newly constructed each week. It is a marked out sacred time; and the act is a sacred act, with the desire to create a space for deep interaction through sustained singing of worship songs.[8] Third, sung worship is a 'place' of God's relating, through a personal encounter of love. It is an embodied experience that can be expressed in 'soaking prayer', which is when a person lies down while sung worship happens.[9] Again, this draws on the notion of spiritual intimacy in the worship space, which is both individual and communal. There is clearly a communal, inter-personal dynamic among the people present, as well as a deep sense of communion with God through the Spirit.[10] From this place of intimacy with God, Pentecostals are empowered to go out in service and mission to the world. So, sung worship also has a missional outcome, it is intrinsic to what can be called 'doxological mission': the Spirit draws us into that moment of adoration via doxology, when hearts are changed and spiritual energy is renewed, so that disciples of Christ are empowered by

---

[7] Andy Lord, 'A Theology of Sung Worship'. Neil Hudson, 'An Ever-Renewed Renewal: Fifty Years of Charismatic Worship', in Mark J. Cartledge and A.J. Swoboda (eds.), *Scripting Pentecost: A Study of Pentecostals, Worship and Liturgy* (London: Routledge, 2017), pp. 87-92.

[8] For example, David's Tent, which is a three-day, non-stop worship camp meeting, is designed to enable worshipers to go deeper in their spiritual lives by means of sustained sung worship. See https.//www.davidstent.net/. For an explanation of the significance of the concept of 'David's Tent' (= 'tabernacle') for a Pentecostal understanding of doxology, see Ruth and Hong, *An Introduction*, pp. 46-65.

[9] Michael Wilkinson and Peter Althouse, *Catch the Fire: Soaking Prayer and Charismatic Renewal* (DeKalb, IL: Northern Illinois University Press, 2014), pp. 40-44. Also see Miranda Klaver, *This is My Desire* (Amsterdam: Amsterdam University Press, 2011), pp. 195-99, for a discussion of music as an aesthetic form, where she discusses the embodied processes of learning or socialization, meaning making through the act of performance (musicking), and the relationship of the words to the music.

[10] Steven Félix-Jäger, *Renewal Worship. A Theology of Pentecostal Doxology* (Downers Grove: IVP Academic, 2022), pp. 94-100, argues that music can be 'sacramental' in Pentecostal worship.

the same Spirit to live life to the glory of God, witnessing to the kingdom of God with passion and purpose.[11] These themes will be noted as the discussion progresses and the idea of 'place' will be developed by means of the concept of 'hybrid space'.

Blurring the Public/Private Distinction in Hybrid Worship

It could be said that the demarcation of social spheres into 'public' and 'private' is a mark of modernity.[12] The public realm was regarded as the domain of truth and facts, the private realm of beliefs and values. Since God could not be verified empirically, beliefs in God were relegated to the private domain of beliefs and values. It was once thought that religion would either disappear entirely or be relegated to the domain of the purely personal and private, perhaps expressed in small groups or the privacy of one's own home, but having little or no influence in the public life of society. However, full scale theories of secularisation have themselves proved to be false and religion of many kinds has shown itself to be a stubborn presence, even in the public domains of society. This has led to the idea that there is something called the 'post-secular' society, which includes religion as an element within it. It is not that religion came back, rather it never went away, but it is configured and accessed somewhat more individually and fluidly.[13] Alongside this post-secular account, we have the invention of the internet and the use of social media, such that the demarcation between what is public and private has been blurred significantly. Now, millions of people around the world, armed with smart phones, share their personal information in a public way while accessing all sorts of content from many different sources. Indeed, the public of the Church has embraced this new digital age, especially among Pentecostals, who are always open to the use of technology for pragmatic reasons.

---

[11] Steven J. Land, *Pentecostal Spirituality: A Passion for the Kingdom* (JPTSup 1; Sheffield: Sheffield Academic Press, 1993).

[12] José Casanova, *Public Religions in the Modern World* (Chicago: University of Chicago Press, 1994), p. 211; however, these distinctions are questioned by Grace Davie, *The Sociology of Religion* (London: Sage, 2007), p. 64, among others.

[13] Marcel Barnard, 'Flows of Worship in the Network Society', *In die Skriflig* 44.1 (2010), p. 78, notes that liminality has been used to describe the threshold between secular and sacred places.

During Covid-19, many churches broadcast their worship services and people participated in digitally mediated doxology from the comfort of their living rooms. They sang along, clapped, raised their arms, and some even danced. I remember watching the Zoom Image of an African Pentecostal woman singing and dancing along to one song during an online service. We were separated by space, she in her home and me in mine, but we were both connected by a corporate worship event, which was hosted via Zoom, and it enabled people from different parts of the country, if not the world, to join together at the same time. The private worlds of our homes were joined together to become a new public, a digitally constructed public, which was also still private, such that once the service was over, it remained a private, personal space. For the duration of the service, however, the public/private divide was blurred and necessarily so. Indeed, it felt as though we had moved beyond this distinction to some extent at least.

In Pentecostal congregational sung worship, there is often an 'affective alliance' among worshippers because of their desire to encounter God through the practice of singing.[14] In addition, worshippers connect with each other emotionally through the inter-personal dynamic of the embodied action of the group of people moving in sync with the beat of the music. By contrast, at home there may be one or two people, or a few more, who sing together and perhaps move around together, but the connectivity and inter-personal dynamic is very different. During the Covid-19 pandemic, Pentecostal churches attempted to recreate their worshipping experiences via different platforms, such as Zoom. Addo observes that for African Pentecostals there were real challenges.

The incorporation of traditional instruments such as drums, congas, or rattles, as well as melodic vocalisations from choir members, all contribute to the multisensory experience of worship. However, this distinctive cultural element loses its value when transferred to the online environment, as it becomes virtually impossible to synchronise instruments and voices from multiple

---

[14] Pete Ward, 'Affective Alliance or Circuits of Power: The Production and Consumption of Contemporary Charismatic Worship in Britain', *International Journal of Practical Theology* 9.1 (2005), p. 39.

devices. Issues of sound lag, delays, and distortions represent technical stumbling blocks for believers. When asked what significant changes they noticed as a result of liturgy moving online, believers expressed the difficulty of engaging in the task of singing collectively.[15]

It is important to acknowledge this challenge at the time, but post-pandemic when the norm became livestreaming hybridity, the issues became somewhat different because synchronization from multiple devices was not the main experience. When everyone was online the public space was a collective of private spaces, with no corporate, concrete in-person space in use. In the congregational-home hybrid space the doxological dynamic is obviously different.

Now, with the resumption of in-person, concrete worship services post-pandemic, the use of digital technology to mediate the public nature of ecclesial worship practices to private homes has, in effect, left the Zoom participants largely 'faceless' to people in the physical, in-person congregation.[16] Typically, people at home watch and listen to the music via their computers or smartphones. They can see the musicians and may be able to see some of the congregational members in their actions of singing, clapping, dancing, and moving, depending on the type of church and its performative culture. They may be alone, or they may be with others in the same physical room in their home. But their space is private space not public space, and they access the public space in a limited manner, perhaps contributing to it when facilitated by the tech people in the concrete setting. It is inevitable that a tension exists for Pentecostals between the dynamics of the public, in-person congregational space, and the private space of a believer's own home. Once again, for the duration of the service, the public/private space is blurred, this time between the in-person congregation and the believer at home (rather than believers each in their own homes). This development, at least for the duration of the experience, also constitutes a form of hybridity that helps move the

---

[15] Giuseppina Addo, 'Join the Holy Spirit on Zoom', *Approaching Religion* 11.2 (2021), p. 51.

[16] Mark Cartledge, 'Worship and the Digital Church', *Preach Magazine* 40 (2025), pp. 32-33.

home-based worshipper beyond the public/private divide.[17] It is this congregational-home hybrid space that invites further analysis,[18] which I turn to now using the ritual elements noted above and analyze it through the conceptual lens of liminality.

Ritual Elements and Liminality

In this public/private digital interface there is created a liminal space, a third space,[19] which may be regarded as ancillary to concrete, congregational spaces, but it is essential to online spaces used in this manner. Schmidt argues that this digital space may be the context for 'virtual communion', that is, it can mediate grace to worshippers in an ancillary manner.[20] While Schmidt's discussion is focused on the nature of the Eucharist in a digital setting, it is also worth exploring in more detail the nature of this space and the experience it provides to worshippers through the practice of 'sung worship' or doxology. This ancillary space is important because of its link to the notion of threshold.[21] An ancillary space is connected but also distinct, it is linked but not fully within the congregational worshipping space. In other words, it is a liminal space.

The concept of liminality is an important one in worship studies as well as practical theology.[22] Anthropologically, it refers to transitions between different stages of life, or the transition between different locations. It also refers to the notion that one is in the process of change, for example, having moved from one place but not having fully arrived in another. It connotes the idea of being 'between and betwixt'. Such an experience is often described as a 'threshold

---

[17] John Dyer, 'Exploring Mediated *Ekklesia*', in H.A. Campbell and J. Dyer (eds.), *Ecclesiology for a Digital Church* (London: SCM Press, 2022), p. 13.

[18] Oliver, 'From In-Person', p. 7, suggests digital hybridity will continue in church life and become established.

[19] See S.M. Hoover and N. Echchaibi, 'Introduction', in S.M. Hoover and N. Echchaibi (eds.), *Finding Religion in the Media: Case Studies of the 'Third Spaces' of Digital Religion* (Boulder, CO: University of Colorado, 2012), for a discussion of third space and digital religious practices.

[20] Katherine G. Schmidt, *Virtual Communion* (London: Lexington Books, 2020), pp. 133-55.

[21] Mark J. Cartledge, 'Virtual Mediation of the Spirit: Prospects for Digital Pentecostalism', *PentecoStudies* 21 (2022), pp. 44-46.

[22] Marcel Barnard, 'Flows of Worship in the Network Society', *In die Skriflig* 44.1 (2010), p. 69.

experience'.[23] Often in this in-between state there is a sense of po-rousness, that things from one place or state connect to another and *vice versa*. It is transitional and temporary such that in this liminality there is a reconfiguring of reality or life experience, the person is both connected and disconnected to the old and to the new at the same time.[24] The boundary lines are blurred, and this blurring is important because, in the context of a discussion of Pentecostal spirituality, it facilitates the divine-human encounter at both individual and corpo-rate levels.[25]

Therefore, it could be suggested that hybrid Pentecostal worship-pers are liminal worshippers, they are in both liminal space and limi-nal time. Liminal space is the ancillary space of the intersection of concrete in-person praise space located in the physical space of a church sanctuary with the personal space of the individual in their home location. Both are embodied, it is not that one is embodied and the other is not; rather they are linked by digital media, such that only sight and sound are mediated, and this restricted mediation has an impact from one to the other. Liminal time is also a form of ritual time, since they are inextricably linked. The corporate worshipping time of the congregation is expanded by hybridity to include the an-cillary space at the same time: synchronicity is important here. Each of these aspects contribute to the multiple dimensions of liminality, and each aspect is a means of divine-human encounter, which to-gether provide a rich experience.

Obviously, worship as an event occurs 'in' time, which is regarded as sanctified time, set apart for that purpose. Typically, this is weekly time when the main Sunday morning worship service gathers people together, and this includes online worshippers. It gives a rhythm to the life of the worshipper. This time is structured according to the foundational macro rites as noted earlier (sung worship, sermon, and altar ministry). The ritual space is provided by a physical location, a

---

[23] See the discussion in Timothy Carson et al., *Crossing Thresholds* (Cambridge: Lutterworth, 2018), especially chapter 5, 'Liturgy, Ritual, and Worship through the Liminal Lens', pp. 84-100.

[24] Scott, 'Worship', pp. 2-3, understands the post-pandemic social context as a 'post-liminal' state. While I agree that the Covid-19 pandemic was a liminal state, I am using the concept in a specific liturgical sense rather than a macro-level social one.

[25] See the discussion of the role of music in Pentecostal worship and mystical experience by Poloma, *Main Street Mystics*, pp. 37-58.

building often called a 'sanctuary', which helps to shape the kinds of rituals found in Pentecostal worship. These spaces can be very different in design and location, but they provide a 'micro-world' in which the worshippers experience God and his creative presence and 'place' of action.[26] For Pentecostals, God can be worshipped anywhere, and the Christian life should be expressed beyond the walls of the church building. Nevertheless, place is important, and the congregational space is especially important for the 'body' of believers, even though these members spill out from their designated space marked by the seating into the aisles and move around the wider space. The leaders occupy the platform, while the altar space (between the first row of chairs and the platform) is the place of meeting,[27] where the Spirit is encountered in prayer. It is 'an *axis mundi* in Pentecostal spirituality', a 'temporary "container"' of sorts for the sacred', which includes a 'liminal dimension', setting 'a boundary between ritual life and daily life'.[28] The congregational roles include those of (1) worshipper, performed in concert with others while retaining individuality (e.g. via speech, posture, and levels of participation), (2) prophet, providing approved contributions to the charismatic dimension of worship, and (3) minister to others through prayer. Congregants also listen to the sermon, seeking to learn more from the Bible, to put what they have learned into practice as disciples of Jesus Christ.

Linked to this liminality of time and space is the worshipping experience as a form of liminality itself. It is possible to lose a sense of place and time in and through intense experiences of sung worship, such that the Holy Spirit, the great mediator of the Godhead, initiates and sustains liminality both to enable the quality of the encounter and the outcome in the transformation of the person/s so engaged.[29] In this sense, it is like the role that sacramentality plays in the Pentecostal church, where anything can mediate the presence of God for the purposes of God.[30] In this case, it is the worshipping life of the Church through her sung doxology that enables the Holy Spirit to lift

---

[26] Albrecht, *Rites in the Spirit*, p. 127; Lord, 'A Theology of Sung Worship', pp. 86-90.

[27] This is the most common designation of the altar space, but see Vondey, 'Pentecostal Sacramentality', pp. 98-99, for an appreciation that the designated 'space' can be more fluid in a congregation setting.

[28] Albrecht, *Rites in the Spirit*, pp. 133-34.

[29] Cartledge, *The Mediation of the Spirit*.

[30] Cartledge, 'Digital Pentecostal Sacramentality', p. 4.

hearts to heaven, such that the liminality is not just at the immanent level between people, or between the physical and the digital, but also at the transcendent level between God and the community of the Church.[31] This liminal 'between and betwixt' event is also eschatological, as the kingdom of God is realised in digital doxology, anticipating the *eschaton*, when doxology will not only be the continuing and primary mark of the Church but her ultimate preoccupation (Rev. 4.8-11; 7.9-17).

The Implications of Hybridity and Liminality for Pentecostal Ecclesiology

Now I turn to how hybridity and liminality in relation to doxology to explore how it may contribute to digital dimensions of ecclesiology from a Pentecostal perspective. It needs to be acknowledged at the outset that most contemporary Pentecostal ecclesiology does not address the digital dimension explicitly. Indeed, this is something that is only beginning to be explored within the wider literature.[32] My own work has investigated methodology,[33] worshipping practices,[34] pneumatological mediation, the Eucharist, and sacramentality more broadly.[35] As yet, I have only addressed sung doxology very briefly, so let me develop four implications more specifically.

First, it can be suggested that doxology is the first mark of the Church.[36] On the day of Pentecost, when the 120 were filled with the Holy Spirit, they spoke with other tongues (Acts 2.4) and 'declared the wonders of God' (2.11). The declaration was heard in multiple languages by those who witnessed this event in the public space, as the 120 spilled out from a semi-private space into a fully public one. We do not know the precise content of this declaration, but it is fair to assume that it was doxological since God was being praised for his

---

[31] Cartledge, 'The Holy Spirit and the Digital Church'.

[32] See Campbell and Dyer, *Ecclesiology for a Digital Church*.

[33] Cartledge, 'Studying Digital Pentecostalism;' and Cartledge, 'Empirical Theology as Theological Netnography'.

[34] Cartledge, 'The Holy Spirit and the Digital Church;' and Cartledge, 'Worship and the Digital Church'.

[35] Cartledge, 'Virtual Mediation of the Spirit', pp. 30-50. Cartledge, 'Pentecostalism and the Eucharist in a Digital Age'; and Cartledge, 'Digital Pentecostal Sacramentality'.

[36] Cartledge, 'The Holy Spirit and the Digital Church'; cf. Mike Higton, *Christian Doctrine* (London: SCM Press, 2008), pp. 311-14.

mighty act of pouring out the Holy Spirit upon the newly reconstituted Israel. Peter explains that this outpouring of the Holy Spirit was from the Father and through Jesus Christ, thus giving it a trinitarian dynamic (Acts 2.33). Therefore, in doxology, one can expect that such declarations be given to the Father, through the Son, in the power of the Holy Spirit. Often Pentecostals focus on the empowerment of the Holy Spirit for witness, which came next, as Peter explains to the crowd the meaning of the event in a way that was understandable to them. But the actual first expression by the people in response to the manifestations of God's presence through wind and fire was speech directed to God himself. This is an important ecclesiological point: the people of God find their primary identity as worshippers first before anything else is or can be said or done.[37] If the chief sin of humanity is idolatry (worshipping the wrong thing), then its counter is worshipping the right person in praise (orthodoxy), made possible by the presence and power of the Holy Spirit. It is through this very act that one's identity is formed and sustained as an individual believer in the context of the Church and her corporate life.

Second, given the experience of Anna noted above, it could be argued that this kind of digital ancillary space is a legitimate extension of the in-person community of the 'temple of the Holy Spirit' (1 Cor. 3.16). The Zoom software allows for the home participant to experience worship by digital extension in real time. The person can hear the music, sing along to it and participate in movement and gesture and even use the chat function to express feelings and thoughts that are shared with others on Zoom, if not others in the in-person communal space. Although, where there is a greater interface between the Zoom participants and the in-person group then a stronger sense of participation may be witnessed.[38] It is clearly not the 'same experience', but it can be a similar experience in relation to sung doxology. The nature of the 'auditory icon' of the people singing around the person will be different.[39] The kinaesthetic dimensions will also

---

[37] It could be noted, of course, that the early Church, because it was still embedded in Judaism, but clearly moving in a new direction, was in a liminal relationship to Israel.

[38] Dawn, 'Worship', p. 185, observes that to create 'an environment for prayer and worship, leaders, preachers, pastors and musicians need to speak directly to online participants as well as those they can see physically'.

[39] Albrecht, *Rites in the Spirit*, pp. 142-44, 155-60.

be different because the person is on her own in her home rather than being in a group of people moving together in response to the musical beat. Nevertheless, there is a sufficient sense of the sung worship sequence that the digital participant can experience the shape, flow, and dynamic of the doxology for themselves. It is somewhat akin to being in the foyer space of a church sanctuary, open to the senses of sight and sound, if not taste, touch, and smell.[40]

Third, it has been observed that the internet blurs the public/private divide of social space, as we invite various public domains into our private world of home life. This was noted in relation to worship during the pandemic when clergy led services from their own homes, inviting congregants into their private spaces via Zoom and other software. The Archbishop of Canterbury even celebrated a service of Holy Communion from his kitchen![41] Since the pandemic, this public/private blurring has continued in worship with the use of livestreaming and participation via Zoom software. It is often said that the Church is a community that has a hard core and a fuzzy edge. The fuzzy edge is how enquirers enter into the space of the Church to observe her life before committing themselves to it through conversion, Baptism and participation in worship, the Eucharist, and the life of discipleship and mission. The Church is a missiological community, and the pull into doxology and worship is the centripetal force that joins her members both to God, whom they serve, and to each other in the family of God. Following this pull towards the centre, the members of the community are then pushed out into service towards the world, experiencing the centrifugal force of the Spirit, empowered for witness. The uniting of the space of the concrete in-person community and the home setting provides the liminal context for people to transition into the community and for the community to transition into service. This blurred, hybrid digital space also allows for a missiological outcome as homes become places for individuals to invite neighbours into a space that is accessible for guests.[42]

---

[40] See Cartledge, 'Virtual Mediation of the Spirit', p. 33, for a discussion of the role of the senses in worship; although my view regarding 'touch' was further developed in Cartledge, 'Digital Pentecostal Sacramentality'.

[41] See, https://www.youtube.com/watch?v=6bmhRCJ3YAI.

[42] Tihomir Lazić, 'An Abductive Study of Digital Worship through the Lenses of Netnography and Digital Ecclesiology', in G. Corbett and S. Moerman (eds.), *Music and Spirituality* (Cambridge, UK: Open Book Publishers, 2024), p. 343, states:

Thus, the home digital space becomes a missiological resource in the life of the Church for the sake of the kingdom of God.[43]

Fourth and finally, doxological liminality is an eschatological foretaste of the banquet at which many tongues across the ages will be united in the eternal song of heaven (Rev. 4.1-11). We live between the times of Christ's first and second coming, which is also a liminality reality. We live 'between and betwixt' heaven and earth, the present and the future, and the now and the not yet of the coming of the kingdom of God. God's inaugurated reign can be experienced through sung doxology as mediated digitally. This is because the Spirit can effect change in the hearts and lives of worshippers as they sing praise to God. Digital doxology, therefore, can also have a sacramental quality, as it participates in that which it signifies.[44] It mediates the heavenly reality that acknowledges and celebrates the kingship of Jesus Christ and the universal presence of the Holy Spirit, anticipating when God will be 'all in all' (1 Cor. 15.28). It is especially through music and its ability to raise our hearts to heaven that we find its eschatological liminal quality. It can bring us to the threshold of heaven, while we remain in our own physical, earthly, and digitally mediated reality. This threshold experience can transform us, enabling us to have a stronger, clearer passion for the kingdom of God.[45] Therefore, the use of digital media extends this eschatological liminal experience to a greater number of Pentecostals around the world.

Conclusion

In this study I have considered the practice of sung worship or doxology as an important aspect of Pentecostal spirituality. I have explored this practice by placing it in the research context of existing Pentecostal scholarship, while also developing this scholarship by viewing the subject through the concepts of hybridity and liminality as mediated digitally. Both concepts when brought together have implications for Pentecostal ecclesiology. In particular, (1) doxology is

---

'As worshippers are uplifted, they are compelled to interact with, support, and stand in solidarity with wider humanity'.

[43] See Hengki Wijaya et al., 'Virtual Worship and Spiritual Growth in Digital Church Era', in S.E. Zaluchu et al., *Proceedings of the International Conference on Theology, Humanities and Christian Education 2022* (Paris: Atlantis, 2023), p. 337.

[44] Félix-Jäger, *Renewal Worship*, pp. 94-100.

[45] Land, *Pentecostal Spirituality*.

the first mark of the Church, as on the day of Pentecost; (2) digital hybridity is an ancillary, liminal, ecclesial space; (3) the blurring of the public/private divide is a liminal aid to mission, not just a social and technological development; and (4) digital, hybrid doxology mediates an eschatological foretaste of the kingdom of God, sustaining the Church in her life. In this way, it can be argued that *hybrid doxology is a legitimate dimension of Pentecostal spirituality because it enables worshippers to connect with God and belong to an ecclesial community in an authentically Pentecostal manner.*

It could be argued further that a practical-theological account of Pentecostal ecclesiology needs to adopt this kind of research using empirical methods to explore the nature of not just concrete ecclesiology, but digital ecclesiology as well. This is an area that needs to be developed because the Church has already embraced digital media in her life, as it is embedded in society that has and is experiencing a fast-moving digital revolution. It does not embrace this research because it is a fad but because it needs to maintain its theological identity in relation to the drive to be relevant. Now the challenge for churches to be relevant is greater than ever, especially in places where the state of Christianity is precarious. For Pentecostalism, with its intuitions to be primitive and pragmatic,[46] this approach draws on its primitivism (doxology as on the day of Pentecost) while being critically constructive in its assessment of its pragmatism (the use of digital media). A digitally informed approach to practical theology is essential to address these questions, engaging in deeper and broader academic conversations for the benefit of the Church and her mission in the world.

---

[46] Grant Wacker, *Heaven Below: Early Pentecostals and American Culture* (Cambridge, MA: Harvard University Press, 2001).

6

'ANTHEM OF GRACE': A THEOLOGICAL EXPLORATION OF DIVINE GRACE IN CONTEMPORARY CONGREGATIONAL SONGS WRITTEN BY NEW CREATION CHURCH, SINGAPORE

H. LENG TOH[*]

Introduction

Established in 1983, New Creation Church (NCC) in Singapore has, over the past four decades, emerged as one of the region's most prominent independent, non-denominational megachurches.[1] Despite its non-denominational classification, NCC is characterized by a distinctly Pentecostal orientation, marked by a Trinitarian theology that affirms God as Father, Son, and Holy Spirit.[2] As Goh observes, the church regularly attracts a weekly attendance of approximately

---

[*] H. Leng Toh (PhD, Alphacrusis University College, Australia) is Honorary Postdoctoral Associate at Alphacrusis University College.

[1] For a broader discussion on Singapore's religious landscape, New Creation Church, and its distinctive emphasis on the theology of grace, see my co-authored chapter with Thornton, which provides an overview and contextual analysis. H. Leng Toh and Daniel Thornton, 'Understanding "Love" in the English Lyrics of the Original Songs by the Multilingual New Creation Church Singapore', *Religions* 15.5 (2024), p. 603. https://doi.org/10.3390/rel15050603.

[2] Daniel P.S. Goh, 'Grace, Megachurches, and the Christian Prince in Singapore', in Terence Chong (ed.), *Pentecostal Megachurches in Southeast Asia: Negotiating Class, Consumption and the Nation* (Singapore: ISEAS Publishing, 2018), p. 182.

30,000 congregants, underscoring its significant influence within Singapore's religious landscape.[3] Central to NCC's doctrinal emphasis is the transformative power of the gospel of grace, which it positions as the primary catalyst for spiritual renewal, personal empowerment, and divine encounter. This theological focus is encapsulated in the church's belief statement, which asserts: 'When we catch a revelation of this truth, we are transformed by His grace from the inside out. That's the beauty of believing and living in our heavenly Father's love and grace'.[4] Through this framework, NCC advances a vision of Christian life that foregrounds grace as both a theological principle and a lived experience.

The senior pastor of NCC, Joseph Prince, presents a ministerial profile on the church's official website that encapsulates both his theological convictions and his leadership ethos. The profile introduces him as 'a leading voice in proclaiming the gospel of grace around the world through his books, teaching resources, and television ministry', and affirms that 'he has impacted church leaders worldwide by preaching the unadulterated gospel of Jesus with boldness'.[5] This portrayal highlights the centrality of grace theology not only in Prince's ministry but also in the broader ecclesial identity of NCC. As a theological cornerstone, the message of God's grace shapes the church's preaching, teachings, and communal life. Crucially, this doctrinal emphasis finds poetic and affective expression in NCC's original worship music, which functions as a dynamic vehicle for articulating and transmitting its theology to the congregation.

Pentecostal systematic theologian Tony Richie defines 'grace (charis)' as 'the sense of a gift of kindness and favor', a characterization that underscores Paul's view in Ephesians 2 of grace as 'unearned, undeserved, unmerited'.[6] Richie argues that humanity's salvation rests solely on God's 'divine grace' emphasizing that this salvation operates entirely through 'divine favor'.[7] He contends that while salvation by grace is accomplished exclusively through an act of divine favor, it

---

[3] Chong, *Pentecostal Megachurches in Southeast Asia*, p. 182.

[4] New Creation Church, 'Who We Are', http.//www.newcreation.org.sg/about-us.

[5] New Creation Church, 'Pastor Joseph Prince and Wendy Prince'. http.//www.newcreation.org.sg/about-us.

[6] Tony Richie, *Saved, Delivered, and Healed: Introducing a Pentecostal Theology of Salvation* (Eugene, OR: Wipf and Stock Publishers, 2022), p. 46.

[7] Richie, *Saved, Delivered, and Healed*, p. 46.

nevertheless manifests as a grace that functions through faith and is subsequently evidenced by 'good work' (Eph. 2.8–10), thereby linking it to the broader framework of 'salvation by grace through faith'.[8] Richie insists that no act of 'righteous work' can precondition or ground the reception of salvation; rather, such works must follow the re-creative and transformative impact of experiencing saving grace.[9] In his view, grace embodies 'divine power' and holds an equivalence to 'divine favor'.[10] Ultimately, Richie asserts that God's favor, imparted through faith, initiates spiritual transformation, and that the consequent divine power equips believers to live out their faith through action.

Joseph Prince articulates a theological vision in which grace is not a detached or 'abstract concept' but is fully embodied in the person of Jesus Christ.[11] He teaches that grace represents the supreme unmerited gift of God, extended freely to all who turn in faith to Jesus, the Son of God. Through belief in Christ's finished work on the cross, individuals receive forgiveness, righteousness, and reconciliation with God – none of which is achieved through human effort but rather granted as a divine gift. As stated on NCC's official website, grace is conceived as an active and transformative strength, one that enables believers to grow in faith, walk in righteousness, and live with divine purpose and joy (2 Cor. 5.21; Rom. 5.17).[12] For NCC, grace is not merely foundational but catalytic – it serves as the cornerstone of the Christian life and the energizing source of spiritual transformation. It fosters authentic spirituality, facilitating intimate encounters with Jesus and guiding believers in a faith journey marked by unmerited favor and divine love.

Beyond formal theological teaching, NCC's original congregational songs function as a vital medium for theological reflection and formation within the congregational context. These songs reinforce doctrinal themes and facilitate an affective and experiential engagement with the church's core theological convictions. When grace emerges as a central motif within the lyrics, it deepens the

---

[8] Richie, *Saved, Delivered, and Healed*, p. 48.

[9] Richie, *Saved, Delivered, and Healed*, p. 48.

[10] Richie, *Saved, Delivered, and Healed*, p. 48.

[11] New Creation Church, 'True Grace Vs Counterfeit Grace', https.//www.new creation.org.sg/true-grace-vs-counterfeit-grace.

[12] New Creation Church, 'Transforming Power of Grace', https.//newcrea-tion.org.sg/whatwebelieve.

congregation's internalization of the church's message, shaping both spiritual understanding and devotional practice. This chapter focuses specifically on the lyrical content of NCC's original compositions to examine how the theme of grace is expressed theologically and creatively by its in-house songwriters. These compositions, situated within the genre of contemporary congregational songs, mirror the church's theological priorities and communal ethos.

A close analysis of NCC's four full-length albums, released between 2014 and 2024, offers valuable insight into the evolution of the church's musical and theological expression over a decade. These albums showcase the creative maturation of NCC's songwriting ministry and serve as a theological archive, reflecting the church's enduring emphasis on grace as a central doctrinal theme. Across the four albums, which together comprise thirty-one original songs, twenty-three explicitly feature the keyword 'grace', while eight do not. This distribution raises important questions for theological analysis: How is the concept of grace articulated in the song lyrics that directly reference the term, and in what ways might the remaining songs, while not using the word 'grace', still convey its theological dimensions?

By tracing lyrical patterns and theological motifs across this ten-year span, I explore how grace is expressed both explicitly and implicitly within NCC's contemporary congregational songs. These compositions not only reinforce the church's proclaimed message of unmerited favor and divine love but also function as a formative medium for congregational identity and spiritual encounter. In this way, NCC's worship repertoire becomes a dynamic space where theology is joyfully taught, wholeheartedly sung, and deeply embodied and internalized.

The genre of contemporary congregational songs outlined by Thornton is 'songs that are popular music oriented, written by Christian worshippers, relatively easily replicable in vernacular contexts, memorable, containing lyrics that are theologically resonant to their performers (congregation), and are personally meaningful'.[13] The theology embedded within contemporary congregational songs often reflects a convergence of personal conviction and institutional direction – shaped either by the individual beliefs of the songwriters or by

---

[13] Daniel Thornton, *Meaning-Making in the Contemporary Congregational Song Genre* (New York: Palgrave Macmillan, 2021), p. 6.

the doctrinal emphasis imparted by church leaders commissioning the compositions. As such, these songs function as expressions of worship and as powerful instruments of theological formation and spiritual imagination within the life of the congregation. What is proclaimed about God through sung lyrics actively shapes – either faithfully or inadvertently distorts – the community's theological understanding and doctrinal development.[14] In this light, worship music becomes both a mirror and a mold of a church's lived theology.

This article, therefore, offers a critical theological investigation into how New Creation Church articulates its understanding of divine grace through its original songs. By analyzing both the lyrical content and thematic emphasis of NCC's worship repertoire, the study aims to uncover the underlying theological currents that inform the church's spiritual identity.

Methodology

This chapter examines the centrality of grace within NCC's theological framework, with particular attention to its expression in original song compositions. Employing a textual analysis methodology, the study identifies and categorizes lyrics according to four theological dimensions of grace: prevenient, salvific, sanctifying, and sustaining. The analysis draws from a corpus of thirty-one songs released between 2014 and 2024, spanning four albums – *Grace Revolution* (2014), *Encounter* (2017), *As He Is So Are We* (2020), and *Face-To-Face* (2024).

To ensure a comprehensive understanding, the analysis is structured around four distinct yet interconnected perspectives of grace. This chapter acknowledges that while God's grace is unified, it manifests in multi-dimensional ways, addressing diverse human needs.[15] However, it is the Holy Spirit's work that 'prepares and leads humans' to their salvation.[16]

Prevenient Grace: God's grace working in the human agents before their salvation and conversion (1 Jn 4.10).[17] Studebaker refers

---

[14] Brian A. Wren, *Praying Twice: The Music and Words of Congregational Song* (Louisville, KY: Westminster John Knox Press, 2000), p. 1.

[15] Richie, *Saved, Delivered, and Healed*, p. 49.

[16] Steven Studebaker, *From Pentecost to the Triune God: A Pentecostal Trinitarian Theology* (Grand Rapids, MI: Eerdmans, 2012), p. 241.

[17] Richie, *Saved, Delivered, and Healed*, p. 49.

to it as 'common grace', alluding to 'the various ways God influences the lives of people in a non-salvific way'.[18]

Salvific Grace: Divine grace as the foundation of salvation and redemption in Christ emphasizes 'forgiveness of sins and the gift of eternal life' (Tit. 3.4–7).[19] Richie denotes this as 'God's grace at conversion' or 'saving grace'.[20]

Sanctifying Grace: The term 'sanctification' derives from the Greek word '*hagiadzo*' meaning to 'set apart'.[21] As Gause aptly observes: 'this separation is intrinsic to one's initial experience in coming to know Christ as Savior'.[22] Sanctifying grace separates believers from the guilt of sin (1 Cor. 6.11; Eph. 5.26; Heb. 10.10) and nurtures a deepened awareness of righteousness, fostering spiritual renewal and transformation throughout their post-conversion journey. It empowers believers 'to cultivate and nourish grace in their lives, confirming and strengthening them in the faith and their faith walk'.[23] John 17.17–19 reveals the sanctifying power of God's Word, setting believers apart for his purpose.

Sustaining Grace: Grace as divine power that empowers the believers as 'divine aid in crisis', conforming them to walk by faith in God.[24] As the term implies, sustaining grace refers to God's ongoing provision and empowerment for the believer's journey of faith. This dimension of grace is exemplified in 2 Cor. 12.9, where the apostle Paul recounts God's assurance: 'My grace is sufficient for you, for my power is made perfect in weakness'. Here, grace is portrayed not merely as the means of salvation but as a continuous, empowering presence that upholds the believer in times of trial, enabling perseverance, dependence, and spiritual resilience.

---

[18] Studebaker, *From Pentecost to the Triune God*, p. 246.

[19] Richie, *Saved, Delivered, and Healed*, p. 49.

[20] Richie, *Saved, Delivered, and Healed*, p. 49.

[21] Hollis Gause, 'Pentecostal Understanding of Sanctification from a Pentecostal Perspective', *Journal of Pentecostal Theology* 18.1 (2009), p. 96, https://doi.org/10.1163/174552509X442174.

[22] Gause, 'Pentecostal Understanding of Sanctification from a Pentecostal Perspective', p. 96.

[23] Richie, *Saved, Delivered, and Healed*, p. 51.

[24] Richie, *Saved, Delivered, and Healed*, p. 51.

The methodology considers the role of poetic creativity in shaping the theological articulation of grace within congregational songs. Songwriters at New Creation Church draw from diverse sources – scriptural inspiration, personal encounters with grace, and pastoral theology – to craft lyrics that are both theologically rich and experientially relatable.

This chapter positions these compositions as expressions of NCC's theological identity and as vehicles for communicating its broader message of grace-centered living to the congregation and beyond. The findings offer significant contributions to the study of sung theology, shedding light on how worship music functions as a medium for theological formation and reflection. Additionally, this analysis highlights the implications of these songs for ecclesial identity and community, illustrating their role in shaping both individual spiritual lives and the collective faith of the church.

Analysis

Table 1 highlights twenty-three song lyrics extracted from the thirty-one NCC song corpus that explicitly use the 'grace' keyword, listing their album names and song titles.

Table 1: NCC's Songs with Usage of 'Grace' Keyword

Number	*Grace Revolution* Album Song Title	Lyrics on Grace
1	Grace Revolution	Grace resounds all across the world Your love is a grace revolution
2	Hearts On Fire	Faith is arising as I look upon Your grace Pour out Your grace like a flood Your grace has set my heart on fire
3	Anthem of Grace	As an anthem of Your grace
4	Sweeter than Wine	Lord, my heart's surrendered to Your grace Your lovingkindness and grace for me
5	Forgiven Much	By Your grace, in Your arms I am found

6	Restore	Your <u>grace</u> will pour
7	I Surrender	To the fullness of Your <u>grace</u> I stand justified by Your <u>grace</u>
8	I Will Follow After You	For Your <u>grace</u> and mercy

Num-ber	*Encounter* Album Song Title	Lyrics on Grace
9	Love Burns Bright	Justified, Your <u>grace</u> my story
10	Wonderful (Grace Made Real)	O how beautiful Your <u>grace</u> unending Grace made real in every weakness
11	Shadow Of Grace	Shadow of <u>grace</u>
12	All Of You	Take my heart, surrendered to Your <u>grace</u>
13	For You So Loved Me	Breathing in Your <u>grace</u>
14	Letting Go	<u>Grace</u> now overflows in me

Num-ber	*As He Is So Are We* Album Song Title	Lyrics on Grace
15	As He Is So Are We	Your <u>grace</u> and truth declared
16	Your Lavish Love	Though one drop of Your <u>grace</u> was enough Just one drop of Your <u>grace</u> was enough Jesus
17	YHVH	Your hand of <u>grace</u> was nailed in <u>grace</u>
18	Trust In The Lord	Acknowledge Your <u>grace</u>
19	For My Good	God of glory and <u>grace</u>

Num-ber	*Face-to-Face* Album Song Title	Lyrics on Grace
20	No Longer I	Surrendered to Your <u>grace</u> Your <u>grace</u> is all I need
21	Father	Your glory and <u>grace</u>

22	Call Upon Your Name	There's a fountain of <u>grace</u> I know
23	Embraced	By the passion of Your <u>grace</u> By Your goodness and Your <u>grace</u>

The subsequent Results and Discussion sections analyze and discuss the specific aspects of grace – prevenient grace, salvific grace, sanctifying grace, and sustaining grace – in detail.

Results and Discussion

Although many contemporary congregational songs implicitly reflect grace through their emphasis on God and Jesus, NCC's lyrics uniquely foreground grace as a central theological theme. They consistently interweave this concept with notions of unmerited favor, freedom from condemnation, and transformative love, distinguishing NCC's sung theology from the broader traditions.

This analysis underscores NCC's multifaceted theology of grace as reflected in thirty-one songs examined, twenty-three of which explicitly include the keyword 'grace'. Pie Chart A visually summarizes the percentage distribution of these aspects. Among these, nine songs (eight with the keyword and one without) address all four aspects of grace (29%), nineteen songs (fourteen with the keyword and five without) emphasize three aspects (61.3%), two songs (one with and one without the keyword) highlight two aspects (6.5%), and one song (3.2%) focuses on a single dimension of grace without using the keyword.

Additionally, Tables 2–4 outline the specific dimensions of grace within songs using the keyword, while Table 5 highlights eight songs that convey grace without explicitly mentioning it. Together, these visuals and tables underscore the theological thematic emphasis within NCC's sung theology.

Pie Chart A: Aspects of Grace Percentage Distribution

Distribution of Aspects of Grace Addressed in NCC Songs

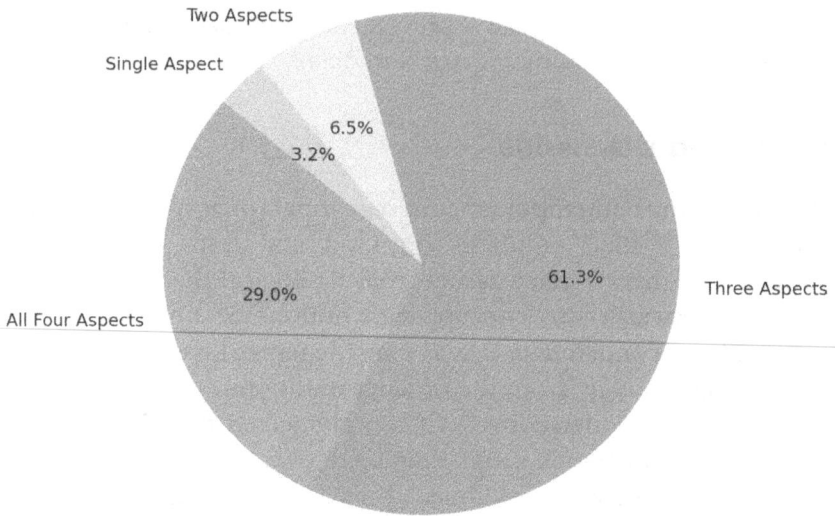

Accompanied by Pie Chart A, Tables 2 to 5 provide a comprehensive overview of the diverse expressions of grace in NCC's theology. These tables offer both quantitative and qualitative insights, detailing each song's album, title, and the specific aspects of grace highlighted. Together, they illuminate the theological emphasis within the songs, showcasing the depth and breadth of grace as a central theme in NCC's musical composition.

Table 2: Songs With Explicit 'Grace' Keywords And Convey Four Aspects of Grace

Album	Song Title	Preveni-ent	Salv ific	Sancti-fying	Sus-taining
Anthem Of Grace	Anthem of Grace	X	X	X	X
Anthem Of Grace	Forgiven Much	X	X	X	X
Anthem Of Grace	I Surrender	X	X	X	X
Encounter	Wonderful (Grace Made Real)	X	X	X	X
Encounter	For You So Loved Me	X	X	X	X
Encounter	Letting Go	X	X	X	X
Whom Jesus Loves	Father	X	X	X	X
Whom Jesus Loves	Call Upon Your Name	X	X	X	X

*Big cap 'X' denotes songs with 'grace' keywords.

Table 3: Songs With Explicit 'Grace' Keywords And Convey Three Aspects Of Grace

Album	Song Title	Preve-nient	Salvifi c	Sancti-fying	Sus-taining
Anthem Of Grace	Grace Revolution	X	X	X	
Anthem Of Grace	Hearts On Fire	X	X		X
Anthem Of Grace	Sweeter than Wine	X	X		X
Anthem Of Grace	Restore	X	X		X
Encounter	Love Burns Bright	X	X		X

Album	Song Title	Prevenient	Salvific	Sanctifying	Sustaining
Encounter	Shadow Of Grace	X	X	X	
Encounter	All Of You		X	X	X
As He Is So Are We	As He Is So Are We		X	X	X
As He Is So Are We	Your Lavish Love	X	X		X
As He Is So Are We	YHVH		X	X	X
As He Is So Are We	Trust In the Lord		X	X	X
As He Is So Are We	For My Good		X	X	X
Whom Jesus Loves	No Long I		X	X	X
Whom Jesus Loves	Embraced		X	X	X

*Big cap 'X' denotes songs with 'grace' keywords.

Table 4: Songs With Explicit 'Grace' Keywords And Convey Two Aspects Of Grace

Album	Song Title	Prevenient	Salvific	Sanctifying	Sustaining
Anthem Of Grace	I Will Follow After You			X	X

*Big cap 'X' denotes song with 'grace' keywords.

Table 5: Songs Without 'Grace' Keywords Yet Convey Aspects Of Grace

Album	Song Title	Pre-venient	Salvific	Sancti-fying	Sus-tain-ing
As He Is So Are We	Supply	x	x	x	x
Anthem Of Grace	Finished	x	x	x	
Encounter	Sons & Daughters		x	x	x
Encounter	Sky	x		x	x
As He Is So Are We	Give Me This Mountain	x	x		x
Whom Jesus Loves	Whom Jesus Loves		x	x	x
Anthem Of Grace	Refuge		x		x
Whom Jesus Loves	Face to Face			x	

*Small cap 'x' denotes songs without 'grace' keywords.

The lyrical examination reveals the distribution of grace's theological dimensions across the analyzed songs. Prevenient grace is featured at 61%, 19 out of 31 songs, highlighting its role in God's initiating work in humanity before salvation. Salvific grace dominates at 90%, 28 out of 31 songs, underscoring its centrality of salvific grace in NCC's theology of redemption. Sanctifying grace appears in 77%, 24 out of 31 songs, reflecting its significance of God's progressive sanctification in the believers' spiritual transformation. Lastly, sustaining grace, present in 87%, 27 out of 31 songs, emphasizes God's provision of grace for empowering and sustaining the believers' faith journey. This distribution illustrates a balanced yet salvation-centered theological narrative in NCC's lyrical compositions.

The *Anthem of Grace* album (2014) explores grace theologically through eight songs, each featuring lyrics with the explicit keyword 'grace'. The song 'Grace Revolution'[25] captures a dynamic journey through prevenient, salvific, and sanctifying grace. Prevenient grace is portrayed as a global invitation to Christ: 'Running to the cross – Where your mercy pours' and 'Grace resounds across the world'. Salvific grace shines through in the liberation and renewal at the cross: 'All my shame is gone – You have won it all'. Sanctifying grace emerges in the believer's position of righteousness: 'Favour is my crown – Christ who reigns in me', reflecting Rom. 5.17.

The song 'Hearts On Fire'[26] showcases grace's transformative, sustaining, and empowering work in the believer's life. The line 'Faith is arising as I look upon Your grace' emphasizes how grace strengthens faith, fostering renewal and confidence in God. Explicit mentions of grace, paired with imagery like 'You shine Your light into my night' and 'Jesus, Your name shattering chains', depict prevenient and salvific grace, highlighting God's initiative in drawing individuals to him. Phrases such as 'Pour out Your grace like a flood' convey grace's sustaining abundance, while 'Your grace has set my heart on fire' reflects its empowering and igniting nature. The imagery 'You raised my soul from ashes into life' illustrates redemption and restoration through salvific grace.

'Anthem Of Grace'[27] celebrates God's salvific grace, focusing on the believer's response to experiencing this gift. The lyric, 'Let my life resound Your praise–As an anthem of Your grace', highlights a life of worship and gratitude, transformed by salvation. The 'anthem' metaphor reflects both personal devotion and communal proclamation, emphasizing grace's impact on identity and worship. The song presents a holistic journey through grace's dimensions: prevenient grace in 'a hope that's so secure' and fearless love; salvific grace in the cross's imagery, where 'sins are washed away'; sanctifying grace in Christ's 'obedience' and the believer's righteousness – 'I am righteous through the One'; and sustaining grace in the dependence on Christ's sufficiency – 'I believe You are everything I need'. Together, the lyrics celebrate grace's transformative power, shaping worship, identity, and daily life.

---

[25] New Creation Worship, 'Grace Revolution', Track 2 on *Anthem of Grace*. Released 2014, https://newcreationworship.sg/albums/anthem-of-grace#grace-revolution.

[26] New Creation Worship. 'Hearts On Fire', Track 3 on *Anthem of Grace*.

[27] New Creation Worship, 'Anthem Of Grace', Track 4 on *Anthem of Grace*.

'Sweeter Than Wine'[28] portrays grace as prevenient, salvific, and sustaining, capturing its multifaceted work in the believer's life. Prevenient grace shines in 'Before the earth's creation – You knew me as I was – And even then You chose me to be Yours', emphasizing God's sovereign choice and calling. Salvific grace is celebrated in 'Lord, my heart's surrendered to Your grace' and 'I receive Your lovingkindness and grace for me', where the believer embraces God's redemptive work. Sustaining grace is reflected in 'Never will You leave me – I'm safe and secure – Forever in Your arms I will abide', expressing ongoing assurance in God's presence and care. Though some phrases do not explicitly mention 'grace', they embody its essence – God's pursuit, redemption, and faithfulness. The song weaves these aspects into a holistic depiction of grace that initiates, redeems, and sustains the believer throughout their spiritual journey.

The song 'Forgiven Much'[29] highlights salvific grace through lines like 'Lamb of God – You're my sin offering' and 'At the cross, there Your will is revealed – Every sickness and pain You have healed', emphasizing Christ's redemptive and healing work. Sustaining grace shines in 'Your love will never fail' and 'You've removed all my fears – All my doubts', portraying God's ongoing comfort and assurance. Sanctifying grace is captured in 'Now and evermore I say – You are my righteousness' and 'I am forgiven much – Your mercy knows no end', reflecting grace's sanctifying and empowering effect. Prevenient grace is subtly expressed in 'By Your grace, in Your arms I am found', revealing God's initiating love. Together, these elements depict grace as redemptive, sustaining, and sanctifying, shaping and transforming the believer's life.

'Restore'[30] highlights prevenient grace in 'You are light – You draw us', illustrating God's initiating love that calls believers into a deeper relationship. Salvific grace is reflected in 'The prodigal – Embraced in love by the Father', symbolizing redemption and restoration for the lost. Sustaining grace emerges in 'Restore us – Darkness turns to light' and 'In You I rest, my heart confess' conveying renewal, peace, and ongoing support. The line 'For what was lost – Your grace will pour – You give so much more' emphasizes grace's restorative and sustaining power to heal and renew. The song situates restoration as

---

[28] New Creation Worship, 'Sweeter Than Wine', Track 5 on *Anthem of Grace*.
[29] New Creation Worship, 'Forgiven Much', Track 7 on *Anthem of Grace*.
[30] New Creation Worship, "Restore', Track 8 on *Anthem of Grace*.

a post-salvation experience, where grace continues to revive and redeem. Themes of spiritual renewal, restored vitality, and redemption of 'wasted years' before knowing Christ underscore the depth of sustaining grace. Through its message, the song affirms that no loss is beyond the reach of God's love, inviting reflection on his continual work of restoration and hope.

'I Surrender'[31] offers a holistic portrayal of grace, intertwining prevenient, salvific, sanctifying, and sustaining aspects. Verse 1 highlights prevenient grace as God's love awakens the sinner – 'Chose me even when You knew – I was tainted by sin'. The chorus celebrates salvific grace through surrender, reflecting Christ's sacrificial love and the believer's yielding response. Verse 2 expresses sanctifying grace – 'To the fullness of Your grace' – and affirms justification in 'I stand justified by Your grace'. Sustaining grace empowers the believer to live as an heir of God's kingdom with awe and devotion. The song narrates the journey of grace, inviting listeners to embrace the freedom and assurance found in surrendering to Christ's redemptive work.

The theme of 'I Will Follow After You'[32] centers on sanctifying and sustaining grace. Verse 1 highlights God's faithfulness as the foundation for continual praise and devotion. Verse 2 conveys joy and security under God's protection, celebrating his lovingkindness. Verse 3 reflects a longing for God's presence – 'Seek Your face, O my Lord – In the morning light' – illustrating grace that sustains through spiritual thirst and darkness. Verse 4 celebrates assurance in God's love and guidance, emphasizing his sanctifying and sustaining grace. The lyric 'In Your holy sanctuary – Will I behold Your face' evokes sanctifying grace, depicting a transformative encounter with God in a sacred space of communion and worship. The subsequent line, 'Your loving right hand – Guides and covers all my ways', affirms God's sustaining grace, symbolizing his strength and tender care. This imagery reflects the psalmic tradition of God as protector and shepherd, offering guidance and protection throughout life's journey. The recurring chorus, 'For Your grace and mercy – Is more than enough', highlights the inexhaustible nature of God's sanctifying and sustaining grace. It deepens this theme by coupling grace with the believer's

---

[31] New Creation Worship, 'I Surrender', Track 10 on *Anthem of Grace*.
[32] New Creation Worship, 'I Will Follow After You', Track 11 on *Anthem of Grace*.

response: 'So let me give You glory – Pour my life upon Your feet'. Here, sustaining grace inspires a life of worship and surrender, as the believers acknowledge their dependence on God's grace and mercy. This depiction underscores grace as a sanctifying and sustaining force and the foundation for wholehearted devotion and faithful following after Christ.

The next six songs from the *Encounter* album (2017) explore the theme of grace. 'Love Burns Bright' [33] radiates God's multifaceted grace through vivid imagery and declarations. Prevenient grace appears as God's love, the sole light in darkness, awakening hearts and the world. Salvific grace is expressed in 'Paint the sky with truth and mercy' and 'Justified – Your grace my story', reflecting how grace redeems and redefines the believer's life. The phrase 'Set a fire deep in (me)' symbolizes personal transformation through justifying grace, igniting change that mirrors God's truth and mercy. Sustaining grace is evident in God's ever-brightening presence, continually filling hearts with his glory.

'Wonderful (Grace Made Real)' [34] encapsulates the multifaceted nature of God's grace. Prevenient grace is seen in 'Heaven come into this moment' and 'You are singing o'er my life', highlighting God's initiative to draw near and breathe life into broken hearts. Salvific grace is expressed in 'Mercy found me in my failings' and 'Freedom paid with arms wide open', reflecting Christ's sacrificial love and forgiveness. Sanctifying grace emerges in 'Take these shattered pieces, mend them in Your nail-scarred hands', while 'Grace made real in every weakness' conveys sustaining grace, offering strength for each challenge. Finally, sustaining grace is seen in the ongoing cry for Jesus and unceasing praise, affirming God's enduring presence.

The song 'Shadow Of Grace' [35] portrays grace as multifaceted, encompassing prevenient grace that imitates God's calls by drawing hearts and breaking 'walls of silence', salvific grace that forgives sins and restores life through Jesus' sacrifice, and sanctifying grace that transforms brokenness and empowers believers to grow in the trust of God. It opens with grace as the ultimate sacrifice – 'Eternity hung on the cross – Looking at me – Eyes brimmed with love', embodying

---

[33] New Creation Worship, 'Love Burns Bright', Track 3 on *Encounter*. Released 2017. https://newcreationworship.sg/albums/encounter#love-burns-bright.

[34] New Creation Worship, 'Wonderful (Grace Made Real)', Track 4 on *Encounter*.

[35] New Creation Worship, 'Shadow Of Grace', Track 5 on *Encounter*.

Jesus' selfless act of love and freedom. The phrase, 'Shadow of grace' illustrates how Christ's salvific grace covers human shame through his sacrificial death, offering an exchange for sin.

The song 'All Of You'[36] begins with an act of surrender, capturing the yielding of self and the believer's response to God's salvific grace. The bridge – 'Take my heart, surrendered to Your grace' – reflects sanctifying grace, emphasizing the transformative work of grace in the believer's life. The desire for God to use one's life for his glory demonstrate ongoing spiritual renewal and alignment with God's will. Additionally, the plea for God's light to illuminate the heart reflects the sustaining grace, nurturing and strengthening the believer. The song's progression from surrender to communion reflects the relational dynamic of salvation, where God's grace saves, sanctifies, and sustains, completing the work of redemption in the believer's life.

The song 'For You So Loved Me'[37] portrays grace in its various aspects: prevenient grace, seen in God's initiative to remove guilt and draw the believer into his love; salvific grace, exemplified in Jesus' sacrifice that justifies and redeems, restoring brokenness; sanctifying grace, reflected in the transformation of a stony heart and surrender to God's trust for ongoing spiritual growth; and sustaining grace, revealed in Jesus as the guiding light through life's uncertainties. The bridge – 'Breathing in Your grace – Trusting in Your love – Calling on Your name, Jesus' – emphasizes sustaining grace, highlighting God's ongoing presence and love.

The imagery of walking upon waves in the chorus of 'Letting Go'[38] illustrate how God's sustaining grace empowers and sustains believers through challenges, providing peace and calm. Verse 1 highlights God's enduring peace and perfect love: 'In the tempest's roar – Still Your peace endures forever – Certain as the dawn – Perfect love has won my heart'. Verse 2 deepens this, expressing trust and surrender: 'Casting all my cares – To the One who holds tomorrow – Resting in Your love – Grace now overflows in me'. The song weaves the four aspects of grace: prevenient grace in God's love reaching out, salvific grace through trust in Christ's work, sanctifying grace in spiritual growth and surrender, and sustaining grace in resting in God's

---

[36] New Creation Worship, 'All Of You', Track 6 on *Encounter*.
[37] New Creation Worship, 'For You So Loved Me', Track 7 on *Encounter*.
[38] New Creation Worship, 'Letting Go', Track 9 on *Encounter*.

peace. Together, it paints a theological narrative of God's comprehensive and continuous grace in the believer's life.

Five songs from the *As He Is So Are We* album (see Table 3) explore different aspects of grace. The title track, 'As He Is So Are We',[39] reflects the scriptural truth of 'grace and truth' from John 1.14–17, highlighting Jesus as the Word made flesh. The song emphasizes God's salvific grace through Christ's sacrifice, portraying rescue from darkness, fear, and death, and securing victory. Salvific grace is depicted in Christ's shed blood, bearing grief, and healing. Sanctifying grace appears in the believer's transformation, captured in lyrics like 'Seated in Christ' and 'As He is, so are we'. Sustaining grace is shown in the assurance that Jesus has the 'final say', renewing hope and dispelling fear. The bridge emphasizes the enduring impact of grace, proclaiming freedom and restoration.

This chorus passage in 'Your Lavish Love'[40] reflects prevenient, salvific, sanctifying, and sustaining grace. Prevenient grace is reflected in the repeated embraces, symbolizing God's pursuit of the lost before they are aware – 'As I took one step to You – Lord, You came running – Leaving heaven behind'. The lyrics – 'Here I stand, I am caught in Your lavish love' and 'Carried home through repeated embraces' – highlight the ongoing, sustaining nature of God's love and grace. At the same time, the phrase 'How You gave it Your all just to find me' speaks to the salvific grace of God, where Jesus' sacrifice and grace rescue and redeem the believer. 'Jesus Your touch heals the broken' encapsulates the essence of God's sanctifying grace. Together, these aspects show how God's grace seeks the lost, saves, sanctifies, and sustains, enveloping the believer in his love and mercy.

The song bridge of 'YHVH'[41] portrays salvific, sanctifying, and sustaining grace. It declares salvific grace by identifying Christ as 'The Lamb of God who bore my shame' and emphasizing his atoning sacrifice: 'On the cross You died to take my sins away'. Sanctifying grace is reflected in 'Your hand of grace was nailed in grace', symbolizing renewal through Christ's crucifixion. Sustaining grace is evident in 'Jesus, risen King, we call upon Your name', as believers rely on

---

[39] New Creation Worship. 'As He Is So Are We', Track 2 on *As He Is So Are We*. Released 2020. https://newcreationworship.sg/albums/as-he-is-so-are-we#as-he-is-so-are-we.

[40] New Creation Worship, 'Your Lavish Love', Track 4 on *As He Is So Are We*.

[41] New Creation Worship, 'YHVH', Track 5 on *As He Is So Are We*.

Christ's resurrection power. The lines 'God is the strength of my heart' and 'my portion forever' highlight his enduring presence, providing spiritual sustenance and support. Together, these elements demonstrate the multifaceted workings of divine grace in the believer's life.

'Trust In The Lord'[42] captures salvific, sanctifying, and sustaining grace. Divine grace is seen in the call to 'Trust in the Lord with all my heart', reflecting God's guidance in shaping the believer's path. Salvific grace shines in 'All of my hope is in You, Jesus', affirming reliance on Christ's saving work. Sanctifying grace is expressed in 'I'll walk by faith and not by sight', highlighting God's transformative work in developing trust. Sustaining grace is seen in 'Every breath is held in Your hand' and 'Whenever I call, You will rescue'. Together, these themes reveal the multifaceted nature of divine grace in the believer's journey.

'For My Good'[43] reflects the themes of salvific, sustaining, and sanctifying grace through imagery and declarations of faith. Salvific grace is evident in 'Jesus, my stronghold and shelter' and 'You are my shepherd', reflecting God's redemptive care. Sustaining grace is evident in 'You walk every step by my side', underscoring his constant presence, and in the commitment to 'walk by faith, not by sight' and 'With every step I will rise', highlighting sanctification and trust.

'No Longer I'[44] from the 2024 *Whom Jesus Loves* album captures themes of salvific, sanctifying, and sustaining grace. Salvific grace is proclaimed in 'How You loved me and gave Your life' and 'You are my salvation – You are my redemption', emphasizing Christ's redemptive work. Sanctifying grace emerges in 'You've brought me out of the valley, changed my life completely', and 'No longer I, but Christ in me', reflecting ongoing spiritual renewal. Sustaining grace is seen in 'Your grace is all I need' and 'I will boast in my weakness – For there Your strength is perfect', highlighting God's provision in times of frailty. Together, these themes celebrate God's transformative and sustaining grace in the believer's journey.

---

[42] New Creation Worship, 'Trust In The Lord', Track 6 on *As He Is So Are We*.

[43] New Creation Worship, 'For My Good', Track 7 on *As He Is So Are We*.

[44] New Creation Worship, 'No Longer I', Track 1 on *Whom Jesus Loves*. Release 2024. https://newcreationworship.sg/albums/whom-jesus-loves#no-longer-i.

The song, 'Father',[45] encapsulates prevenient, salvific, sanctifying, and sustaining grace. Prevenient grace is shown in 'You loved me forever from the start' and 'Embraced me with mercy from Your heart', highlighting God's initiating love. Salvific grace is depicted in 'Lord, You surrounded me with Your light', symbolizing deliverance and illumination through Christ's redemptive love. Sustaining grace is seen in 'You go before me – You never leave me' and 'You are the constant that never changes', emphasizing God's unwavering support. Sanctifying grace is expressed in 'Here in Your presence is where I belong', signifying the transformative power of God's presence. Together, these themes celebrate the comprehensive and life-changing grace in the believer's journey.

'Call Upon Your Name'[46] reflects prevenient, salvific, sanctifying, and sustaining grace. Prevenient grace is captured in 'There's a voice stirring deep within – Calling me to Your secret place', illustrating God's invitation. Salvific grace is expressed in 'There's a fountain of grace I know – Blood that washed all my filth and shame', symbolizing Christ's redemptive sacrifice. Sanctifying grace appears in 'I call upon Your name – Forever I am changed', showing the believer's transformation. Sustaining grace is seen in 'Your mercies flow', highlighting God's ongoing support. Together, these themes illustrate the multifaceted of God's grace, guiding, saving, transforming, and sustaining the believer.

'Embraced',[47] reflects salvific, sanctifying, and sustaining grace. Salvific grace is expressed in 'This life I live – By Your blood I've been redeemed', affirming Christ's sacrifice and the believer's redemption. The line 'And now I'll praise – The name of the One who has set me free' reinforces this freedom. Sanctifying grace emerges in 'I will arise – Shine with the light of Your freedom' and 'My soul revived – As I hear that voice of my Saviour', highlighting transformation. Sustaining grace is seen in 'Forever I'm embraced – By Your goodness and Your grace', symbolizing God's ongoing support. Together, these themes highlight grace's work of redemption, transformation, and endurance in the believer's life.

Eight other songs, though not explicitly mentioning the keyword 'grace', subtly embody multifaceted essence. They reflect prevenient

[45] New Creation Worship, 'Father', Track 2 on *Whom Jesus Loves*.
[46] New Creation Worship, 'Call Upon Your Name', Track 3 on *Whom Jesus Loves*.
[47] New Creation Worship, 'Embraced', Track 10 on *Whom Jesus Loves*.

grace in God's invitation to intimacy or restoration. Salvific grace is conveyed through redemption, forgiveness, and the restoration of the lost. Sanctifying grace is implied in themes of transformation, spiritual dependence, and continual renewal. Sustaining grace is seen in lyrics that offer spiritual sustenance, peace, and strength. Together, these songs portray the powerful, ongoing work of grace in the believer's journey, even without explicitly naming it.

The song 'Refuge'[48] from the *Anthem of Grace* album intertwines sustaining and salvific grace. Sustaining grace is seen in affirmations like 'No fear comes', 'I will not grow faint', and 'Your faithful love endures age to age', emphasizing God's enduring strength. Salvific grace is conveyed through imagery such as 'You delivered me from harm' and 'In the shadow of Your wings', highlighting God's protective presence. The refrain 'I run to You, my refuge' reflects trust and reliance, encapsulating grace as both redemptive and sustaining. Together, the lyrics portray grace as protective, redemptive, and empowering in the believer's journey.

'Finished'[49] captures prevenient, salvific, and sanctifying grace. Prevenient grace is reflected in 'Relentless love pursued my soul – Till condemnation lost its hold', illustrating God's love breaking the enemy's condemnation. Salvific grace is emphasized in 'You took my sin – The just for the unjust' and 'You paid in full salvation's price', highlighting Christ's redemptive sacrifice. 'Through Your redeeming blood' underscores this grace's power to redeem. The breaking of condemnation also points to sanctifying grace, transforming the believer's heart with the liberating truth of God's love. Together, these elements highlight grace as loving, redemptive, and sanctifying.

Without the explicit usage of 'grace' in the song, 'Sons And Daughters'[50] reflects salvific grace. Verse 1 speaks to the redemptive power of grace, highlighting the transformation into a 'new creation'. Verse 2 emphasizes being 'born again' through Christ's sacrifice, affirming both salvific and sanctifying grace in the believer's identity as God's child. The chorus celebrates freedom and forgiveness in Christ's love, while the bridge highlights sustaining grace, reinforcing God's favor and the unity that empowers believers to live with faith and purpose.

---

[48] New Creation Worship, 'Refuge', Track 6 on *Anthem of Grace*.
[49] New Creation Worship, 'Finished', Track 9 on *Anthem of Grace*.
[50] New Creation Worship, 'Sons And Daughters', Track 2 on *Encounter*.

'Sky'[51] conveys the various aspects of God's grace through imagery of divine restoration, and divine calling. Prevenient grace is seen in God's stirring of creation, drawing believers into God's presence. Sanctifying grace is symbolized by rain on the heart, representing transformation and renewal. Sustaining grace emerges in the anticipation of miracles, the restoration of the broken, and the longing for God's will and kingdom, offering hope and purpose. Together, these elements emphasize grace as both a renewing and empowering force creatively.

From the *As He Is So Are We* album (2020), 'Give Me This Mountain'[52] encapsulates God's grace through triumphant faith, renewal, and victory. Prevenient grace is reflected in the call to rise and follow God, with love breaking obstacles and leading the believer forward: 'Your love is calling me onwards, I'm moving'. Salvific grace shines in the victory of Christ's cross: 'Jesus, You've conquered all' and 'The cross proclaims, the victory is ours', emphasizing redemption and God's unshakable promises. Sustaining grace is seen in daily renewal and transformation: 'Each day I wait on You, my strength in You renewed', while the repeated affirmations of God's unwavering promise reinforce trust in his ongoing support. Together, the song powerfully testifies to grace's role in initiating, saving, and sustaining the believer's journey.

'Supply'[53] conveys prevenient grace through Christ's sacrifice, which removes sin and brings peace, healing brokenness, and fear. Salvific grace is reflected in the acknowledgment of Jesus' redemptive work, making all things whole. Sanctifying grace is symbolized by drinking from the wellspring of life and lifting hands in worship, depicting ongoing transformation. Sustaining grace is found in the assurance of Jesus as the constant supply in every season, offering peace and calm in times of need. Together, the lyrics highlight grace as the source of redemption, transformation, and sustenance without explicitly naming it.

'Face-To-Face'[54] reflects sanctifying grace through the transformative power of God's presence, which heals, restores, and completes

---

[51] New Creation Worship, 'Sky', Track 8 on *Encounter*.

[52] New Creation Worship, 'Give Me This Mountain', Track 1 on *As He Is So Are We*.

[53] New Creation Worship, 'Supply', Track 3 on *As He Is So Are We*.

[54] New Creation Worship, 'Face to Face', Track 5 on *Whom Jesus Loves*.

the believer. The imagery of being drawn into God's loving embrace and experiencing healing through his touch symbolizes the ongoing sanctification process. In the chorus, the encounter with God's presence causes fear to fade and tears to be wiped away, illustrating grace's purifying and restorative nature. Ultimately, the believer is made whole and transformed in God's presence, creatively expressing the continuous work of grace, even without explicitly mentioning the term.

The last song, 'Whom Jesus Loves',[55] though absent of the word 'grace', powerfully conveys salvific grace through its focus on God's sacrificial love and the redemptive work of Jesus Christ – 'On Calvary, You took my sin – My soul, my life, set free'. The acknowledgment of Jesus bearing sin and setting the believer free speaks to the salvation through grace. The declaration, 'I am the righteousness of God' points to sanctifying grace, affirming the believer's new identity in Christ. Additionally, sustaining grace is evident as God's love is described as ever-present, protecting the believer, and continually unfolding miracles and blessings. The certainty of salvation and promises exemplifies grace that saves, sanctifies, sustains, and assures the believer of their beloved status in Christ.

Insights

NCC's lyrical analysis highlights the theological perspectives of grace articulated within their compositions. The examination reveals the distribution of grace's theological dimensions across the analyzed songs: prevenient grace highlighting God's initiating work in humanity before salvation; salvific grace underscores its centrality in NCC's theology of redemption; sanctifying grace reflects the significance of God's ongoing sanctification in transforming believers; and sustaining grace emphasizes God's provision for empowering and sustaining the believers' faith journey. This distribution showcases a balanced yet salvation-centered theological narrative in NCC's lyrical compositions.

The portrayal of grace in these songs is rarely confined to a single perspective. Instead, grace is presented as multifaceted, showcasing God's work in individuals through various dimensions – drawing

---

[55] New Creation Worship, 'Whom Jesus Loves', Track 8 on *Whom Jesus Loves*.

them to Jesus Christ, redeeming, and restoring, sanctifying and empowering believers for transformed living. This layered depiction emphasizes the richness and depth of God's grace, highlighting its continuous and holistic impact on the believers' lives through the songs of NCC. It reveals grace as a dynamic and continuous work of God within believers, mediated and empowered by the Holy Spirit, often referred to as the 'Spirit of Christ', shaping their faith journey and spiritual formation.[56]

Theologically, NCC's song lyrics align with the Apostle Paul's doctrine of grace, which forms the cornerstone of the church's message of salvation. Paul emphasizes that grace precedes faith, functioning as the divine means by which salvation is made accessible to humanity (Eph. 2.8–9). In this framework, grace is the unmerited favor of God that removes condemnation, not through human effort but through the redemptive work initiated and sustained by God himself (Rom. 8.1–4). Prevenient grace, as portrayed in Paul's writings, reflects God's initiative in reaching out to lost humanity, drawing them toward reconciliation (Rom. 5.8; Titus 2.11).

Salvific grace is central to Paul's gospel, encapsulating God's restorative power to redeem and justify sinners through faith in Christ's atoning sacrifice (Rom. 3.24–26). This grace secures believers' status as children of God and heirs of eternal life (Gal. 4.6–7). Furthermore, sanctifying grace, which Paul describes as the transformative work of the Spirit, renews believers, and liberates them from sin's dominion (2 Cor. 3.17–18; Rom. 6.14). The Spirit's empowering presence enables believers to live holy lives and faithfully fulfill God's call (Phil. 2.13).

Finally, sustaining grace, a recurring theme in Paul's epistles, empowers believers to endure trials and remain steadfast in their faith (2 Cor. 12.9–10; 1 Cor. 10.13). This grace underscores God's ongoing provision of grace, enabling believers to trust him continually as the source of their strength in the journey of faith (Phil. 1.6; Heb. 12.1–2). These theological dimensions – prevenient, salvific, sanctifying, and sustaining – form the theological backbone of NCC's songs, aligning with the church's gospel teachings and Paul's doctrine of grace. The study illustrates how God's grace is presented as an

---

[56] Studebaker, *From Pentecost to the Triune God: A Pentecostal Trinitarian Theology*, p. 263.

ongoing, transformative force in believers' lives, enabling their spiritual growth and ongoing relationship with Christ.

Conclusion

This study affirms that NCC's song lyrics effectively articulate the church's 'gospel of grace', aligning with the church's teachings and the Apostle Paul's theology. The thematic depth and creative expression of grace in their music reflect the church's core beliefs and shape the spiritual lives of its congregation. Through contemporary congregational songs, NCC continues to emphasize the centrality of grace, inviting worshippers into transformative encounters with God's abundant grace.

7

A DIVINE INVITATION OF WORSHIP: THE INTERSECTION AMONG SPIRITUAL DIRECTION, TRAUMA, AND HOPE

ALAINE THOMSON BUCHANAN*

Introduction

This chapter explores how Spiritual Direction is an act of worship that can provide hope in the midst of dealing with trauma. Spiritual direction is an opportunity for a director and directee to explore what 'is' today, where and how God is present in the midst of what 'is', and how God may be inviting the directee to respond. The Polyvagal theory is one way to explore how trauma affects the nervous system. When a spiritual director becomes familiar with this theory, they have a greater opportunity to understand where a directee is coming from and to help a directee explore how God might be at work in the midst of addressing their trauma. The process of earning trust and helping a directee grow in their relationship with God may take weeks, months, or years, and it is an act of worship to God because the director and directee come as they are, explore the realities of what 'is', and create space to listen to what God wants to say and to how God is inviting the directee to respond.

---

* Alaine Thomson Buchanan (PhD, Regent University) is Dean of Graduate Studies at North Central University, Minneapolis, MN.

Trauma

According to Bessel Van Der Kolk, trauma is both an event or series of events that took place sometime in the past, as well as the imprint of that experience on the brain, body, and mind.[1] Stephen W. Porges and Seth Porges describe trauma as experiencing something that 'our neuroception interprets as so scary or life-threatening that it triggers our ANS (autonomic nervous system) to enter a survival mode, and shifts the goalposts on our body's concept of how safe the world is'.[2] Janyne McConnaughey describes trauma as 'anything that causes an individual to feel threatened emotionally or physically, feel powerless, and/or affect their capacity to cope while overwhelmed'.[3] A traumatic event is when a painful experience or series of painful experiences take place where a person cannot control what is happening, and their body responds by fighting, fleeing, or shutting down. When a person remembers or recalls the traumatic event or events, their body may respond similarly to when the remembered event or events took place.[4]

When trauma occurs, it affects 1) the R-Complex brain, which controls reflex, muscle control, balance, breathing, and heartbeat and is reactive to direct stimulation;[5] 2) the Limbic Brain, which is the source of emotions, instincts, attachment, and survival, and focuses on pleasure and pain; and 3) the prefrontal cortex, which controls functions such as skills, reason, speech, meaning, and wisdom.[6]

[1] Bessel Van Der Kolk, *The Body Keeps the Score: Brain, Mind and Body in the Healing of Trauma* (New York: Penguin Books, 2015), p. 21.

[2] Stephen W. Porges and Seth Porges, *Our Polyvagal World: How Safety and Trauma Change Us* (New York: W.W, Norton & Company, 2023), p. 92.

[3] Janyne McConnaughey, *Trauma in the Pews: The Impact on Faith and Spiritual Practices* (Glendora: Berry Powell Press, 2022), p. 3.

[4] Van Der Kolk, *The Body Keeps the Score*, pp. 2, 43.

[5] Van Der Kolk, *The Body Keeps the Score*, pp. 58-60.

[6] Peter A. Levine, *In An Unspoken Voice: How the Body Releases Trauma and Restores Goodness* (Berkeley: North Atlantic Books, 2010), Diagram A, used with permission from Netter Illustrations, www.netterimages.com (Elsevier Inc).

Polyvagal Theory

The Polyvagal theory was developed by Dr. Stephen Porges in 1994.[7] At its basic core, Polyvagal theory helps with understanding how the brain and body work together in stressful, danger-filled, or safe situations.[8] The vagus is the tenth cranial nerve that runs from the base of the brain to the gut, connecting the brain to the body.[9] It regulates one's heart rate and their breathing, digestion, and emotional state.[10] It includes the following systems.

1. Ventral Vagal – System of Connection (Engages with life)-home-core self; heart regulation, bronchi, facial muscles, and head[11]
2. Sympathetic – System of Action (Anxious, Angry, Escapes)[12]
3. Dorsal Vagal – System of Shutdown (Disconnected, hopeless, drained)[13]

When trauma is experienced, a person generally moves from the ventral vagal system to either the sympathetic space or through the sympathetic space to the dorsal vagal space, which is when the prefrontal cortex shuts down. In order to return back to the ventral vagal system, someone in the dorsal vagal space must move back through the sympathetic space first.[14]

---

[7] 'What is Polyvagal Theory?' https.//8e115b39-c03a-4d76-acda-c7be1a334bf8.usrfiles.com/ugd/8e115b_f83c8b6cb81948e7aca99db83c8946a7.pdf, retrieved December 15, 2024.

[8] Stephen W. Porges, *The Pocket Guide to the Polyvagal Theory: The Transformative Power of Feeling Safe* (New York: W.M. Morton & Company, 2017), pp. 5-6.

[9] Porges, *The Pocket Guide to the Polyvagal Theory*, 31; Levine, *In An Unspoken Voice,* Diagram B.

[10] 'What is Polyvagal Theory?' https.//8e115b39-c03a-4d76-acda-c7be1a334bf8.usrfiles.com/ugd/8e115b_f83c8b6cb81948e7aca99db83c8946a7.pdf, retrieved December 15, 2024.

[11] Porges, *The Pocket Guide to the Polyvagal Theory*, pp. 5, 30-31.

[12] Porges, *The Pocket Guide to the Polyvagal Theory*, pp. 5, 29.

[13] Porges, *The Pocket Guide to the Polyvagal Theory*, pp. 12-13.

[14] Tracey Busse, 'Walking Alongside Trauma', Companioning Center, Spring 2022, Zoom.

Spiritual Direction, Trauma, and the Polyvagal Theory

Spiritual direction, in regard to trauma, is meant to help directees discover where and how God might be at work in the midst of how their previous trauma affects the present time and place in which they currently find themselves, whether they be in the dorsal, sympathetic, or ventral space. This means a spiritual director needs to be prepared to observe facial expressions, tone of voice, and other nonverbal cues to understand if a directee is operating the dorsal, sympathetic, or ventral space. When the time is right, the director could offer an exercise to help create space and an opportunity in which a directee might hear from God more clearly.

Both listening and creating space for God to interact with the directee promote peace and hope for those who have experienced trauma. In a spiritual direction session, the spiritual director needs to listen to the Spirit of God, the directee, and themselves at the same time. While the Spirit of God is truly directing the session, the director's role is to 'be' with the directee and serve as a witness as the directee shares what is on their heart, mind, and soul, and when God responds to the directee's heart cries.

There may be times in a spiritual direction session when the director is triggered by something the directee expresses. If and when this happens, it is critical for the director to recognize what is happening, internally acknowledge their feelings and what is happening in their body, and place this experience and feeling off to the side, with the understanding that the director will come back to this experience later. By doing so, the director creates space for themselves to continue being present with their directee, all the while addressing their own heart later.

In order for the spiritual director to provide safe space, trust, and kindness for their directees, they need to discover the particular directee's language for God and how they most easily connect with God. It is necessary to recognize when the directee is open to sharing part of their story, understand when to refer to other professionals, and for the director to allow their own past suffering to create a peaceful, safe space for directees to talk with God about how their trauma affects their life today.

Trust is earned, and it may take quite a bit of time for trust to develop when trauma is present.[15] In some cases, trust may not develop at all. If this happens, it is the director's responsibility to help connect their directee with a different spiritual director, if this is what the directee prefers.

Trauma oftentimes affects a person's image of and relationship with God.[16] In some cases, God may seem to be impotent and powerless, and some people may even feel like God has abandoned them.[17] Because of this, it is important to discover 1) if a person believes in the divine, 2) how they understand the divine, 3) how they refer to the divine, and 4) their current perception of God. The reasons for this are because God meets people right where they are, regardless of their belief system.

A spiritual director's respect of a directee's understanding of God creates an even greater opportunity for both the director and directee to see and understand how the Holy Spirit is in the midst of drawing that person closer to God, all the while providing hope and peace in and through the spiritual direction process. Even though perceptions of God may differ between the director and directee, it is critical for the director to understand the reality that God 'is'. God, the creator of all living things and the giver and sustainer of life, is with the director and directee, undergirding the entire encounter and drawing the director and directee closer to the core of God's heart.

At some point in the session (and if the timing is right), a director may ask something along the lines of 'What is it that you need or desire from God today?' or 'Where and how might God be at work in the midst of what 'is' in your life today?' or 'How is God inviting you to respond?' These questions engage the heart, mind, soul and body of the directee and allow the directee to have an opportunity to explore their needs and desires, as well as how God might be reaching out to them both in response to them for in requesting a response from them.

---

[15]Annemarie Paulin-Campbell. 'Teaching Spiritual Accompaniment in the Context of Trauma', *The Way* 53.4 (2014), p. 35; Anne Richardson, 'Spiritual Direction with Trauma Survivors', *Presence: An International Journal of Spiritual Direction* 25.3 (2019), p. 15.

[16]Paulin-Campbell, 'Teaching Spiritual Accompaniment', p. 33.

[17]Paulin-Campbell, 'Teaching Spiritual Accompaniment', pp. 33-34.

For spiritual directors, a crucial step in helping those who have experienced trauma is creating an environment of trust and safety.[18] If a directee is in the dorsal space, then they are 'shut down' and may need their director simply to be present and to listen attentively. When the survivor is ready, he or she may want to share part of their story with the director. The pacing and timing of their story may be unpredictable, and it is critical for the director to pay attention to facial expressions, body language, and tone of voice. In doing so, God may give the director an idea of when to keep moving forward with the directee's story, when to take a pause, when to take a step back, or when to stop.[19]

This second stage, the sympathetic vagal space, is when a directee senses they can address part (or all) of what happened in their trauma by sharing whatever part of their story they would like to share, allowing themselves to 'be' with God and the director to 'be' with them, as they witness the directee's story alongside them. This is when the body may react similarly to when the initial trauma took place. The director will need to use discernment and interact with the directee to see how they are doing and react accordingly.

Gradually, a directee may reframe their story and realize the trauma is part of their story, yet it does not define the entirety of who they are. Judith Herman writes, 'Perhaps the trauma is only one part, and perhaps not even the most important part, of their life story'.[20] In this third space, the Ventral Vagal Space, a directee reconnects with ordinary life, emerges from isolation, and considers a shifted framework for understanding life, the trauma that happened, and how that trauma influences what 'is' now.[21]

Conclusion

If the spiritual director has basic familiarity with how the 10th cranial nerve connects the brain with the body, alongside a basic understanding of the polyvagal theory, they are better able to recognize the

---

[18]Robert W. McChesney, 'The Morally Injured Inigo de Loyola: New Insights for Ignatian Spiritual and Pastoral Care', *The Way* 61.4 (2022), p. 63.

[19]McChesney, 'Morally Injured', p. 63.

[20]Judith Herman, 'Recovery from Psychological Trauma', *Psychiatry and Clinical Neurosciences* 52 (1998), p. 148.

[21]McChesney, 'Morally Injured', p. 64.

physical and verbal responses of the directee during the session. The spiritual director can help the directee take a necessary step backward, forward, pause, or to stop and take a few deep breaths, as they listen to and watch the directee and listen to the Spirit of God at the same time. In this way, spiritual direction is an act of worship that can bring peace and hope to those who experience trauma.

Addendum

At this time, I would like to share some exercises that have been helpful to some of the directees I have the privilege of walking alongside. We will start with lamenting and then move into a grounding exercise, a breathing exercise, and imaginative prayer. We will conclude with a Lectio Divina-type exercise of reading Mt. 11.28-30. These practices can help with calming the heart and soul of those who are traumatized and provide hope and movement towards healing in the dorsal or sympathetic, and even the ventral, spaces.

Lamenting

1. Using whatever words you prefer to use to describe God, ask for God's attention to be turned towards you.
2. Let God know what is on your heart and mind. What isn't as it should be?
3. Ask God to hear and respond.
4. Express your trust in who you hope God is and what you hope for God to do.

Grounding

1. Notice five things you can see.
2. Notice four things you can touch and touch them.
3. Notice three things you can hear.
4. Notice two things you can smell.
5. Name one thing you can taste.

Breathing exercise

1. Breathe in for 5-10 seconds.
2. Hold it for 5-10 seconds.
3. Exhale for 5-10 seconds.
4. Relax for 5-10 seconds.

*Repeat at least three times.

Imaginative Prayer

1. Think of something you want to ask God. It could be a concern, a need, or even something you might just want to tell God.
2. Take a few deep breaths. Imagine yourself in a space that brings you peace or joy. Spend a couple moments in this space.
3. You notice someone coming closer and close to you, and you recognize it is God. As God comes to you, God invites you to ask your question or say whatever you need to say. It's okay to take some time with this and tell God as much as you can about what is on your heart and mind.
4. When you are ready, let God respond to whatever you shared.
5. Take a few moments to remain in God's presence, thanking God for the time God has shared with you, expressing gratefulness for this space that brings peace or joy, and thanking your mind, heart, and body for their willingness to engage in this space.
6. Return back to your physical space, doing a grounding exercise or two to reorient yourself, if you would like to do so.

Lectio Divina

Read a passage four times:

1. Listen and notice if there is a word or phrase that sticks out to you.
2. How does this word speak to you in this moment?

3. How is God inviting you to respond?
4. Rest in the presence of God.

'Come to me, all who labor and are heavy laden, and I will give you rest. Take my yoke upon you, and learn from me, for I am gentle and lowly in heart, and you will find rest for your souls. For my yoke is easy, and my burden is light' (Mt. 11.28-30 ESV).

PART 2

WITNESS IN THE PUBLIC

8

Insights to the Nature of Worship and How to Avoid Worshiping Nature: At the Crossroads of Ecotheology and Theology of Worship

Sanna Urvas[*]

Introduction

Pentecostals are well known for their lively and participatory worship. They are less known for their concern for the environment and climate issues. This chapter brings these two topics together by comparing views from other faiths and proceeding to view a Christian approach to worship as an activity which bears the fruit of loving the creation. The aim of this study is to understand, how Pentecostals should and should not construct approaches to worship and creation care.

Daniela Augustine has written a groundbreaking essay 'Liturgy, *Theosis*, and the Renewal of the World'.[1] Augustine constructs a vision of creation as a temple and an arena for humanity to find its place as a mediator and a bond between cosmos and its creator. Additionally, her message is to explain how worship is a pedagogical tool to guide us towards creation care.[2] There is a need to create a greater

---

[*] Sanna Urvas (PhD, University of Helsinki) serves as Professor of Systematic Theology in the Theological School of Finland.
[1] Daniela C. Augustine, 'Liturgy, *Theosis*, and the Renewal of the World', in Lee Roy Martin (ed.), *Toward a Pentecostal Theology of Worship* (Cleveland, TN: CPT Press, 2020), pp. 216-36.
[2] See Augustine, 'Liturgy, Theosis, and the Renewal of the World'.

understanding of this connection which will further encourage us to protect the planet.

Jeffrey Lamp lists various reasons for Pentecostals as being indifferent to ecological concerns and creation care. Adoption of dispensationalist beliefs is mentioned as one of the reasons. The dispensationalist paradigm which envisions the church as raptured up and the earth as left down for destruction is central.[3] This did not encourage giving a second thought to the overuse and exploitation of natural resources. Instead, Pentecostals were generally emphasizing individual salvation and empowerment of the Spirit and neglecting the ecological, social, and political soteriology as noted by A.J. Swoboda.[4] The roots of dispensationalist thinking can be located in the theological writings of John Nelson Darby. Dispensationalism has never been a coherent set of theological claims, and it has been developed and contextualized in communities which adopt this eschatological scheme.[5] However, it created a stark dualism by separating theologically the heaven and the earth.[6] This dualism together with doom's day pop culture has created a tendency to ignore what is happening in the environment.

Peter Althouse has elaborated transformational eschatology in dialogue with Jürgen Moltmann. He acknowledges the dissonance of Pentecostal expectation of outpouring of the Spirit with the expectation of the doom.[7] Therefore, to create the bridge across this mental divide between strong pneumatology and Doom's day eschatology, we can turn back to the creation and the covenant God made

---

[3] Jeffrey S. Lamp, 'Ecotheology. A people of the Spirit for Earth', in Wolfgang Vondey (ed.), *The Routledge Handbook of Pentecostal Theology* (London: Routledge Francis and Taylor, 2020), pp. 358-59.

[4] A.J. Swoboda, *Tongues and Trees. Towards a Pentecostal Ecological Theology* (Blandford Forum: Deo Publishing, 2013), p. 193.

[5] Norman Gulley names four stages of development as the Pre-Scofieldian, Scofieldian, Essentialist, and Progressive. Norman Gulley, 'Progressive Dispensationalism. A Review of Recent Publication', *Andrews University Studies* 32.1 (1994), pp. 41-46. This is a division based on historical development but additionally there are variations based on the cultural and geographical diversity.

[6] David G. Hummel, *The Rise and Fall of Dispensationalism: How the Evangelical Battle over the End Times Shaped the Nations* (Grand Rapids: Eerdmans, 2023), pp. 11, 21.

[7] Peter Althouse, 'Pentecostal Eco-Transformation: Possibilities for a Pentecostal Ecotheology in Light of Moltmann's Green Theology', in A.J. Swoboda (ed.), *Blood Cries Out. Pentecostals, Ecology, and the Groans of Creation* (Eugene, OR: Pickwick, 2014), p. 122.

with Adam. Together with this vision of creation as a temple in which the worship takes place, and as such the dwelling place of the sacred, and the covenantal obligation given to us as descendants of Adam, it is possible to imagine a different kind of relationship between creation and the people of God. Due to the fall of Adam grace is needed to reach this place. Worship as a sacramental act between Christ and the community can create a platform for this union in spiritual, experiential, ontological, and in cognitive level even before the final consummation.

Christian theology is devoted to proclaiming a sovereignty of triune God who created the world. Therefore, to combine two concepts, worship and ecology, it is essential to clarify the foundation of the Christian understanding of the ontological reality of cosmology. Thus, discourse about worship and ecology is not to converse about worshiping nature as divine, it is very much about worshiping only the Creator God. This clarification is a necessity and relies on the Christian confession of transcendent God and a panentheistic worldview. Equally, it is vital to understand the status of believers as part of that created nature.

The Pentecostal understanding of worship includes the notion of transformation. Participation in the divine sphere through the Holy Spirit will generate a change due to the life-transforming nature of the Spirit. This transformation is not an abstract concept rather, it can be experienced emotionally, spiritually as well as in a cognitive level. Furthermore, the covenantal relationships between God and humanity are combined by grace, promises, and obligations which are valid already in this age. This combination will be discussed below.

Religion and environment have been paired in the academic discourse, for example, by putting religions in the dock. This discourse will be visited first. Additionally, worship and nature as a combined topic has a hidden twist to point towards themes that may break the boundaries of the Christian kerygma of the sovereignty of God. This is evident, for example, in the message of a certain kind of environmentalism which projects nature as divine, or even as a Goddess.[8] I am aware that there is a danger for misunderstanding my message, so I will begin by providing insights to two faith traditions and the

---

[8] See, for example a philosophical study of the subject. Paul Reid-Bowen, *Goddess as Nature* (London: Routledge, 2007).

relationships between divinity and created order according to their cosmology. This will then be reflected with the Adamic covenantal relationship with the Christian worldview, and how worship has a role in this bond.

Theoretical Observations on Religions and Environment Crisis

There are several disciplines which have studied the relationship between religiosity and environment. Environmental philosophers have pondered which are the primary reasons for the current environmental crisis. One crucial question is whether religious views are a primary reason or only a secondary. If religiosity was the primary reason, religious leaders could be key players to change the current decline. If those are secondary and only explanatory, it will be a harder task. The latter model presents a materialistic approach which reasons that ecological-economic activities of humanity is the primary reason for the current environmental crisis. According to this model, worldview conceptions related to the natural world have developed to support and promote these currently exploitative activities. The former model takes religious kerygma seriously.[9]

Matthew Foster has labored an ethical philosophical study on human–nature relationships and presents three categories: first, humans as overpowering the otherkind, secondly, a balanced relationship which he has named as stewardship ethics and thirdly, the needs of otherkind and nature over humanity. The key concept to argue any requirements for actions are discussed with the concept of justice.[10] This approach could lead to the search of a possible righteous way to treat the environment. However, Foster explains that it is an impossible task to solve that question realistically because non-human nature cannot be an actor in a justice system.[11]

Michael Levine has provided a helpful comparison between theistic, pantheistic, and atheistic environmental ethics. For example, the

---

[9] Heikki Pesonen, 'Kristinusko ja ympäristökriisin "syylliset"', in Heikki Pesonen (ed.), *Uskonnon luonto. Ihmisen ja luonnon suhde uskonnollisessa ajattelussa* (Jyväskylä: Atena Kustannus Oy, 1999), pp. 13-14.

[10] Matthew Foster, *The Human Relationship to Nature: The Limit of Reason, the Basis of Value, and the Crisis of Environmental Ethics* (Lanham, PA: Fortress Academic, 2016), pp. 353-55.

[11] Foster, *The Human Relationship to Nature*, pp. 353-55.

pantheistic ecological ethics will not be anthropocentric theoretically because it is metaphysically based in terms of the divine unity. However, a theistic view will not prevent a deep concern of environment either.[12] He concludes that at the end the crucial question is not about the philosophical worldview of the cosmos but rather whether people simply care to listen to other voices in the first place.[13]

Therefore, in order to influence the current crisis, religious actors have at least in principle the means to influence the situation, because any materialistic reasoning for ethical behavior is bound to crumble in front of the greedy selfish humanity. Thus, God and religion are needed to point humanity to its place in this cosmological system and to its role in the world as a piece in a balanced whole. This is the reason why we need to view the Adamic covenant. Now it is time to look at the attitudes of two faith traditions.

Environmentalism in Islam and Hinduism, and Some Insights to the Finnish Forest Relationship

Lynn White was one of the first writers in the late 1960's who connected Western Christianity with the humanity's problematic relationship with nature. Christianity was to blame for the environmental degradation. Interestingly, one defender of Christianity was a Muslim philosopher Seyyed Hossein Nasr. He wrote that it was not the Christian theology to blame but the rationalism, humanism, and renaissance which de-sacralized nature and gave the right to dominate the environment for the sake of a worldly wealth.[14] Since, there has been a debate about the roles of humanity and nature before Allah and in the Islamic law.[15] Tuula Sakaranaho writes that in Turkish traditional understanding the Quran presents humanity not as above nature but rather in an equal position. Humans were not offered the dominion singlehandedly, but it was equally offered to nonhuman nature, but they did not take it. It is notable that according to the Quran, the

---

[12] Michael P. Levine, 'Pantheism, Ethics and Ecology', *Environmental Values* 3.2 (1994), pp. 131-32.

[13] Levine, 'Pantheism, Ethics and Ecology', pp. 121-38.

[14] Seyed Hossein Nasr, *Man and Nature: The Spiritual Crisis of Modern Man* (London: Unwin Chapterbacks, new edn, 1990), p. 96. Quoted in Emmanuel Karagiannis, *Why Islamists Go Green. Politics, Religion and the Environment* (Edinburgh: Edinburgh University Press, 2023), p. 3.

[15] Karagiannis, *Why Islamists Go Green*, pp. 3-4.

natural environment carries the sign of the invisible God, which therefore, requires attention and care.[16] Islamic beliefs have roots in Judaism and in the Christian tradition, and it is not surprising to find similarities between these two worldviews. Hinduism, however, is another case which requires attention.

Christopher Framarin argues for the direct moral standing and the intrinsic value of animals, plants, and all-natural environment based on scholarly writings of Hinduism and their philosophy. Per Framarin, Hindu texts and tradition present a plausible base for environmental ethics. This implies the proper treatment of nature. The base argument for this human–nature relationship is built on the foundation of ontological connection and similarity between these two, or alternatively, the sacred essence of all nature. Additional remarks reveal the cosmological claims of Hinduism that nature has an *atman* (an eternal and immaterial self) and it is identical with *brahman* (God) and/or it emanates from *brahman*.[17] Framarin quotes O.P. Dwivedi who claims that 'veneration, respect, and acceptance of God in nature is required of Hindus in order to maintain and protect the natural harmonious relationship between human beings and nature'.[18] It is notable that Framarin does not express the relationship between humanity and the natural environment with the concept of worship but as veneration and respect even if there is this ontological connectedness with divinity involved. However, the common assumption regarding Hinduism and Hindu beliefs includes the worship of nature or natural objects.

Radharani P. explains that, for example, tree worship is a common tradition in Hinduism but that it is an expression of a lower form of religion. The development commenced from the reverence of trees as a necessity for human survival and flourishing. Trees were considered the choicest gift from God to humanity. Trees represented symbols of gods and deities and were endowed a personality. Therefore,

---

[16] Tuula Sakaranaho, 'Pyhyyden taju. Tieto, ihminen ja luonto islamissa', in Heikki Pesonen (ed.), *Uskonnon luonto* (Jyväskylä: Atena Kustannus Oy, 1999), pp. 45-47.

[17] Christopher G. Framarin, 'Hinduism and Environmental Ethics: An Analysis and Defense of a Basic Assumption', *Asian Philosophy* 22.1 (2012), pp. 75-91.

[18] Dwivedi, O.P. 'Dharmic Ecology', in Christopher K. Chapple & Mary E. Tucker (eds), *Hinduism and ecology* (Cambridge, MA: Harvard University Press, 2000), pp. 3-22. Quoted in Framarin, 'Hinduism and Environmental Ethics: An Analysis and Defense of a Basic Assumption', p. 5.

the environmental concern in Hindu tradition has a magico-ritualistic origin.[19] Naturally, there is a highly diverse spectrum of worldviews in modern India, but the incentives to preserve the natural environment which are rooted in cosmological understanding of the sacred and divinity are inevitable.

There are also other cultures in which trees have a considerable major role for the culture. For example, trees and forests are considered the security of life and source for living in Finnish culture. Forests cover more than 75% of Finland. Forests are an important part of the cultural identity for Finns and has been considered also a place in which humanity can experience divine presence, either the traditional religious deities according to ancient Finnish primal religion or Christian God. An old saying expresses that 'Forest is a Finn's church'.[20] Forest is a place for worship, not the trees but rather to meet the sacred and one's God, whomever it is. Finnish largest denomination Evangelical Lutheran Church is a major owner of forest areas and active in preservation projects.[21] Finnish Pentecostals are unfortunately less known for their environmental advocacy.

Islamic tradition directs worship only to the almighty God, Allah. Fazlun Khalid explains that the Qur'an offers a holistic view of a created order and humans are expected to be submissive which in turn is understood as a conscious act of worship. Allah creates a balance in the universe, and men should obey and maintain that balance.[22] Natural environment mirrors the nature of divinity because God has placed all of God's attributes or his names on the created order. Syafaatum Almirzanah explains in turn that creation is a self-disclosure of God. He writes about the interconnectedness of

---

[19] Radharani P., 'Hinduism and Natural Environment', *Journal of Dharma: Dharmaram Journal of Religions and Philosophies* 31.4.(2006), pp. 497-504.

[20] One survey of the meaning of forest to the forest owners was titled 'Forest is a church, gym and a bank'. See Anna-Kaisa Asikainen, *Metsä on kirkko, kuntosali ja pankki. Pohjoissavolaisten metsänomistajien näkemyksiä erikoisluonnontuotteiden tuotantoketjuun osallistumisesta* (Master of Business and Administration, thesis. Savonia, University of Applied Sciences, 2024).

[21] Luomakunnan metsät hanke, (Forests of creation project). See more https://luontoliitto.fi/luontoliitto-ja-kirkko-kaynnistavat-yhteistyon-seurakuntametsien-luontoarvojen-kartoittamiseksi/.

[22] Fazlun M. Khalid, 'Exploring Environmental Ethics in Islam: Insights from Qur'an and the Practice of Prophet Muhammad', in John Hart (ed.), *The Wiley Blackwell Companion to Religion and Ecology* (Hoboken: John Wiley and Sons Ltd, 2017), p. 132.

humanity with the created order. Creation can survive without humanity but humans cannot live without plants and animals. Simultaneously humans are at the top but without a proper respect they will neglect their responsibility to act according to their given role.[23] Nawal Ammar and Allison Gray argue that 'To respect God means one has to respect and glorify all Creation, including environment'.[24] They continue by explaining that environmental attitude should have a devotional dimension as a worship of God through rituals and reverence, and generate activity towards God's creation. However, they admit that statistics show how Muslim countries are not following their own religious ethos, and they are failing to follow this ideal.[25]

The Islamic concept of worship has similarities with a Christian one; worship is directed towards a sovereign divinity which is simultaneously transcendent and imminent.[26] However, a Christian, and especially a Pentecostal, understandings of worship have a sacramental character which enlarges this act towards more participatory activity rather than being only as devotion by submission. Therefore, a Pentecostal understanding of worship has more potentiality to influence the worshipping community – not only morally but also affectively – to engage in creation care activities. In order to understand this connection and causality from worship to activity, it is necessary to observe the theology of worship, some metaphysical aspects of reality, and the agency of humanity. The background is the Adamic covenant and a pneumatic element of worship.

Worship as a Sacramental Relation Between God and the Church

Steven Félix-Jäger writes, 'Christian worship has two principal aims: to glorify God and to help people enter into God's presence'.[27] He

---

[23] Syafaatum Almirzanah, 'God, Humanity and Nature: Cosmology in Islamic Spirituality', *HTS Teologiese Studies/Theological Studies* 76.1 (2020), pp. 6-7.

[24] Nawal H. Ammar and Allison Gray, 'Islamic Environmental Teachings: Compatible with Ecofeminism?' in John Hart (ed.), *The Wiley Blackwell Companion to Religion and Ecology* (Hoboken: John Wiley and Sons Ltd, 2017), p. 302.

[25] Nawal H. Ammar and Allison Gray, 'Islamic Environmental Teachings', pp. 304-305.

[26] See the Muslim view. Khalid, 'Exploring Environmental Ethics in Islam', pp. 135-36.

[27] Steven Félix-Jäger, *Renewal Worship. A Theology of Pentecostal Doxology* (Downers Grove: IVP Academic, 2022), p. 3.

defines worship as an act in which a person's heart is turned towards God because of God's self-revelation. Therefore, worship is an active and participatory activity which has both human and divine elements. God is the primal mover but without a human activity, it cannot be called worship.[28] This relationality needs to be seen both on the ontological level as well as a spiritual act. To view worship as a transformative event it requires this ontological dwelling of the Spirit within an individual, and in a worshipping community. Félix-Jäger reminds us that Christ's mission on earth was to bring humanity and creation back to life by restoring the relationship, and the outpouring of the Spirit was the means for that end. Worship holds this eschatological hope by renewal in the Spirit. The mission of the church is to make this as a wider reality via Spirit empowerment. Félix-Jäger extends this renewal to include creation.[29] This ontological and participatory activity is directed towards Jesus as the King but this communal and relational dimension invites the attention to be enlarged. Therefore, the understanding of the reality is the key.

The comparison with other faith traditions that teach us that humanity is part of creation, as claimed by both Islamist and Hinduist beliefs, but ontologically separated from the divinity (and such disagreeing with Hinduism) but still having a potentiality which Islamic ethos does not offer. This is the renewed bond and relation between humanity and the otherkind because of the mysteries of Incarnation, the redemption, and headship of the cosmic Christ as the ultimate telos of all existence. Paul describes this eschatological hope and reveals this cosmic redemptive plan for the church (Col. 1:15–20). It is an absolute plan of God which has been proclaimed to us but, he waits for us to participate in this process. Individuals need to accept the salvation prepared and offered through the Christ's work on Calvary, and communities are called to be united by the Spirit. This makes the church and the community of believers different from other faiths. The key is the participatory union with the cosmic Christ through worship today; and one day in full reality. The transformative nature of worship is part of this eschatological hope. Félix-Jäger writes, 'As God reconciles us in worship, we receive a foretaste of the total reconciliation that awaits all of creation at the eschaton'.[30]

---

[28] Félix-Jäger, *Renewal Worship*, p. 5.
[29] Félix-Jäger, *Renewal Worship*, pp. 37-40.
[30] Félix-Jäger, *Renewal Worship*, p. 48.

Félix-Jäger writes that healing is one essential dimension of sacramental encounter between God and the worshipper.[31] Therefore, we need to be agents of this reconciliation towards the created order, and not to work against the flow of the Spirit that ongoingly sustains, renews, and feeds the creation. The healing union that is materialized for us in worship needs to generate concrete and extended acts of healing as part of our obedience as reconciled people. Healing is a manifestation of God breaking into the present reality, and as stated by Félix-Jäger, it is a promise of the coming kingdom.[32] 2 Chronicles 7.14 states clearly that the healing of the land is included in the process of renewal of the relationship between God and the people who humble themselves. This healing is an act of God, but again, the people were not passive spectators in the covenant which Jahve made with the people of Israel. They were to obey the will of the protector, their God.

The Covenant Between God and His People, in the Garden and Today

The idea of a covenant is one way to observe the relationship between God and humanity. There are several covenants clearly mentioned in the Bible, and for the Christian faith the new covenant is the fulfilment of all the promises given through earlier covenants. The first covenant was made between the Creator and Adam and Eve as representatives of humanity even if the actual word covenant is not mentioned in the Genesis text. A pneumatological reading of covenants acknowledges that each covenant was a combination of requirements of obedience, and aspects of grace, power, and promise, which were then all completed in the new covenant.[33] Adam and Eve were given the mandate and a promise of abundant life together with a close relationship with God but it was dependent on their obedience to the rules, or a singular rule. This rule was broken, and so

---

[31] Félix-Jäger, *Renewal Worship*, p. 48.

[32] Félix-Jäger, *Renewal Worship*, p. 49.

[33] I follow here Stephen Wellum's idea of Progressive Covenantalism which is reconstructed with my pneumatological reading. See Stephen J. Wellum, 'Progressive Covenantalism', in Brent Parker & Richard Lucas (eds.), *The Covenantal and Dispensational Theologies. Four Views on Continuity of Scripture* (Downers Grove: IVP Academic, 2022), pp. 74-75. God has always promised his power to his followers; he has never left his people alone.

was the closeness and the fullness of life; buthe solution was already promised before the doors of the Garden were closed. Christ is the fulfilment of those promises, and the new covenant has all the grace but the requirements of obedience hold still. God's people have not yet the full access back to the Garden but worship is the means to enter this realm through the Holy Spirit. If we have received the grace and the fullness of life through the sacrifice of God, we are obliged to be obedient to the first command given to humanity to work for the land as to serve it[34] and to protect it.[35] It is only logical that if the new covenant is restoring what was broken, it will not negate the required obligation of the original first covenant. People of God do not yet live in full and free obedience because humanity is still bound by its sinful instincts but with the power of the Spirit the body of Christ should be able to remain in the obedient relation to the King, if they only understand the requirements.

The Adamic covenant is related to The Garden of Eden. This garden has been a symbol of various divine dimensions. David Taylor notes how the garden was not a farmland but an archetypal sanctuary. Those Hebrew words, 'to work' and 'to protect', are the same language as used in Exod. 3.12 and Num. 28.2 to describe sacrificial offerings.[36] There is yet another connection with the Garden and worship service. However, the creation is told to be anxiously longing and waiting for the revelation of the sons of God (Rom. 8.19). This creates a vision of three parties in the covenant which all have their positions but the creation does not have the agency other than to remain patiently waiting. The hidden message of the Genesis story and the Garden proleptically points to the present in which the worshiping community can visit this sanctuary in the spiritual realm. Alexander Schmemann points out that worship, or liturgy, does not create a new reality; it celebrates what is already existing but hidden.[37]

---

[34] The Hebrew word לְעָבְדָהּ can be translated with the meaning of working as a servant. Strong's lexicon 5647. 'abad' עָבַד.

[35] וּלְשָׁמְרָהּ means to guard and protect. Strong's lexicon 8104. 'shamar' שָׁמַר.

[36] Taylor quotes Gordon Wenham's 'Sanctuary Symbolism in the Garden of Eden Story', in *Proceedings of the 9th World Congress of Jewish Studies* 9 (1986). See David Taylor, 'Creation and Worship', in K.J. Williams and M.A. Lamport (eds.), *Theological Foundations of Worship: Biblical, Systematic, and Practical Perspectives* (Grand Rapids, MI: Baker Academic, 2021), p. 39.

[37] Ivana Noble, 'Mystery and Worship', in K.J. Williams and M.A. Lamport (eds.), *Theological Foundations of Worship: Biblical, Systematic, and Practical Perspectives* (Grand Rapids, MI: Baker Academic, 2021), p. 160.

This unites the acts of knowing as a cognitive dimension, and participatory dimension of unity with God in a mysteriously metaphysical level. This cognitive choice to direct the attention in worship should, therefore, embrace the future reality in which the creation does not need to remain anxious. This forms and extends the requirements of obedience outside of the church service to our daily life choices. Christ is the centre of the worship, and the mystery of the cosmic Christ invites the church to the mystery of eternity and the present united. Ivana Noble writes that worship teaches the church 'how to hold together the relationship between the world, the church, and the kingdom of God'.[38] The worshiping community participates both in God and in the world via the kingdom of God. This enforces the transformative aspect of worship.[39]

Beauty and the Holiness of the Garden Visited Through Worship

The essence of the Garden is from one hand the ontological reality present but hidden. Furthermore, this hiddenness communicates symbolically the harmony of the kingdom which is present in the worship. This age we see this reality as in the mirror.[40] God's creation has an ability to speak through this mystery, this mirror. The last point of this study is to understand this secret by visiting the philosophy of icons which helps us to relate to the divine beauty which is hidden in the nature; not to be worshipped but to direct our devotions and actions correctly.

Serafim Seppälä approaches this hiddenness with the philosophy of icons. The Greek word for icon (εἰκών) did not mean only sacred pictures painted on the wood. Anything that represented the message and the presence of the divine was considered an icon in Byzantine theology. Ultimately, the whole universe is an icon. Spiritual eyes allow a person to see the world as an interconnected whole with layers which have relations and structures of meanings. These layers are not separated realities but each penetrating and reflecting others by forming icons in which the lower may mirror the higher in the perfect

---

[38] Noble, 'Mystery and Worship', p. 164.
[39] Noble, 'Mystery and Worship', p. 165.
[40] 1 Corinthians 13.12.

order. Incarnation is the most beautiful example of this, the representational relationship between the Son and the Father. Son is not ontologically lower than the Father but kenotic two-nature Christology describes this relation. Humanity as Imago Dei is another example. Thus, we are a reflection point of divine beauty in a material way, as is the whole creation.[41] Therefore, the stark difference between devotion of the sacred in Hinduism and the respect for the hidden God reflected in the natural environment is, first, this cosmological order. Second, it is to understand the act of worship correctly when we are connected to this natural sphere.

Worship as a participatory activity and the meeting point of God can be seen through the phenomenon of resonance described in the natural sciences. Seppälä writes. 'According to scientific definitions, a vibratory system resonates when it is influenced by an external force whose oscillation frequency is approximately the same as the system's natural frequency of vibration. Resonance amplifies the vibration to a particularly large extent.'[42] The pneumatological reading of this revels that creation is formed with this potentiality of vibration which resonates the hidden beauty and holiness of God. It is hidden in humanity, it is hidden in nature. This vibration becomes an experiential reality of the presence of God when the church gathers in worship. The Holy Spirit is the vital force which amplifies the presence of the divine, and the body of Christ can enjoy the presence of their King. But it is the same Spirit dwelling in us when we go to the forest and see the beauty of the creation. The same vibration can be experienced again, and this unites the people of God with the nature which resonates the hidden beauty of the Creator. This experience of interconnectedness between God, nature and humans has been misinterpreted in, for example, Hindu cosmology. Therefore, the correct teaching of the nature and direction of worship is vital. But Pentecostal worship has neglected the kerygma of this connection and it has not directed the worshippers to love the created order.

Worship at the church context should encourage us to fall in love with God. Our hearts enlarged by the divine love enable as to be united with the cosmic Christ. But if our spiritual eyes remain blind to the hidden beauty of the creation we fail to remain obedient to the

---

[41] Serafim Seppälä, *Ikonin filosofia* (Helsinki: Kirjapaja, 2014), pp. 17-19.

[42] Seppälä, *Ikonin filosofia*, pp. 26-27.

covenant of the original, and now restored humanity, as people of God. Through the power of the Holy Spirit we have spiritual access to the Garden in worship even if ontologically, the veil is still present. Thus, our act of worship becomes prophetic which points to the future fulfilment in the everlasting abundance and happiness in that Garden if we are united to look after our planet.

9

¡GLORIA A DIOS! PENTECOSTAL SEMINARIANS READING THE BIBLE TO GLORIFY GOD

LAURA JEAN TORGERSON*

Introduction

The seeds of my research into Pentecostal biblical interpretation were planted when I was teaching a NT survey course at an ecumenical Protestant seminary in Nicaragua to a group of students who were mostly Pentecostal. At the time of the class, the students were in their second of five years working towards a *licenciatura* – an undergraduate degree in theology. These students were incredibly kind and respectful towards me, and so I was very surprised by their mutiny – when they refused to do an exercise I assigned in class – staging a debate about faith and works between Paul and James – because they insisted that 'the Bible does not contradict itself'.

Students who have learned how to read the Bible in their churches often feel disoriented when they enter a biblical studies classroom, whether they are coming from Pentecostal churches in Nicaragua or from Pentecostal, Baptist, Lutheran, Presbyterian, Episcopal, or other churches in the United States.[1] To understand better the challenges that theological students face (in Managua and elsewhere), I

---

* Laura Jean Torgerson (PhD, Graduate Theological Union) is Associate Professor of NT at Berkeley School of Theology, Berkeley, CA.

[1] Laura Sterponi, 'Literacy Socialization', *The Handbook of Language Socialization* (2011), pp. 227-46. Caroline Zinsser, 'For the Bible Tells Me So: Teaching Children in a Fundamentalist Church', *The Acquisition of Literacy: Ethnographic Perspectives* (1993), pp. 55-71. Mary M. Juzwik, 'American Evangelical Biblicism as Literate Practice: A Critical Review', *Reading Research Quarterly* 49.3 (2014), pp. 335-49.

conducted a multi-site ethnographic study, based in three Pentecostal congregations that have sent their students to this seminary, and in the seminary classrooms. In each of these settings, I observed how biblical interpretation was taught and practiced, with a primary focus on religious education of adults.[2]

My research considers the interpretive practices of some Nicaraguan Pentecostals through the lens of ethnography of literacy, which understands reading, recitation, and writing as culturally specific practices.[3] This methodology sheds light on the relationships between literacy practices and the ideologies they enact, and does so via microanalysis – honing in on specific instances that connect to larger themes and phenomena, to understand better why students engage biblical texts in certain ways in specific moments. This perspective explicitly rejects a deficit model, in which academic modes of study of biblical texts provide something that was lacking, instead adopting a cultural model, in which different interpretive communities have different purposes and practices for reading.

The Nicaraguan Pentecostals in this study, like other Christians, learn about the Bible through worship. Their initial formation guides believers to read the Bible for many devotional purposes that overlap with worship: praising God, thanking God, experiencing God's presence, hearing a word from God, and giving God glory. The theme of this year's conference, 'More Than a Song: The Public Witness of Pentecostal Worship' presented an opportunity to go back and look at the data from this study with a different lens, one focused on devotional reading.

Some students resist academic biblical interpretation as antithetical to faithful practice, others integrate the various tools they are given into a new perspective, and still others use academic tools for devotional purposes. Most students will manage the tensions between the divergent norms of the spaces they inhabit using all of the listed approaches at one time or another. To my surprise, my latest

[2] Laura Jean Torgerson, 'Crossing Contexts: Nicaraguan Pentecostal Biblical Interpretation in Church and Seminary' (PhD dissertation, Graduate Theological Union, 2022).

[3] Jonathan Boyarin, 'Voices around the Text: The Ethnography of Reading at Mesivta Tefereth Jerusalem', *Cultural Anthropology* 4.4 (1989), pp. 399-421. James Collins and Richard Blot, 'Literacy and Literacies: Texts, Power and Identity', (2003). Marcia Farr 'Essayist Literacy and other Verbal Performances', *Written Communication* 10.1 (1993), pp. 4-38.

reading of the data focused on the complexity of these tensions sur-
faced ways that two female seminary students engaged problems with
the Bible and its applications in their church communities by using
academic methods. Rather than devotional reading methods or orientations causing problems for academic methods and vice versa, academic methods and orientations allowed women to challenge
church interpretations of a troubling text.

As a supplement to observation of biblical interpretation in congregations, I conducted text-study focus groups, where I had different groups at the seminary read passages and answer open-ended
questions. I had groups of first year students, third year students, and
students in their 4th or 5th year, as well as groups of professors, reading the same texts and answering the same questions.

The two women who are the main focus of this chapter, I call
Mercedes and Damaris.[4] They often had very different perspectives.
Damaris is a lay woman, and a lawyer by profession. Before and during seminary she became very disenchanted with her church, especially when she investigated its bylaws and saw that the concentration
of power and lack of accountability around finances were not as they
should be. At the same time, she had a great love for her work in the
church, especially teaching teenage girls.

Mercedes co-pastors her church together with her husband and
was writing her thesis entitled '*¿Pastora o esposa del pastor?*/ (Female)
Pastor or pastor's wife?' trying to deal with a lack of clarity about the
leadership roles that she and other women play in the church. While
she and her husband generally saw themselves as equal partners in
church leadership, many church members and others saw her as 'the
pastor's wife' rather than a pastor in her own right.

In my first focus group with these women, the fifth-year students
were reading the story of Moses and the burning bush (Exod. 3.1-
14). In that session, a discussion arose about whether Moses truly
had the option to reject God's call, and most of the group – including
Damaris – agreed that this was a fairly bossy (*mandón*) image of God.
Damaris went so far as to say that this story was not part of what she
bases her faith on, that 'Moses is not my reference. For me, Jesus is
my reference / *Moisés no es mi referente. Para mi, Jesús es mi referente*'.
Mercedes responded in protest, 'But it's the foundation, that is

---

[4] All names are pseudonyms.

history, because the Bible is our foundation/ *Pero está el fundamento, eso es historia, porque la Biblia es nuestro fundamento'*. Mercedes goes on to say that from her experience, responding to God's call to serve God's people is something that she does with joy, and not because anyone has obligated her to do it. The story of the call of Moses connected positively with her own sense of vocation and calling to serve as a pastor. Because she imagined herself as being like Moses, she also imagined Moses as being like her, freely and joyfully accepting God's call to lead.

A few weeks later, when the fifth-year students read Mk 7.24-30, the way Mercedes engaged the text was markedly different. Given that her experience of church life included both joyfully pursuing a call to ministry and barriers to that pursuit because of sexism, perhaps this should not have been surprising.

The second question after reading the passage was: Q2: What do you like about this passage? Is there anything you dislike? Mercedes gave the first response to the question.

Excerpt 1	
(1) *Mercedes: La parte donde Jesús, como que es excluyente, que aparta y hace acepción de personas, me parece bien que al final se hace el acto de misericordia.*	(1) Mercedes: The part where Jesus, how he is exclusive, that he separates and shows partiality, I think it's good that at the end the act of mercy is carried out.
(2) Damaris: *No me gusta que Jesús aparece como arrogante.* *Siempre me incomodó ese pasaje, no comprendía como podía ser en ese momento, me desagradaba,* *Así que lo omití durante todas mis lecturas de forma sencilla;*	(2) Damaris: I don't like that Jesus is portrayed as arrogant. That passage always bothered me. I didn't understand how he could be [like that] in that moment; I disliked it. So I just omitted it from all my readings.
y ahora que comprendo que lo escribió alguien, entonces me doy cuenta que, Eso era como una mancha que tenía Jesús ideal, y que fue comprendida nada más, que mi Jesús ideal, no existe y ya. (3) B.: *¡dejaste de creer!* (4) Damaris: *No, (Risas ...) Me tuve que hacer una construcción, no es que dejé*	And now that I understand <u>that someone wrote it,</u> I realize that, that was like a stain on the ideal Jesus, and it was simply understood, that my ideal Jesus doesn't exist, and that's it. (3) B.: You stopped believing! (4) Damaris: No, (laughing) ... I had to construct ... It's not that I stopped

| de creer en *Él, pero en el Jesús ideal que yo me idealicé …* | believing in him, but in the ideal Jesus that I idealized … |

Throughout the different groups of readers, with all the texts read, more advanced students and professors had more to say in response to the question 'Is there anything you dislike about the text?' than newer students. In this group of students in their final year of study, not only is Mercedes willing and able to answer the question about something in the text she dislikes, but she also leads with what she dislikes (turn 1). Damaris also picks up on the 'dislike' part of the question and does not respond to the first part of the question at all (turn 2).

In these and many other instances of talking about texts, speakers may discuss a story as a text, written by someone, and refer to features of the text and its author's intentions. When someone mentions textual features or the author, this indicates that the speaker is operating in a 'text-reading' frame. A very common alternative is to operate in a frame of discussing the story as an account of 'things that actually happened', and to treat even fictional characters as if they are real.[5] The tensions between talking about a story as text or a story as events are present across genres. They are particularly significant when the story being discussed is from the Bible. The movement between these frames can be rapid. The second frame is closely connected with devotional reading, especially two of its aspects: connecting to the person of Jesus and/or God, and obeying instructions based on interpretation of the biblical text.

In her response (turn 1), Mercedes slips from a text-reading frame, referring to the 'part where' Jesus acts a certain way, into a talking-about-events frame, describing his attitude using the verb 'to be' and making him the subject of the verbs 'separate' and 'show' (partiality). While experiencing Jesus in the reading of Bible stories is generally positive, this experience of Jesus is a problem for both women.

This story has long been a problem for Damaris, and before she began her theological studies, the strategy she used for dealing with

---

[5] In her study of women's readings groups, Elizabeth Long, *Book Clubs* (Chicago: University of Chicago Press, 2003), p. 606, noted that readers 'often respond directly to fictional characters as if they were real people, discussing whether they like or dislike, admire or despise them, rather than focusing on how or why authors may have constructed such characters'.

it was simply to ignore it and not read it. Her framing also shifts. Her initial response about how she feels in the moment, is that Jesus 'seems' arrogant (2) – implicitly, that he is portrayed that way by the text and/or author. When she talks about her relationship with this story in the past, however, she describes it as something that happened, rather than as a text or story. As she returns to the present, with the word 'now' she explicitly evokes the text-reading frame with the phrase 'that someone wrote it'. She also seems to be describing a journey of sorts, from the past, when the text 'always bothered' her, to 'now that [she] understand[s]' after almost five years of seminary education. Throughout the groups of different readers, talking about biblical authors was a consistent way of both indexing and practicing academic biblical interpretation.

The brief – and joking – intervention by a young male student (turn 3) presents a tension present in seminaries the world over, including many of my students in Berkeley, California. Will learning too much about the Bible and theology threaten our faith? Despite her disillusionments, Damaris insists that she has not lost faith in Jesus but rather has had to adapt her image of him (turn 4).

This brief excerpt of initial responses to one question brings out some of the broader dynamics at play, especially for the Pentecostal women students. The text of Mk 7.24-30 itself is a problem because it does not conform to the image of Jesus found in other stories. There is a tension between connecting with the events and characters directly. The language used reveals a strong sense of 'before' and 'after' of theological studies and how these students read the Bible.

The following question, Q3, is 'How do you imagine this passage? If you were there, what would you have seen, heard, smelled, and touched?' Damaris doesn't really respond to the question, which invites readers to engage the story as 'something that happened', to consider it as an event more than a text.

Excerpt 2	
(a) Damaris: *Yo le puse una raya a este pasaje, ya te dije que omití ese espacio porque me resultaba grosero ...*	(a) Damaris: I crossed out this passage, I already told you I omitted that space because it seemed rude to me ...
(b) *y la siguiente pregunta que habla ¿dónde lo escuchó?*	(b) and the next question that says, where did you hear it?

| (c) *Haya ... que se exalta la forma que se humilla esa mujer, por la fe, no era necesario humillarme para eso* | (c) Oh ... the way that woman humiliates herself is exalted, because of her faith, it wasn't necessary to humiliate myself for that, |
| (d) *pues, ya le dije que ese era mi Jesús ideal, que tenía una mancha negra, un puntito negro, ya lo borré.* | (d) well, like I said, that that was my ideal Jesus, that he had a black mark, a little black dot, I just erased it. |

Implicit in the response Damaris gives (a) right after the question is posed, is that this kind of imaginative reading belongs to her past rather than her present. Because she had already 'crossed out' and 'omitted' the passage, she claims to have had no experience of imagining the story and has no capacity to generate a response in the present – possibly because she is committed to operating in a 'text-reading' frame.

Damaris moves ahead to the next question (b), skipping over the question about imagining the story, just as she describes having skipped over the story itself in the past and comes closer to a key theme for her that is about her history with the text (c). Not only did she ignore or omit the story from her personal reading, but she also had a negative experience of people telling her what the text meant. This brief phrase, 'the woman who humiliates herself is exalted' represents the church teaching she has heard (c). She gives another reason for her rejection of the passage – not just the image of Jesus it presents, but the way it has been used in her church to dictate a submissive attitude.

Even thinking about herself prior to her studies, she seems to have had internal criteria for rejecting this interpretation: 'it wasn't necessary for me to humiliate myself for that' (c). She then circles back to her omission of the passage. Elsewhere, she talked more about how people in the church and her family would criticize her for speaking her mind, and this story was very much linked with those experiences.[6]

This excerpt shows further evidence of different frames in past and present, and how this text was not a resource available to Damaris for devotional reading or a positive experience of Jesus. In addition, Damaris begins to reveal here what she later expanded upon,

---

[6] There is a certain irony in this text being used to criticize someone for speaking up – when the woman's boldness in talking back to Jesus is one of the most notable features of the story.

that beyond the text itself, its use in her church to praise the submission of women is a big part of what made it painful.

A little later, in response to Q7: 'Does this passage tell us anything about God? Does it how to live our faith?' Mercedes also pushed back against the questions.

Excerpt 3	
(a) Mercedes: *Es que la verdad es que nosotros ya lo miramos <u>más a base de quien lo escribió</u>, y por ejemplo entendemos que ahí, hay una forma excluyente hacia la mujer, y cualquier protagonista es una mujer a quien Jesús le está diciendo esas palabras tan fuertes, y no se las dice por ejemplo a un hombre, Porque no fue un hombre el que llegó a pedir por una hija, por ejemplo,*	**(a) Mercedes**: The truth is that we already <u>look at it more based on who wrote it</u>, and for example we understand that there is an exclusive way towards women, and whoever the protagonist is – it's a woman to whom Jesus is saying such harsh words, and he doesn't say them to a man, for example, because it wasn't a man who came to ask for something for a daughter, for example,
(b) *porque cuando llega Jairo, por ejemplo a Jairo lo trata súper muy diferente de como la trata a la mujer, entonces (.) porque de hecho, estamos viendo un maltrato* [Benjamin cabecea] *palpado ahí, entonces, (que te) pone a esta mujer, a una mujer,*	(b) because when Jairus arrives, for example, he treats Jairus very differently from how he treats the woman, so (.) because in fact, we are seeing a palpable abuse [*Benjamin nodding*] there, so, (what) puts this woman, a woman,
(c) *es más a Jairo <u>le pone nombre</u>, e ella ni siquiera, solo que era Sirofenicia, Entonces ya nosotros <u>ya estamos con nuestra mente trabajada en eso</u>, entonces cuando se nos pregunta, en que nos aporta, como miramos a Dios desde nuestra fe … es como que…*	(c) and even more Jairus <u>is given a name</u>, and she is not even [given one], only that she was Syrophoenician. So then already – We <u>are already with our minds working on that</u>, so when we are asked, what does it contribute to us, how do we see God from our faith … it's like …

Mercedes, too, is indexing an academic approach to this text, one that focuses on human authors (a). By foregrounding this orientation to the text, she implies that academic reading precludes theological and ethical readings. But as she goes on, it becomes clearer that it is actually the sexism in the text that makes it hard to appropriate for devotional and other religious purposes.

She highlights the contrast with how Jesus responds to this woman and to Jairus, a man who comes to Jesus to ask for the healing of his daughter. This intertextual connection considers the harshness of Jesus' words to constitute abuse, and that these words put the woman in a very difficult position (b).

The phrase 'is given a name' (c) indicates an awareness that someone has written this story. She remains in a frame that considers the text as a text rather than a report of 'what happened'. A consistent theme with all students was that newer students and those who were more suspicious of academic study tended to read the Bible simply as a report of what happened. Those who are more advanced and/or more open to the new approaches they are learning are more likely to talk about the texts *as* texts.

Mercedes identifies sexism in the text by contrast, both in the behavior of Jesus and the choice of the narrator not to give the woman a name. When talking about the actions of Jesus – 'saying such harsh words' (a) and 'treats Jairus very differently' (b) – she slips into an 'event' frame even though she has just evoked the 'text-reading' frame. While she seems to attribute the difficulty of this passage to an orientation to 'who wrote it', a text with a human author who had intentions and prejudices, this slippage between frames suggests that the difficulty comes from a more devotional orientation to the text, its content, and the Jesus it portrays. This difficulty is compounded by the choice at the narrative level not to give her a name. So, in this instance, *both* devotional and academic styles of reading and talking about the text reveal sexism.

The phrase 'our minds working on that' (c) refers to both an academic orientation to the text and the elements of the text highlighted by this style of reading. It's hard to capture in a transcript the sense of despair in her voice as Mercedes trails off at the end of this answer, as if to say, 'What can you do?' I got the sense that she was almost offended or hurt that I had asked her to find a theological lesson in this text.

In these examples, we see that academic study can highlight problems in biblical texts, but it also provides tools for engaging texts that were already problematic, and that have been used to insist that these women accept harsh words and demonstrate faith by adapting submissive postures. Reading a painful text in such a way to 'look at it based on who wrote it' may actually have a protective effect for these women readers.

Acknowledging the problems in the texts, however, did not pre-clude this group of students from finding meanings in the text that also have devotional significance. Another group of advanced stu-dents, fourth-year students in 2017, also found important meanings in this text while reflecting on its historical context.

In response to Q9, 'Are there people or actions in this text who serve as examples to follow? Are there actions present in the text that we can follow? Are there actions that we should avoid?' Damaris gave the following response.

Excerpt 4	
Damaris: *Y entonces parece que la conducta y la forma que no debemos seguir, es la forma que dice el escritor que tomó Jesús* …	**Damaris:** And so it seems that the conduct and the form we should not follow is the form that the writer says Jesus took …

Here we can see how what might be a shocking conclusion – we should *not* follow the example of Jesus – is made easier by the engagement of a literary critical frame. It is one of two hedges in the response she gives. The first hedge or softening of her answer is 'it seems'. The second is the phrase, 'the writer says'. This distance makes a judgment about the behavior of Jesus less direct because it judges the narrative presentation. The critical distance that allows Damaris to make this judgment gives her a resource for saying that something in the text is a bad example, where previously her only option was to omit it entirely.

The group of fourth-year students jointly constructed a similar response to this same question (Q9). Their responses are more frag-mentary but highlight another aspect of the way these seminarians have learned to find meanings in biblical texts – collaboratively.

Excerpt 5	
(1) Emilia: *Es que sí ya Oscar dijo algo, que no debemos de ser excluyentes.* (2) Rogelio: *Equitativa*	(1) Emilia: Yes, Oscar already said something, that we shouldn't be exclusive. (2) Rogelio: Equitable

Oscar, Emilia, and Rogelio put their response in a more positive sense than 'we shouldn't do what Jesus did'. They find a lesson about treating others equitably, and not excluding others based on ethnic identity, gender, or even religion.[7] The process of arriving at this lesson involves listening to the perspectives of others, highlighting their agreement by referring back to an earlier comment(1), and chiming in by giving the positive attribute – 'equitable' that corresponds to avoiding exclusivity (2).

The group of fifth-year students also arrived at some conclusions through similar patterns of conversation. In response to Q8, 'Does this passage have any application for you and your community?' an older male pastor gave an extensive response excerpted below.

Excerpt 6	
(0) G: *no valoradas … la iglesia, nuestro contexto hoy en día, tenemos que marcar eso, el valor que realmente Dios le da a la humanidad.*	(0) G: … women who are not valued … the church, our context today, we have to highlight that, the value that God really gives to humanity …
Q9: *...example?* (1) Benjamin: *¡Muy bien eso de defender la dignidad!* [palabras entrecruzadas] (2) Mercedes: *Si, defender la dignidad* (3) Damaris: *¿Cómo defenderíamos nuestra dignidad?*	Q9: ... example? (1) Benjamin: That's great about defending dignity! [cross-talk] (2) Mercedes: Yes, defending dignity (3)Damaris: How would we defend our dignity?
(4a) Mercedes: *si porque está bien la interpretación de que la de la perseverancia, la búsqueda, que al final logramos el objetivo,*	(4a) Mercedes: Yes, because the interpretation of perseverance, the search, that in the end we achieve the goal is fine,
(4b) *pero la parte donde tal vez la mujer fue humillada, maltratada, ósea para <u>llegar al objetivo</u> <u>tenemos que permitir eso en nuestras vidas</u>(.)*	(4b) but the part where perhaps the woman was humiliated, mistreated, in other words, <u>to reach the goal, we have to allow that in our lives</u>(.)
(4c) *Cuando predicamos ese texto, digo predicamos, porque yo lo he predicado, sacamos a relucir el carácter de Jesús.*	(4c) When we preach that text, I say we preach, because I have preached it, we bring out the character of Jesus.
(5) Benjamin: *... El de la mujer.* 6a) Mercedes: *Y tampoco decimos la mujer se humilló, se arrastró,*	(5) Benjamin: ... of the woman. (6a) Mercedes: And we don't say the woman humbled herself, she crawled,
(6b) *No, sino que la mujer tuvo fe, fue guerrera perseverante, No se dejó aplastar …*	(6b) No, but rather the woman had faith, she was a persevering warrior, she didn't let herself be crushed …

---

[7] These themes emerged in their broader discussion.

The group that Damaris and Mercedes were in also co-construct a positive meaning and lesson from the text. The final answer to the previous question included an extensive turn from a male pastor (0), mentioning the importance of valuing women who are often marginalized and dismissed in communities and churches. When we moved to the example question, Benjamin references what the pastor said, summarizing it as 'defending dignity' (1). Mercedes chimes in to echo in agreement (2), and Damaris wants to know how this could be applied (3). All four of these students agree that the text holds an important and relevant lesson about the value and dignity of marginalized women, and they show their agreement with one another by taking up one another's ideas and phrasing.

Mercedes remains unsatisfied with this text, both what she sees as its typical church interpretation – one she herself has preached – (4c, 6b) and how it seems to her now, in the middle of wrestling with what it means to be a woman pastor in her church. She insists that leaving out the negative elements of the story is inadequate. As for Damaris, the application that stings and is unacceptable, is that women should accept abusive behavior from the church and its leaders (4b). Although she agrees with the positive lessons that are available, she insists on the need to deal with the problems in the text that echo in the life of the church.

At the end of the focus group in 2017, students were invited to make any final comments after they had answered all the questions.

Excerpt 7	
Emilia: *la verdad es que a mí me llama la atención, la valentía de esta mujer verdad, en aquel tiempo, digo yo, siendo extranjera, como, como se atrevió a entrar, donde estaba Jesús, a esa casa, a una la casa, quizás conocida por ella, estaba Jesús ahí, estaba Jesús ahí en ese tiempo no era permitido que una extranjera, pues hablará con un judío, si en aquel contexto, y la humildad y persistencia a la vez, de la mujer, además de ser valiente, fue humilde y persistente; porque Jesús le dijo una frase fuerte, verdad, y sin embargo ella, ella se bajó, se humilló, y ella dijo: no, hasta los perrillos dice recogen el pan de la mesa.*	**Emilia:** The truth is that I am struck by the courage of this woman, right, <u>at that time</u>, I would say, being a foreign woman, how, how she dared to enter, where Jesus was, into that house, into a house, perhaps known to her, Jesus was there, Jesus was there at that time it was not permitted for a foreign woman to speak to a Jewish man, yes <u>in that context</u>, and the humility and persistence at the same time, of the woman, besides being brave, she was humble and persistent;

	because Jesus said a harsh phrase to her, right, and yet she, she lowered herself, she [humbled] herself, <u>and she said</u>: no, even the dogs, she says, pick up the bread from the table.

In this response I saw an integration of historical information and the Syrophoenician as a positive example for women and men in faith and life. This summary and retelling of the story centers on the mother who comes to Jesus and her courage both in seeking him out in the first place and in persisting in the face of his initial refusal and insult. It does this without skipping over or excusing the 'harsh phrase' and gives the Syrophoenician woman the final say. Her subtle rephrasing of the saying – that the dogs 'pick up the bread from the table' – places an even stronger emphasis on the woman's worthiness and equality.

In conclusion, I began the research for this chapter looking for elements of Bible reading as worship that might impede academic study for these students. What I found was much more complicated. While students do experience tensions between devotional and academic modes of reading, they have already experienced tensions in reading the Bible and navigating what other people tell them it means – before entering seminary. This was particularly significant for two women students in their final year of study, when dealing with a troubling text.

In addition, both the fourth-year group in 2017 and the fifth-year group in 2019 were able to generate lessons that were spiritually and ethically meaningful for them, even from a difficult text. One of the major insights from the larger research project was that in many and various ways, the Pentecostals in this study embody and live out their interpretations of the Bible. While I started looking for explicitly devotional engagement of the biblical text, I realize that the lessons these groups of advanced theology students perceived – not being exclusive of people who are marginalized because of their ethnicity or gender – and defending the dignity of people who are dismissed and undervalued – this too, is a way of reading the Bible to glorify God. It could be theirs, and our, reasonable worship.

10

Worship as Discovery: Martin Heidegger's *Dasein* and the Pursuit of Knowledge

Christain M. Teachout[*]

Introduction

When one considers worship as more than a song, one must first recognize what it means to worship. This chapter defines worship in terms of two aspects. First, worship directs one toward God in reverence, gratitude, and joy. It calls one to acknowledge God's sovereignty, his beauty, and his wisdom. More than this, though, worship is also a matter of God revealing himself – not in the sense of where he is not otherwise present, but in the sense of where he makes himself known. At no point can anyone claim God's absence from the discovery process, as he remains omnipresent. The discovery process does not occur without connection, even if only to time and space. Most often it entails a communal act, which invites humanity to greater communion with God and to participate in communion with others. It is this which makes Martin Heidegger's concept of *Dasein* relevant to this year's theme.

* Christain M. Teachout, PhD, is Adjunct Professor at Assemblies of God Theological Seminary, Springfield, IL.

Heidegger defines *Dasein* as a matter of being in time.[1] More than this, it also incorporates space.[2] It is a matter of existence, but additionally, one must consider how this impacts human existence, especially as it relates to understanding. God is pleased to reveal himself through the pursuit of knowledge. People celebrate and glorify Him through intellectual discovery.

When one considers discovery as worship, one must recognize not only how God is glorified in the discovery process, but also how it is a communal act. Even as corporate singing is edifying to the body of Christ as all members participate together, as multiple individuals share of themselves in the development of knowledge, this also is edifying and life-giving to the body. In the act of discovery, believers share truth. They help others see what God has revealed to them in their specific existence in experience.

Yet discovery is not only a matter of individual learning. From the beginning, God intended discovery as a deeply communal act. He did not place Adam and Eve in Eden and ignore them after this. He walked with them in the cool of the day. He let them work the Garden that they might participate in the pleasure of the creative process. With all of creation pointing toward God and magnifying his glory, everything around them continually directed toward God. They had the pleasure of discovering while communing with God and each other. Humanity was meant to discover in relationship with God.

Additionally, both Adam and Eve existed in perfect communion with the other. Sharing in everything together was good, perfect, and came from the overflow of love that each had for the other. Adam saw Eve as part of himself. Both equally loved and served the other. This would have impacted the discovery process, as well.

When sin entered the world, it impacted more than simply humanity's relationship with God. It impacted their intimacy with one another and their relationship with creation. Discovery became an act of the will and no longer about God. The service and perfect communion of Eden gave way to the off-centered worship of self. Exploring Heidegger's *Dasein*, as viewed through the lens of faith, invites a restored union with God and others, as well as a chorus of

---

[1] Martin Heidegger, *Being and Time* (trans. by Joan Stanbaugh; New York: State University of New York Press, 1996), pp. 15-17.

[2] Heidegger, *Being and Time*, p. 50.

communal discovery as the voices of each generation blend together harmoniously in discovery applicable to their specific time and place.

The Formation of *Dasein*

Heidegger was deeply impacted by the ideas of Edmund Husserl. Husserl, the founder of phenomenology, did not publish much during his lifetime, but after his death he left thousands of pages of unedited manuscripts in shorthand, which have shed light on his philosophy.[3] 'Husserl's goal was to develop a new philosophical science as the radical critique of the possibility of experience, a science that did not take the possibility of cognition for granted.'[4] Husserl believed that essence is defined not only by itself but by the perception of those outside it and by one's prior experience with it. This means that perception is organized prior to sight. Stephen Plant describes Husserl's phenomenology as essentially accusing philosophers before him of failing to consider adequately how cognition impacts perception and encounter. 'Even before I *sense* the world, Husserl thought, my experience of it is already organizing itself in my mind.'[5] In this way, Husserl's primary concern focused on transcendental consciousness. His emphasis on experience remains important for the understanding projected here regarding worship.

Heidegger considers discovery and observes that *Dasein* has the responsibility to 'appropriate what has already been discovered, defend it *against* illusion and distortion, and ensure itself of its discoveredness again and again. All new discovery takes place not on the basis of complete concealment but takes its point of departure from discoveredness in the mode of illusion.'[6] He goes on to consider the role of being in both concealing and revealing truth in relation to others. He describes this process of discovery in terms of connection with others, so that each discovery is relationally connected to that which preceded it. Discovery provides an objectively present conformity between objectively present things, so that discoveredness or

---

[3] John J. Drummond, 'Husserl, Edmund', in *Encyclopedia of Philosophy Vol. 4: Gadamer – Just War Theory* (Detroit: Thomson Gale, 2006), p. 521.

[4] Drummond, 'Husserl, Edmund', p. 522.

[5] Stephen Plant, 'Heidegger and Bonhoeffer', in Peter Frick (ed.), *Bonhoeffer's Intellectual Formation* (Eugene, OR: Wipf & Stock, 2008), p. 304.

[6] Heidegger, *Being and Time*, p. 204.

truth is related to what is encountered.[7] '*Dasein* understands itself in terms of what it encounters within the world. The world in what has been *expressed*'.[8]

Thus, as one encounters truth in one person's discoveries and ideas, this can lead to another's further discovery. All of this occurs within time and space. All of this occurs as each person learns from another who has produced their works before or sometimes alongside them. Two people who occupy the same time and space can produce different works based on their research, experiences, and questions. At the same time, though, being in precisely the same time and space is not a requirement. Someone can exist in a different time or space and still impact the present if their works move beyond their own limits. In this way learning is a living thing, which transcends the capacity of the person discovering. Even after someone has died and no longer impacts the present physically, someone can read their works and be impacted by them. Someone in a country one may never visit or in a time one may never live can contribute to one's understanding, if one learns from their thought. Additionally, one should not think of this only sequentially, as if one is limited to only interact with one specific individual. Rather, in scholarship, one also might engage the works of those who influenced the work in question. Additionally, other works will be considered by one author that another author did not access. Each author brings their own discoveries and research to the table. In so doing, they share not only facts, but their own perspectives, questions, and experiences. In this way, the experiences of one are interrelated to those of another.

Important here, discovery is much more than acknowledging the existence of facts without any relationship with or response to them. Knowledge translates into experience. The data and discoveries of today build upon the ideas of yesterday, and tomorrow someone else will continue to further the quest for knowledge. Each generation works within its own paradigm of time and space. While research can be either an individual or corporate effort, in either case, one must engage the work of others. One must also consider data in terms of experience. This also is one reason academic integrity is so important. It is not just about the right person receiving credit but understanding

---

[7] Heidegger, *Being and Time*, pp. 205-206.
[8] Heidegger, *Being and Time*, p. 207.

the context, perspective, and layers of discovery associated with learning.

Introduction to Sociality

The sharing of knowledge both in utilizing the work of others and in creating new content calls one to give of oneself. Not everyone who shares knowledge does so through a lens of faith or even out of concern for others. Yet, in these things, one does incorporate the work of others and in sharing one invites others to grow alongside oneself, bringing others to the point of discovery, so they too can experience the joy in revelation. In this, God receives honor and glory.

Discovery is deeply related to being and existence. Yet, to understand this idea truly, it is helpful to consider sociality, especially as Dietrich Bonhoeffer considered it. The term 'sociality' is not original to Bonhoeffer. In his notes in the English translation of *Sanctorum Communio,* Bonhoeffer expert Clifford Green defines it as a 'complex category comprising several specific views of person, community, and social relations'.[9] It involves a way of seeing and interacting with others caused by a work of God's Spirit in one's heart at salvation. Only through the Holy Spirit can one truly love others as oneself.

This work of the Holy Spirit in one's heart serves as the foundation for sociality. Love enabled by the Spirit of God quickens in one's heart authentic love for the other so that the good of the other genuinely matters, and one's entire perception of the other changes (Rom. 5.5; Gal. 5.22). Thus, apart from a relationship with God, one's ability to show agape love to another remains decidedly broken. Only the Holy Spirit can enable one to love others in the example of Christ, and only in a healthy Christ-centered community can one rightly love God and others (Phil. 2.1; Col 1.8).

This is not at all to suggest that people outside of Christ cannot love others. That would be ludicrous. I do suggest, though, that as far as exhibiting and experiencing a love, which overflows out of relationship with God, this requires the presence of salvation. This love

---

[9] Clifford Green, 'Preface', in *Sanctorum Communio: A Theological Study of the Sociology of the Church*, vol. 1, of Dietrich Bonhoeffer, *Dietrich Bonhoeffer Works (DBW)* (ed. Clifford Green; trans. by Reinhard Krauss and Nancy Lukens; Minneapolis, MN: Fortress Press, 2009), p. 21.

impacts discovery and the pursuit of knowledge. It helps establish the community and cultivate an entirely different mindset than one would have without the presence of faith.

The question of being in relation to sociality is where Bonhoeffer found Heidegger's *Dasein* helpful. Aside from this, though, when one starts considering the relationship between Heidegger and Bonhoeffer, one begins to consider two very different individuals. In *Being in Time*, one observes that for Heidegger, one must always understand *Dasein* as 'being in this world'. He means this as more than mere existence. While existence does define *Dasein*,[10] it is greater than this. He sees this in terms of complexity within spatial relationships and location. Environment and interconnection with the world are part of *Dasein*.[11]

Jens Zimmermann explains that Bonhoeffer took the idea of *Dasein* and made it a theological one, because for him self-understanding required the presence of faith. Therefore, Bonhoeffer's understanding of this proves critical for this study. Heidegger, as an unlikely ally, gave him a good starting point since he recognized the temporal-historical nature of humankind and how self-knowledge unfolds within history, culture, and tradition. Bonhoeffer appreciated this about his thought.[12]

With these things in place, one should now begin to consider the implications of these things for community and theology. As one does this, it should be understood that Bonhoeffer gathered from a variety of important perspectives from philosophy, sociology, and theology – not just from Heidegger. These other perspectives would absorb the entirety of this chapter, though, if they were brought into focus. When it comes to *Dasein*, let us return to the previous notion of discovery in Eden.

---

[10] Heidegger, *Being and Time*, p. 11.

[11] Heidegger, *Being and Time*, p. 50.

[12] Jens Zimmermann, 'Dietrich Bonhoeffer and Martin Heidegger: Two Different Versions of Humanity', in Brian Gregor and Jens Zimmermann (eds.), *Bonhoeffer and Continental Thought* (Bloomington & Indianapolis, IN: Indiana University Press, 2009), pp. 111-12.

Discovery in Eden: The Fall and the Implications of It

> The Lord God took the man and put him in the garden of Eden
> to work it and keep it. And the Lord God commanded the man,
> saying, 'You may surely eat of every tree of the garden, but of the
> tree of the knowledge of good and evil you shall not eat, for in
> the day that you eat of it you shall surely die' (Gen. 2.15-17).

The entire Garden of Eden was available for discovery. Adam had
been set in Eden with the understanding that he would work and
keep it. עָבַד ('ā·ḇaḏ) is to 'work or serve. [13] The word שָׁמַר (šamar) is to
'keep, watch, preserve'.[14] The idea of dominion granted to Adam earlier was not a position designed to gratify him from a selfish standpoint. God gave Adam and Eve permission to enjoy the Garden, but
part of this enjoyment meant tending to and caring for it. God says
here that Adam may eat of the fruit of the Garden. Yet, Adam also
had an important job of protecting and keeping watch, as well as
serving. To work was to participate in the work of God. He would
learn, discover, and engage with God's design for life as he worked.

In Scripture, keeping is a matter of stewardship. They were not
owners of Eden. Rather, they had been placed there to steward it. 1
Kings 22.14 describes Tikvah, son of Harhas as the keeper of the
wardrobe. This meant he cared for everything that went into it. Keeping is not just a matter of protecting. It requires preservation and
implies responsibility.

Importantly, Adam's role as keeper set him in a specific place with
the responsibility of stewardship. This stewardship only could be
done according to God's design as it occurred within the parameters
God had established in place. Discovery was good, as it occurred
within God's design. Both Adam and Eve, entrusted with the responsibility of stewardship, also received the benefit of communion with
the one who had ownership.

When Satan tricked Adam and Eve to step outside this in Gen.
3.1-8, that discovery failed to be worship but became about themselves. While discovery done according to God's design drew them
near to God and each other, discovery that reached out for what God

---

[13] 'עָבַד', Enhanced Brown, Driver, Briggs Hebrew-English Lexicon, Logos Bible Software.

[14] 'שָׁמַר', Enhanced Brown, Driver, Briggs Hebrew-English Lexicon, Logos Bible Software.

did not offer led to estrangement from God and caused Adam and Eve to feel the need to hide from the one who made them. The relationship had with each other was negatively impacted by discovery through disobedience, as well. Thankfully, it does not end there.

Christological Implications of *Dasein*

Galatians 4.4 reads, 'when the fullness of time had come …' and goes onto describe Christ's mission of redemption. Christ came into a specific time and place to live among humanity and die. There is nothing random about Christ's work or the choices he made as the second Adam. Where the first Adam took discovery and made it about self, the second Adam redeems discovery through his life, death, and resurrection.

The events which led up to Christ prepared for his arrival, and that which occurs after his ascension remain impacted by the reality of salvation found in Christ. The timing of Christ's arrival in this world was not at all accidental. He came into time and space bringing revelation of God, his kingdom, and the salvation available for all humankind. In his death, he makes life possible for all.

As discovery relates to identity and personhood, Christ's restorative work first occurs in the transformation he makes possible through the Cross. Through Christ, the last Adam, discovery once again occurs in relationship with God. Yet, more than only restoring relationship with God, the corporate dimension of discovery also is restored.

Christ came in 'the fullness of time' into the reality of sin and brokenness, so that where the first Adam made community impossible, the last Adam made way for hope and restoration of community. In doing this, Christ also reestablished the relational aspect of discovery. When discovery centers on self, it is corrupt and even crippled by selfishness. When discovery is re-oriented in Christ, it becomes healthy and oriented according to God's design.

Pneumatological Aspects of *Dasein*

From a Pentecostal standpoint, this should lead to a consideration of these things in light of Pneumatology. Pentecostal Theology is based upon Theological understanding, but experience also is a vital aspect of our faith. Veli-Matti Kärkäinnen describes this in terms of the Spirit at work within the body of Christ. He considers the importance of equipping and empowering each member of the community. His focus goes to personhood and the vital role of diversity of voices within the body.[15] While his focus does not go to discovery specifically, what he observes about the work of the Spirit is important for a Pentecostal understanding on this topic within the body of Christ. If people of other cultures, backgrounds, and beliefs are being equipped, strengthened, and served, it makes sense that they also will contribute to the discovery process as equals.

Daniela Augustine also considers the deliberate inclusion of others. She observes that at Pentecost each heard the proclamations in their own language. This demonstrates the hospitality of God, again meeting people in their time and space, so they might know and experience him. This is a divine embrace, which the community cannot ignore.[16] When it comes to discovery, though, even as the Spirit used care to invite hospitably all nations to hear, in the body of Christ, all nations and voices should be permitted to participate in the discovery process.

Nimi Wariboko considers this from the perspective of Pentecostal epistemology. His work considers the idea of sense and spirit. Something can fail to make intellectual sense, but it can make Spirit, as it coincides with the will of God. Discovery is significantly more than a matter of data. The data and facts matter, but a vital experiential component in relationship with the Spirit layers Pentecostal research and translates the data in ways which impact life itself. This allows for depth, creativity, and various possibilities, even as discovery also looks to the facts. Everything must be centered on Christ, and discovery also looks to the Spirit of the Lord both in the development and sharing of knowledge.[17] This sharing of perspectives is not merely about including various ethnicities or perspectives, but it comes to a sharing of experiences. Discovery does not set aside the

---

[15] Veli-Matti Kärkkäinen, *Spirit and Salvation, A Constructive Christian Theology for the Pluralistic World* (Grand Rapids, MI: Eerdmans, 2016), p. 188.

[16] Daniela C. Augustine, 'The Empowered Church: Ecclesiological Dimensions of the Event of Pentecost', in John Christopher Thomas (ed.), *Towards a Pentecostal Ecclesiology: The Church and the Fivefold Gospel* (Cleveland, TN; CPT Press, 2010), p. 159.

[17] Nimi Wariboko, *The Pentecostal Hypothesis: Christ Talks, They Decide* (Eugene, OR: Cascade Books, 2020), pp. 111-12.

intellect, but it also recognizes revelation as more than this. Returning to *Dasein* specifically, being in time looks to the present reality but also the future horizon. One can argue that as one considers discovery at present one must realize tomorrow will be made different by the discoveries of today. This goes for that which is discovered through the leading of the Spirit and intellectual perspectives.

Discoveries, which incorporate into one's experiences, often come as a result of one's own story. The background one brings to a subject, the experiences one has, and the questions that inform one's lens of engagement are further enhanced by an encounter with the Spirit. The Spirit leads into truth. In this way, pneumatological discovery is also an encounter with the Spirit. Discovery, which is led by the Spirit provides a taste of what Eden was. Even as Adam and Eve equally discovered in the very first community alongside one another, in a restored community centered on Christ, all believers equally have a voice at the table. One learns of this world that God has designed – one learns of Him and in this case the sharing with others is life-giving. Where Eve's sharing with Adam brought death and destruction, sharing with one another discovery centered on Christ uplifts the body and brings greater understanding. God is exalted in this sharing of discovery.

Conclusion

Were this chapter to continue, it could further consider the implications of this restorative process for every area of theological thought. While one might initially imagine discovery as an individual act, the fact that the work and experiences of others, as well as the work of God, have an essential part to play in the process, makes discovery a deeply communal act. Christ made it possible for discovery to move away from the self to opportunity to interact with God and worship him in the process. Once again, discovery becomes a matter of honoring God – not just honoring self.

Additionally, in discovery, one listens to the voices of others who also invite yet others to engage in what they have learned. Whereas without Christ, this can be an egotistical act, in Christ, discovery calls brothers and sisters to participate in an ensemble of knowledge directed back toward Christ and his Kingdom. He is exalted in the discovery and presentation of knowledge. He is known through the perspectives of various members in his body who operate in the gifts and skills he has given. This is done, within time and space, as each generation builds upon the thought of those before them. In this way, in Christ, discovery once again occurs, so that God is honored and exalted. His body participates in restored communion with God and each other. This certainly is worship – not in the sense of music, as one might normally imagine, but absolutely in the sense of exalting and fellowshipping with God and sharing in him alongside others.

11

A SONG IN THE NIGHT: AFRICAN AMERICAN PENTECOSTAL WORSHIP AS RECLAMATION AND RESISTANCE

JOHNATHAN E. ALVARADO*

Introduction

Effervescent singing, passionate prayer, tongue speech, hand clapping, 'catching' the Holy Spirit, and communal rites, are central features of African American Pentecostal worship. The worship of African Americans has been forged within the crucible of degradation and subjugation, in secret, with muted voices singing in hushed tones. This same worship found its voice in brush harbors on plantations and in the livery stables of Azusa Street and beyond. African American worship in general and African American Pentecostal worship in particular has historically had a repealing effect upon the ontological terrorism that sought to dehumanize blackness.[1] This chapter suggests that a careful exploration of the rites and rituals of African American Pentecostal worship, as a corporate expression, reclaim black spirituality, black personhood, and resists the orchestrated,

---

* Johnathan E. Alvarado (ThM, Columbia Theological Seminary; DMin, Regent University) is President of Greater Atlanta Theological Seminary, Atlanta, GA.
[1] Craig Scandrett-Leatherman, 'Rites of Lynching and Rights of Dance', in Amos Yong and Estrelda Alexander's (eds.), *Afro-Pentecostalism: Black Pentecostal and Charismatic Christianity in History and Culture* (New York: New York University Press, 2011), pp. 95-99.

systemic, socio-cultural degradation forcibly imposed upon every aspect of black life in America.

Building and organizing this chapter principally upon the work of
Jon Michael Spencer, I will seek to follow his example of 'Protest and
Praise'[2] as a two-fold motif for understanding the nature of African
American Pentecostal worship. As protest and praise were the de-
scriptive methodological framework within which Spencer depicted
black religious life; reclamation and resistance are the specific goals
of that depiction. Collaterally, as African American Pentecostal worship has influenced the variegated musical, creative, cultural, phenomenological, enchanted spiritualities within the Pentecostal orbit,
it has also reverberated with the sounds of freedom, liberty, and spiritual self-agency that should be enjoyed by all. Informed by the scholarship of Estrelda Alexander, Obery Hendricks, Jr., Jermaine Marshall, James Cone, James Abbington, Alisha Lola Jones, and Clifton
Clarke, *inter alia*, the goal of this small contribution is to highlight the
ways in which African American personhood can be reclaimed
through worship, and to encourage vociferous resistance to the deaf-
ening silence of the so-called allies of oppressed persons in general
and African Americans specifically.

African American Pentecostal Worship as a Protest Movement

Ensconced within the particularities of Black Pentecostal religious
life are the liturgical markers, rites, rituals, and practices that make
African American Pentecostal worship 'more than a song'. Black worship has always been typified by its liberative praxis. The way African
Americans read sacred scripture, preach, sing, pray, and dance,
demonstrates the spiritual vitality of a people and how they thrive,
despite the enormous oppressive forces against them. African American Pentecostal worship has been the continuation of protest and
resistance to several aspects of white dominance over African American vitality from our inauspicious beginnings in this country, up until
now. The scope of this chapter does not allow for me to explicate
fully the nuanced ways in which African American Pentecostal

---

[2] John Michael Spencer, *Protest & Praise: Sacred Music of Black Religion* (Minneapolis, MN: Fortress Press, 1990).

worship reclaims personhood and resists oppression, but at least two dimensions of its appearance require focused attention. It emerged in the early part of the 20th Century as a polemic against the social status quo, the notion that black lives were then and are now assigned to a particular station in life without the hope of elevation, enhancement, upgrade, or improvement. Secondly, African American Pentecostal hermeneutical method, which informs the preaching of the gospel to African American Pentecostal communities, has been built upon a particular hermeneutics of suspicion and a Theo-musicological interpretive praxis worthy of deeper investigation.[3]

Hopelessness and the Status Quo

From the beginning of the 20th century, African American Pentecostal adherents were frustrated by the sense that they were unable to experience the promise of freedom and the upward mobility enjoyed by their white counterparts in segregated America. They were frustrated with white Christian complicity with the systems of injustice, of which Dr. Martin Luther King, Jr. wrote in his Letter from a Birmingham Jail.[4] They were frustrated with the length of time it was taking for them to realize the promises of a better life for themselves and their children, for they had been prophetically preaching and praying for a day of deliverance.[5] Instead of despair, their frustration fueled their proleptic vision of hope and the eschatological in-breaking of the Kingdom of God. Though their condition had only improved slightly, their hope burned brightly in large part because of the preaching, praying, tarrying, dancing, and celebration they experienced within their sacred spaces. Their celebrative worship amid life-negating circumstances was a statement of defiance and resistance to the principalities and powers that fueled systems of injustice and racist behaviors. African American Pentecostals believed and celebrated the coming Kingdom and its equalizing effect upon all flesh. African American Pentecostal worship spaces were

---

[3] Braxton D. Shelley, *An Eternal Pitch: Bishop G.E. Patterson, Broadcast Religion, and the Afterlives of Ecstasy* (Oakland, CA: University of California Press, 2023), pp. 1-3.

[4] Jermain J. Marshall, *Christianity Corrupted: The Scandal of White Supremacy* (Maryknoll, NY: Orbis Books, 2021), p. 210.

[5] Kenyatta R. Gilbert, *A Pursued Justice: Black Preaching from The Great Migration to Civil Rights* (Waco, TX: Baylor University Press, 2016), p. 3.

empowerment zones designed to bring deliverance from trouble, healing to bodies, joy in sorrow, and hope for a better day.

African American Pentecostalism(s) and African American primal spirituality in general, did not comport with the cessationist dogma that mired so many mainline and denominational churches in the early 1900's. African enchanted spiritual sensibilities both informed and aligned with the 'deeper life' emphasis of the Holiness-Pentecostal Movement. That emphasis made room for and celebrated the spiritual particularities of African American Pentecostal worship in ways that most white denominationalism at that time did not accommodate. African American Pentecostals were more inclined toward enchanted experiential engagement with the Holy Spirit as an immanent and invasive force into their lives, not just a propositional truth to be understood. Thus, African American Pentecostals largely took the shape of continuationist theology and embodied, emotive, affective spirituality.

Douglas Jacobsen articulates it in this way, 'In a general sense, being Pentecostal means that one is committed to a Spirit-centered, miracle-affirming, praise-oriented version of Christian faith'.[6] Anything less than a commitment to this style of Christianity was for many Pentecostals, living beneath the spiritual mandate for Christian holiness. The Holiness-Pentecostal movement held firmly to the notions of sanctification and social holiness. Thus, African American Pentecostal preachers and congregations began to preach and lean into a proleptic hope for brighter days ahead. This hopeful preaching and celebration did not necessarily take on forms of public protest, though some did, but it did hold space for community solidarity and the eschatological hope they shared with their enslaved ancestors.

Another way in which African American Pentecostal worship began to reclaim, and resist was in its embodied protest against lynching and violence. You see, lynching and physical violence were the preferred tools of white supremacists who sought to keep blacks, especially black men in a perpetual state of adolescence and boyhood, denying them the prerogatives afforded to a man of full stature. White communities in the south used threats of violence, actual violence, and lynching to break the human spirit of African American

---

[6] Douglas Jacobsen, *Thinking in the Spirit: Theologies of the Early Pentecostal Movement* (Bloomington, IN: Indiana University Press, 2003), p. 12.

citizens, with a view to keeping them docile and subservient. Entire white communities, including children, as a social event, complete with picnic baskets, blankets, and joyful expressions, often gleefully attended these dehumanizing, murderous spectacles. Of this phenomenon, Pentecostal scholar, Craig Scandrett-Leatherman commented, 'Though concentrated on individuals, lynchings were performed against the whole black community and were concentrated against black men to reduce their options, squelch their energy, and threaten their lives'.[7]

Lynching and violence, in addition to their physically harmful nature, are insidious forms of psychological castration as well, denying African American boys the rites of passage into manhood that were once afforded by the community in Africa. Though the acts of violence were then targeted at the men and boys of the community, the entire community, women and girls included, suffered the incapacitating effects of the societal oppression they went through together. The oppression of white supremacy, fueled by demonic institution and ideology, had then and has now, as its core agenda, the suppression of black potential and the reordering of black ontology.

'Principalities and powers', now in the form of institutions and ideologies[8] were exerting themselves against the souls of black folks in America. The visible institution of slavery was no more, but the debilitating effects of invisible institutions fueled by demonic principalities sought to crush the living Spirit of God out of the bodies and lives of African Americans through violence and lynching, at the turn of the century. Fallen powers were not then, neither are they now, myopically beholden to individuals and their singular estate. Principalities and powers were then and are now focused on institutional suppression for the sake of their own survival.[9] But, they sorely underestimated the power African American Pentecostal embodied protest as a means of reclamation from and resistance to the powers that sought to imprison and relegate them to deformation and hopelessness.

---

[7] Scandrett-Leatherman, 'Rites of Lynching and Rights of Dance', p. 95.
[8] William Stringfellow, *William Stringfellow: Essential Writings* (New York: Orbis Books, 2013), pp. 155-57.
[9] Stringfellow, *William Stringfellow*, p. 156.

The Bible We Read and the God We Know

African American Christians, as sons and daughters of the transatlantic slave trade, have historically had an onerous relationship with the bible. Because the book of Christian faith and practice was weaponized against Africans in America through; the omission of liberation passages, the elevation of subjugation passages, and the misrepresentation of Christian virtue by slave overlords and their descendants, African Americans grew suspicious of the sacred text and developed a preferred hermeneutic, one that emphasized liberation and eschatological hope. The tridactic hermeneutic relationality between suspicion, faith, and certitude has required African American Pentecostal adherents to revisit the biblicism, fundamentalism, and Evangelical lenses through which many have come to read and understand sacred scripture.

For one to understand the relationship that African Americans have with the text of sacred scripture, one must first understand that African people and African sensibilities were part and parcel of the characters, construct, and canonization of the text. This is an aspect of reclamation of the self that must be prominently featured in African American worshipping communities. The 'Notoriously Religious' nature of the African spirit, according to John Mbiti,[10] is widely accepted among African scholars even if it is expressed differently among the various religious expressions on the continent. Thomas Oden's assertion that African consensual ethos framed the ante Nicene reading and curation of texts which formed the bible, if taken seriously, should inform how African Americans hear, read, and appropriate the bible as their book of faith and practice.[11] The fact that Africans reencountered the text of scripture on African soil as early as the fifteenth century, prior to the slave trade, opens up different hermeneutical possibilities for hearing scripture in language-worlds that were life-affirming and not centered around enslavement, dehumanization, and domination. It should not be assumed or accepted that African Americans first encountered the text of Scripture through their involuntary arrival in the Americas as slaves.

---

[10] John S. Mbiti, *Introduction to African Religion* (Johannesburg, SA: Heinemann Educational, 1975).

[11] Thomas C. Oden, *How Africa Shaped the Christian Mind* (Grand Rapids, MI: IVP Academic, 2010).

The so-called Christianity of slavers and the hermeneutic of colonizers were undergirded by a material agenda. As Vincent Wimbush posits, 'Their direct or indirect efforts to 'convert' Africans to various forms of Christianity could not ultimately be separated from their attempts to exploit them commercially, to dominate them, and then to humanize and socialize (make it European) them – Africans, who were first deemed different, then inferior'.[12] The Bible was used in this imperial enterprise not only to validate white, European supposed superiority, but also to give authoritative language to the colonizers with which to subjugate the stolen Africans that served them as slaves. Europeans created a Zionistic 'New World' using the Bible as their justification for domination and control, their permission or divine right. With the Bible as their justification, they cast themselves as the pilgrim people of God, the New Israel, who were tasked with Christianizing the inferior and child-like Africans and Native Americans. The savages or rebellious, who would not receive their stultifying catechesis were spiritually, culturally, and physically exterminated, for the sake of the gospel.

It was within this crucible of degradation that the African American slave began to interrogate the form of Christianity taught to them and modeled by the white slavers who held them captive. The problem was that the Bible was the property of the slave owners. It was theirs to use as a socializing agent, a cultural roadmap, and a weapon against African slaves in America. The Reformed, Calvinistic, Puritanical, theological framework out of which Europeans constructed systems of oppression provided them the hermeneutical lenses through which to see Africans as fulfilling their predestined socio-cultural status as slaves, subjects, and recipients of the oversight of benevolent dictators. African Americans were disadvantaged in that few of them were afforded the opportunity to learn to read, to interpret, and even fewer were allowed to prognosticate the gospel to other African Americans. They were, in most cases, thoroughly dominated and controlled by whiteness as a cultural framework, a standard for Christianity, and a hermeneutical lens through which the slaves should read and understand the Bible.

---

[12] Vincent L. Wimbush, *The Bible and African Americans: A History in Six Readings* (Minneapolis, MN: Fortress Press, 2004, 2023), pp. 1-2.

This colonial superimposition of virtue and values share overlapping, anxious, stressful, and apprehensive usage within interpreting communities, particularly Black communities, upon whose backs the American empire was resting. Thus, the tension of African American Pentecostal preaching requires that we be faithful to a text that was used, and in many cases introduced to African Americans, unfaithfully. This requires an African American progressive interpretive prowess, a hermeneutical revitalization that affirms the indigeneity of scripture, and a progressive interpretive framework that makes scripture sacred and safe for all. This is in part what we must reclaim, and this is in part, what we must resist.

Conclusion

Pentecostal worship and the act of preaching therein, has enjoyed primacy within black worship spaces, as acts of resistance to the diabolical, ontological terrorism that African Americans have endured in the Western hemisphere throughout the past four centuries. The primal spirituality that is manifested in our penchant for song, dance, melodious preaching, story, call, and response, have not only been the liturgical markers of African American worship praxis, but they have served as a call to action, birthed in The Spirit, validated in the struggle. The soul force that is exemplified through this liturgical drama is often imitated by our counterpart cultures and stylized for entertainment value to those who do not often recognize its liberative effect. Yet, to African Americans, a song in the night still liberates, empowers, reverses, and forcefully resists the principalities and powers, systems and structures, ideologies, and prejudices that have sought to mute our voices. For African Americans understand that 'Life is Saved by the Singing of Angels …'[13]

---

[13] Howard Thurman, *The Inward Journey* (Richmond, IN: Friends United Press, 1961). On the scriptural theme of leveraging privilege in the service of pursuing racial justice, see Dominique Dubois Gilliard, *Subversive Witness: Scripture's Call to Leverage Privilege* (Grand Rapids, MI: Zondervan, 2021).

12

'SEARCHING THE SCRIPTURES': DAVID S. INGRAHAM'S THEOLOGICAL HERMENEUTICS

JONATHAN D. BENTALL*

Introduction

Worship has a way of unexpectedly inserting itself when one is doing theology. Take the apostle Paul, for example: in what is among the most dense and complex theological arguments found in any of the Pauline epistles, Romans 9–11, the culmination of the discourse is not a concluding propositional claim or a restated thesis but rather a doxological flourish: 'O the depth of the riches and wisdom and knowledge of God!' (Rom. 11.33a, NRSVue).[1] For Paul, it seems, worship belongs to theology – not merely alongside it, nor simply as a practical application or spiritual afterthought, but *embedded* right there within it. Moreover, Paul's blend of theological reflection punctuated by praise emerges within what might appear to be a surprisingly ordinary genre of practical human communication: an ancient letter.[2]

---

* Jonathan D. Bentall (PhD, University of Durham, UK) is Assistant Professor of Bible at Northwest University, Kirkland, WA.
[1] See Jason Byassee, *Surprised by Jesus Again: Reading the Bible in Communion with the Saints* (Grand Rapids, MI: Eerdmans, 2019), pp. 8, 153.
[2] See Nijay K. Gupta, 'The Doxological Apostle', in Jeffrey W. Barbeau and Emily Hunter McGowin (eds.), *God and Wonder: Theology, Imagination, and the Arts* (Eugene, OR: Cascade, 2022).

Something similar happens repeatedly throughout the recently discovered personal journal entries of David S. Ingraham, a 19th Century abolitionist missionary to Jamaica. In the midst of the author's recording of admittedly mundane details associated with church membership, travel plans, and the health concerns of his family and wider community, he is frequently moved to comparable doxological outbursts such as the following: 'O for a heart to praise the Lord who alone has done great things for us' (p. 3).[3] In decidedly less routine portions of his journal, Ingraham bears witness to the both the depths of human wickedness and the acute human suffering embedded within the transatlantic slave-trade and is moved to a blend of theological reflection and raw worship: Added to his deployment of the well-worn lament refrain of the Psalter – 'How Long O Lord?!' – is the author's own searching question: 'O who can measure the guilt or sound the iniquity of this nefarious trafick [*sic*] …' (p. 24).

In these and numerous other examples, Ingraham's journal offers a fascinating and provocative window into the theological convictions, personal piety, and activist ministry of a relatively unknown historical figure. In a manner strikingly reminiscent of many of the epistles of the NT, this seemingly mundane, practical document – a personal diary – reveals a profound and instructive insistence on holding together what the Christian tradition has too often been prone to separate: namely theology, worship, and the pursuit of justice.

The purpose of this chapter is to explore aspects of David Ingraham's use and interpretation of the Bible, as it is on display in the context of his journal, and to propose that his interpretive approach and theological convictions can be instructive for communities of Christian faith today. I begin with a brief introduction to Ingraham as a historical figure, in the context of 19th Century revivalism and abolitionism. Following this, I present a number of examples of the author's interpretive practices, along with my own comments on what these practices seem to reveal about his overarching hermeneutic and

---

[3] Here and throughout, I am citing the primary source manuscript of Ingraham's journal, held at the Adrian College Archives, excerpts of which have been transcribed and published as Appendix C in David D. Daniels III et al., *Awakening to Justice: Faithful Voices from the Abolitionist Past* (Downers Grove: IVP Academic, 2024), pp. 194-208. Below, I will use in-text citations of the handwritten manuscript and endeavor to retain as much as possible the original punctuation in transcribed form.

theological vision. Finally, I conclude by suggesting some of the ways that Ingraham's approach to Scripture might serve as a *resource* and a *prophetic summons* to contemporary interpreters and interpretive communities.

'The Holy Cause': Worship, Holiness, and Justice Among 19th Century Abolitionists

Born in 1812, David Stedman Ingraham was influenced by the holiness tradition and revivalist preaching of Asa Mahan (1799-1889) and Charles Finney (1792-1875), and educated at both Lane Theological Seminary (Cincinnati, OH) and Oberlin Collegiate Institute (Oberlin, OH). Notably, Ingraham was among the famous 'Lane Rebels' who in 1834 held a series of debates and speeches making a Christian case for the abolition of slavery in America, formed an anti-slavery society, and eventually left the institution in protest when the seminary's trustees prohibited such discourse and opposed their activism.[4] Ingraham continued his academic training at Oberlin, where he met and later married his wife Betsey, and in 1837 the couple traveled to Jamaica to engage in ministry, evangelism, and education among recently emancipated people. According to historian Christopher Momany, 'Christian abolitionists like the Ingraham's hoped to repudiate the racist objection to emancipation promoted by proslavery Whites that freed people of color could not advance or govern themselves'.[5]

Ingraham's early commitments as an abolitionist were of a piece with his later missionary activity in and around Kingston, Jamaica. In his personal journal entries, which comprise approximately 100 handwritten pages and span from July 1839 through March 1841, it is abundantly clear that the author sees holiness and piety before God, the worship and witness of Christian communities, and the pursuit of justice for those who are vulnerable to oppression as inseparable aspects of not only his own calling, but also the 'holy cause' of the

---

[4] See Daniels et al., *Awakening to Justice*, pp. 10-11, 30-35. See also Donald W. Dayton, *Discovering an Evangelical Heritage* (New York: Harper & Row, 1976), pp. 35-43.

[5] Christopher P. Momany, '"How Long, O Lord?": A Narrative of Three Christian Abolitionists', in Daniels et al., *Awakening to Justice*, p. 37.

Church.[6] Examples such as the following are peppered throughout, calling attention to the author's heartfelt desire for increased personal devotion and piety: 'O how sweet to feel *perfectly* submissive to all God *says* or *does*' (p. 34), and 'O for *entire submission* + *perfect love* + confidence in God' (p. 36). These references to holistic obedience to God are by no means limited to some reductive account of inner spirituality, but rather they gesture toward what is framed elsewhere as a commitment of active 'labor' and 'consecration' toward the 'cause' to which Ingraham has been called: namely, the liberation of the oppressed via the abolition of slavery and ministry among those recently emancipated. The following example illustrates the author's distinct sense of vocational responsibility against the backdrop of Jamaican emancipation:

> O that the great + glorious changes which have taken place in this Isle during the past year may take place in America, Cuba + wherever the sight of the oppressed is heard. O for the freedom of the *world* For this let me labor – for this let me pray. (p. 4)

Repeated exclamations such as, 'O for more + more of the spirit of consecration till my whole being is lost in God + his cause' (p. 77), reveal that Ingraham's understanding of sanctification refuses any potential dichotomy between the dynamics of personal holiness and piety and those of being set apart for the work of bearing faithful witness to God's liberative kingdom purposes.[7] Thus, in many ways, Ingraham's journal constitutes an illuminating primary source that further reinforces the blend of social and political activism with revivalist spirituality among 19th Century Evangelicals that has been documented by scholars such as Donald Dayton and Douglas Strong.[8]

---

[6] This phrase comes from the autobiography of James Bradley, but variations upon it appear repeatedly in Ingraham's journal, e.g. on pp. 3, 45, 77, signaling a firm insistence on the interrelationship between notions of sanctification and social justice. See Douglas M. Strong, '"This Holy Cause": Revivalist Theology and Justice Advocacy', in Daniels et al., *Awakening to Justice*, pp. 92-109.

[7] In an intriguing section of the journal, the author describes reading and benefitting greatly from a lecture by Charles Finney on the topic of sanctification, and Ingraham's emphasis is not only upon victory over sin and unbelief but also upon 'entire consecration' toward his abolitionist mission (pp. 45-46).

[8] See Dayton, *Discovering an Evangelical Heritage*, and Douglas M. Strong, *They Walked in the Spirit: Personal Faith and Social Action in America* (Louisville, KY: Westminster John Knox, 1997).

Ingraham's previously unknown journal was discovered at Adrian College in 2015 and, alongside two other historical documents from the same period, it is the subject of a recently published book entitled, *Awakening to Justice: Faithful Voices from the Abolitionist Past.*[9] The other documents offer invaluable windows into the perspectives and experiences of two African-American associates of Ingraham, James Bradley and Nancy Prince. Bradley was a formerly enslaved person and, alongside Ingraham, was counted among the aforementioned Lane Rebels.[10] In a brief autobiography published in 1834, he relates his testimony and describes his long, arduous journey to purchase his own freedom. Prince would become a co-laborer in ministry alongside Ingraham in Jamaica, and the details of her own work among emancipated communities in the Caribbean come to us via her 1853 autobiography, 'The Narrative of Nancy Prince'.[11]

'Searching the Scriptures': David S. Ingraham's Biblical Hermeneutics

As I turn my attention to the journal itself, a couple of introductory remarks are in order:

First, it is worth noting right away that Ingraham is not engaging in academic biblical exegesis, nor is he delivering a sermon or a homily with sustained attention to a specific scriptural passage. His interpretive practice consists mainly of brief allusions, partial quotations, and often a blend of interrelated references to different parts of Scripture. As a result, while some remarks may indeed constitute

---

[9] This volume brings together a group of scholars affiliated with the 'Dialogue on Race and Faith Project', which has also produced a documentary film and a number of other resources. See https.//www.awakeningtojustice.com/. This group aims to bring careful scholarship, Christian worship, and committed advocacy for racial justice firmly together in and for our contemporary world, and the impetus for doing so stems in part from the witness of these individuals from the mid-19th Century who likewise refused to separate what ought to be integrated components of faithful Christian witness and beloved community.

[10] Bradley's role in the aforementioned student debates is discussed in Ted A. Smith, 'Introduction', in *The End of Theological Education* (Grand Rapids: Eerdmans, 2023). Also explored here is the founding of Lane Seminary in the context of revivalism and abolitionist sentiments, and the tensions resulting from a network of funding that benefitted from the economics of the slave trade, alongside students and stakeholders committed to its abolition.

[11] Nancy Prince, *A Narrative of the Life and Travels of Mrs. Nancy Prince* (Boston: published by the author, 2nd edn, 1853).

legitimate allusions, or self-conscious references to specific parts of the Bible, others might simply reflect a set of communicative patterns that have been so shaped by Scripture that its own language, imagery, and vocabulary simply become part of the speaker's available lexicon.

Second, because our primary source is his personal journal, a reasonable assumption is that Ingraham himself would be the only intended audience for the words we find there. As a result, it is unsurprising that many of his biblical references consist of brief, and often subtle, remarks that seem to echo or evoke a larger verse, passage, or story from Scripture. Thus, my own account of how he might be using and interpreting the Bible is a self-consciously hermeneutical endeavor: I can't be certain about what he may have meant by specific references, nor can I definitively reconstruct his exegetical reasoning with any kind of precision. What I *can* do, however, is pay close attention to his words, as he weaves biblical allusions throughout his personal recollections and pious exclamations, in an effort to discern core elements of his Scriptural reasoning and theological vision for the Christian life.

Part One: A Sleeping Church

My comments on Ingraham's interpretive practice will revolve around what is easily the most 'chilling' and 'arresting' portion of the journal.[12] On p. 24 of the primary source document, Ingraham relates a harrowing experience that prompts the following remarks:

> O where are the sympathies of christians for the slave + where are their exersians [*sic*] for their liberation. O it seems as if the church were asleep + Satan has the world following him …

> … As I contemplate the awful suffering that these poor creatures must have endured during a passage of 50 days from the coast of Africa my soul is in disbelief + I feel to exclaim How long O Lord How long shall these poor creatures be torn from ~~their coast~~ their homes + made to endure so much for the avarice of men? O who can measure the guilt or sound the iniquity of this nefarious

---

[12] I am borrowing both terms from Chris Momany's discussion in Momany, 'How Long O Lord?', p. 38.

trafick [*sic*] + its twin sister slavery O that I may pray *often* + with more *faith* for the oppressed. (p. 24)

A Portuguese ship, designed for transporting enslaved human beings, was captured near Port Royal in Jamaica, resulting in the liberation of over 500 people. Ingraham's entry from 25 December 1839 is striking for both its description of his experience boarding the now empty vessel, and for the sketch he drew in his journal, detailing the layout of the ship.

One of the scholars responsible for identifying Ingraham as the author of the journal describes this section of its contents:

Ingraham … examined the empty ship and took measurements of its various compartments. He was explicit, almost obsessively so. This ship held 556 people – captured in West Africa, and the voyage took some 50 days.

Ingraham's notes seem to suggest that the height of the space used to transport the captives was but two feet and five inches.[13] The stern included an area that was sixteen by fourteen feet and held 117 girls. The next compartment was twenty by twenty feet and held 107 women. The third was thirty-two by eighteen feet and held 216 men. The fourth, at the bow, was fifteen by twelve feet and held 93 boys. In all 533 people survived the ordeal. Ingraham's response, while documenting the atrocity, was a mix of disbelief and outrage.[14]

As he records these details, Ingraham employs the classic refrain 'How Long O Lord?', found in numerous lament psalms. In the Psalter, these words might appear within an individual lament over the seeming absence of God (Ps. 13.1–2), or in the face of God's apparent failure to rescue the psalmist from their enemies (Ps. 35.17); yet the phrase also features in broader, communal frames of reference in

---

[13] According to Christopher P. Momany, 'The Art of Hearing to Speech: A Story of Discovery', (unpublished chapter), p. 7, n. 20, 'The astonishingly small space receives some confirmation in an entry found among Charlton T. Lewis (ed.), *Harper's Book of Facts* (New York and London: Harper & Brothers, Publishers, 1906), p. 898. This text lists the height as 2 feet, 4 ½ inches. However, note also Momany's comment that the dimensions given here in the journal differ slightly from those described in a subsequently published letter (1840). See Momany, 'How Long O Lord?', p. 38, n. 13.

[14] Momany, 'The Art of Hearing', p. 7. See further developed comments along similar lines in Momany, 'How Long O Lord?', pp. 38-39.

which the seeming persistence of God's anger, or the apparent delay of God's righteous judgment upon the wicked is in view (see Pss. 79.5 and 94.3, respectively). While it is possible that our author has in mind one of these specific Israelite prayer-poems, it is probably more likely that he is simply adopting the common Scriptural expression of agonized questioning regarding God's seemingly delayed or absent kingdom purposes and vocalizing it in the context of his own bewildered response to the grave injustice he has now witnessed. In conjunction with this lament, Ingraham utters this prophetic indictment: 'O it seems as if the church were asleep …' His comment on the body of Christ's apparent slumber is preceded by two rhetorical questions that specifically frame the church's lack of 'sympathies' for enslaved and trafficked human beings and the perceived absence of any meaningful activity oriented toward their 'liberation', in terms of a lack of wakefulness.

In another context, on page 35 of his journal, Ingraham is describing the negative impact of his ill health upon his ability to continue to care for and minister to his congregation. He comments that while he is forced to focus attention on his own physical recovery and well-being, he leaves his 'dear church … in the hands of a merciful shepherd who never slumbers nor sleeps' (p. 35). This allusion appears to combine the imagery of two famous psalms, the Divine Shepherd of Psalm 23 and the Divine Helper of Psalm 121. In both contexts, God is portrayed as one who guides, keeps, and protects God's people, especially in situations of potential crisis or threat.[15] Whereas numerous other psalms call upon the God of Israel to awake, thus apparently presuming that God does sometimes doze off a little (see Pss. 7.6; 35.23; 44.23; 59.4–5), here the decisive theological claim is that YHWH *never* slumbers, nor sleeps, and therefore can be trusted as a helper (from the root עזר) and a protector (from the Hebrew root שמר) no matter what form of life-threatening scenario might arise.[16]

---

[15] It is interesting, but probably coincidental, that these two poems use the same key term associated with *shade* or *shadow* (צל) but in negative (death-shadow from which one needs protection in Psalm 23) and positive (YHWH as shade from elements in Psalm 121) terms, respectively.

[16] See Nancy de Claissé-Walford et al, *The Book of Psalms* (NICOT; Grand Rapids, MI: Eerdmans, 2014), p. 897.

The theological intuition of Ingraham is relatively straightforward here: God can be trusted to provide for and watch over the congregation under his care because God is never found to be dozing off, asleep on the job, unaware of the potential plight of God's people.[17] This image of a God who refuses to slumber connotes an alert and active divine engagement, oriented toward the well-being and protection of human agents, thus providing a striking contrast with the proclamation from a few pages earlier, that the church – those who ideally would function as faithful representatives of God – seems to be sleeping, either unengaged with or perhaps even deliberately unaware of the plight of those most in need of active protection and liberation from dehumanizing and life-diminishing exploitation.

It is not only the church at large, and the God of Israel, that Ingraham has in mind when he applies the imagery of sleep and wakefulness to his particular situation, there is also evidence that he sees remaining awake and alert as a crucial factor of his own personal spirituality. A final noteworthy reference in this regard is Ingraham's emphatic comments on the kind of individual piety and faithfulness to which he aspires as a follower of Jesus. In the entry for March 25th, 1840, our author is brimming with gratitude for at least a momentary respite from his ill health but also is quick to comment that he 'know[s] not what a *day* may bring forth' (p. 38). Given these remarks about the contingencies of life and the unpredictability of his own journey with failing health, Ingraham exclaims, 'O that I may live at the *feet* of Jesus + ever have my lamp trimmed + burning' (p. 38). Here, again, his characteristic approach to Scripture is on display, involving what seems to be a blended allusion to multiple biblical accounts – his reference to *living* at the feet of Jesus is most probably recalling the famous account of Mary and Martha from the Gospel of Luke (Lk. 10.38–42), while the references to a perpetually trimmed and lit flame alludes to the so-called parable of the bridesmaids in Matthew 25 (Mt. 25.1–13).

In the former passage, a contrast is made between the posture of two sisters toward Jesus: Martha is portrayed as 'distracted' (περιεσπᾶτο) by 'many' (πολλὴν) aspects of service and hospitality, whereas Mary is praised for sitting at the feet of Jesus and listening

---

[17] It is worth noting that this particular section of the journal (e.g. p. 58) features numerous references to God's care for the people of Israel in the midst of their oppression, again through a series of biblical references and allusions.

to him, a choice that Jesus commends as 'the better part' (την αγαθην μεριδα).[18] The parable compares the kingdom of heaven to a scenario in which the arrival of a bridegroom is delayed to such an extent that a group of bridesmaids get tired of waiting, become drowsy, and fall asleep. The parable functions both to critique a foolish posture of drowsy inattentiveness and to commend instead one of remaining awake or alert, as well as wisely prepared, given the temporal uncertainties associated with the revelation of God's kingdom purposes, concluding with the imperative to 'Stay awake!' (γρηγορεῖτε, Mt. 25.13; cf. comparable passages in Lk. 12.35–40 and Mk 13.32-37).

The parable conveys the idea that one cannot simply remain idle and unprepared, become preoccupied, or doze off and then expect to be an active participant in God's kingdom purposes; rather, meaningful and active participation in the kingdom of God requires attentiveness, vigilance, discernment, and wisdom, in order to recognize the signs and indications of the kingdom's arrival and align one's own orientation and witness with it. When joined with the allusion to sitting at Jesus' feet, this posture of alertness to God's kingdom purposes takes on an even clearer sense of orientation toward the teaching of Jesus in the context of Christian piety and discipleship. Thus, against the backdrop of formidable health challenges and legitimate logistical concerns associated with caring for his family and congregation, Ingraham draws on these portions of Scripture to convey his desire to remain awake and alert, undistracted and wholly committed to his 'holy cause'.

It is, of course, no secret that metaphors associated with being *awake* have been a live issue in conversations around racial justice in our own very recent contemporary setting here in the U.S. A simple Amazon search utilizing the key terms 'woke' and 'church' will quickly yield titles such as 'White Awake', 'Woke Church', and 'When the Church Woke', composed by authors who seem to find in the metaphor a compelling and provocative image of Christian

---

[18] Note that the narrator's description of Martha as 'distracted' is echoed and perhaps also filled out by Jesus' own comment that she is both 'anxious' (μεριμνάω) and 'troubled' (θορυβάζῃ), whereas the narrator's more explicit description of her distraction in terms of engaging in 'much service' (πολλὴν διακονίαν) may be contrasted with Jesus' more ambiguous comments about her being concerned with 'much' or 'many things' (πολλά).

communities being roused from the slumbers of complacency and compromise with systems that perpetuate injustice and oppression, and thus provoked to respond in resistance to them. Yet interspersed among these very titles, the same search will also yield books that bemoan what is framed as the misguided appeal of a 'Woke Jesus', insisting that 'Biblical Justice' ought not to be confused with 'Social Justice', and calling instead for a decidedly 'Woke-Free Church'. While he is, of course, writing some 180 years before the events that spur this dispute within the subculture of contemporary American Christian faith and its attendant publishing industry, it remains note-worthy that David Ingraham is drawn to this very metaphor. If In-graham found such imagery to be an appropriate way to express both his commitment to the holy cause of abolition and his critique of a defunct or absent Christian witness, then it is worth considering whether the metaphor may indeed have some Scriptural justification and theological purchase.

To summarize, notice that biblical allusions associated with the contrast between falling asleep vs. remaining awake are applied by Ingraham to (1) his own individual piety, (2) the witness of the church, and (3) God's own sovereign care for humanity. To use pre-sent-day parlance, one might suggest that for Ingraham, Scripture portrays a 'woke' (or, perpetually awake) God, who not only watches over human affairs but also expects members of God's covenant community to likewise remain 'woke' (i.e. awake/aware/alert) to his in-breaking kingdom of justice and liberation. Thus, when he is con-fronted with the horrors of the slave trade, on display in all of its grotesque specificity via the logistical details of the transport ship, his theological and ecclesial impulse is to rebuke the body of Christ for being tragically and faithlessly asleep.

Part Two: Satanic Opposition

Ingraham's prophetic lament over the church's negligent slumber is not articulated in isolation but rather paired with the striking com-ment that the entire cosmos has succumbed to a kind of diabolical discipleship. It is not only that God's people have failed to remain awake to the injustice around and among them, but also that Satan appears to have the whole world following him and doing his bidding. In this next section of my comments, I'll explore some of the ways in which the author either explicitly invokes or more subtly alludes to satanic agency in his journal.

On the opening page of his journal (p. 3 in the physical artifact), Ingraham describes the recent addition of new members to his congregation at Cotton Wood, near Kingston, Jamaica. He revels in recording the details of Sunday, 14 July 1839:

> This has been one of my *best Sabbaths* O how unworthy am I of such blessed privileges. We have once more celebrated the Lord's death till he come + our hearts were made glad by receiving new soldiers into our ranks. <u>Twenty two</u> [*sic*] for the first time (most of them) publickly [*sic*] consecrated themselves to God + his cause. O what a glorious sight. I used to think that God would bless my labors in some degree, but I hardly expected to see such a sight – 22 who had a little time since been in the very depths of sin – living in fornication drunkenness + 'such like things' now 'clothed + in their right minds' + taking the vows of God upon themselves O that we may all be encouraged to walk nearer to God + do more for the salvation of the O.[oppressed] Our church now numbers 62 + most seem to be truly the disciples of Jesus. O for more and more of the Holy Spirit to enlighten, lead, strengthen, + <u>sanctify</u> us all, that we may be holy + without blemish before Christ in love. (p. 3)

Ingraham's description of this conversion experience may seem rather straightforward but in fact it involves a fairly complex blend of scriptural allusions. In describing this state of sin, Ingraham lists some fairly predictable ciphers for iniquity, i.e. 'fornication' and 'drunkenness', but then he adds the seemingly innocuous phrase 'and such like things'. If it weren't for his quotation marks within the original document, this might be dismissed as a fairly banal phrase, basically equivalent to using the adverb 'etcetera'. However, the punctuation suggests a likely allusion to Galatians 5 in the KJV, which lists numerous actions that Paul calls 'works of the flesh', uses precisely this phrase to suggest similar behaviors, and then contrasts them with the well-known 'fruit of the Spirit'. The phrase 'and such like things' seems to be Ingraham's way of evoking that entire list of various activities that Paul frames as not only sinful, but also decidedly at odds with the kingdom of God.[19]

This probable allusion is paired with an explicit quotation, this one unambiguously calling to mind the account of the Gerasene demoniac from Mark 5 (see also the parallel account in Lk. 8.26–39). In this episode, we encounter an individual who has been plagued by an 'unclean spirit' to such an extent that he has characteristically engaged in loud wailing and acts of self-harm, needing to be restrained with 'shackles and chains', although even these have proved unsuccessful limitations on the demonically influenced behavior. After Jesus liberates the man from this formidable spiritual oppression, the narrator of the Gospel describes people coming to see what had happened and, to their surprise and even fear, discovering the man previously 'possessed by demons' now, instead, 'clothed and in his right mind' (Mk 5.15).

This network of allusions suggests that Ingraham regards the former condition of these 22 new converts as a kind of holistic blend of sinfulness, demonic agency, and opposition to God's kingdom, and their public consecration to God is akin not only to a set of new beliefs, nor a mere cessation of formerly immoral behaviors, but rather a liberation from demonic possession! Therefore, it is not at all surprising that he follows up his narration with a prayer that the whole community would be encouraged to 'walk nearer to God' in personal piety, and to engage more fully in God's salvific purposes on behalf of the oppressed and exploited (p. 3).

So, for Ingraham, biblical language and imagery associated with 'the very depths of sin' (p. 3) and an immeasurable 'guilt and iniquity' (p. 24) apply as directly and appropriately to personal vices including fornication and drunkenness (e.g. pp. 25-26, 43, 78), as they do to the horrific, systemic exploitation and dehumanizing injustice of the slave trade. It is not one or the other, and both are together the target of scathing critique and a source of profound lament (e.g. pp. 24, 50). Moreover, allusions or explicit references to demonic/Satanic influence are likewise applied *both* to the previous immoral state of new

---

[19] Of course, it is entirely *possible* that Ingraham is merely saturated in scriptural language from the KJV and so the earlier phrase comes naturally as a way of extending his list and stressing the depths of sin; however, the quotation marks and the two particular terms do seem to be indications that he is being deliberate in evoking Galatians 5 more broadly.

converts *and* to the scourge of slavery that Ingraham and other abolitionists are devoted to opposing. For Ingraham, it seems, the iniquity of the slave trade is not simply a set of actions people need deliverance from, but a kind of Satanic mission that must be decisively opposed by the cause of those who follow Christ and participate in his liberative kingdom.[20]

'God Speaks Very Loud': The Need for a Holistic, Prophetic Hermeneutic Today

Despite Ingraham's journal emerging from a historical context very different from our own, it can nevertheless speak to contemporary issues in profound and necessary ways. As Strong and Momany put it, 'Poring over Ingraham's nineteenth-century diary … could be a means through which twenty-first century Christians might address the reality of racism in society today'.[21] In the light of this conviction, I'd like to draw our attention to two aspects of Ingraham's approach to the Bible that might be instructive for us today, and then conclude with a brief reflection on how we might adopt a comparable approach as well.

First, notice that the author doesn't simply quote Scripture, draw upon Scripture, or use the Bible to make his point. Instead, he is *immersed* in it. The Bible forms the lexicon, the grammar, the vocabulary that he uses in his own writing, prayer, and reflection. As the NT scholar Richard Hays has shown to be the case with the use of sacred texts in Paul's Letters and with the Gospels, Ingraham often echoes, alludes to, and evokes numerous scriptural traditions as he develops theological insights of his own.[22] I've tried to show that paying careful attention to how these allusions are combined and invoked can yield insight into the author's theological vision and vocational convictions. In an important sense, for Ingraham, the Bible is less like an external source or convenient resource that one might *apply* to

---

[20] Douglas M. Strong identifies both conversionism and justice advocacy as two markers of revivalist spirituality during this time. See Strong, 'This Holy Cause', pp. 95-97.

[21] Douglas M. Strong and Christopher P. Momany, 'Introduction: Waking a Sleeping Church', in Daniels et al., *Awakening to Justice*, p. 11.

[22] See Richard B. Hays, *Echoes of Scripture in the Letters of Paul* (New Haven: Yale University Press, 1989), and Richard B. Hays, *Echoes of Scripture in the Gospels* (Waco: Baylor University Press, 2006).

contemporary life; it is more like a new and life-giving world of justice and liberation that we might immerse ourselves in and which then re-narrates our own reality around the priorities of God and God's kingdom as a result.[23]

Second, Ingraham's interpretive practices ought to inspire and reinforce our own impulse toward the holding together of committed advocacy for social and racial justice alongside fervent doxology, piety, and devotion. The same language, symbols and metaphors that he draws upon in describing the Christian's calling out of patterns of sin and into a consecrated life before God, are also invoked to furnish an account of the systemic injustice of the slave trade as a twisted work of the devil himself, and the mission of the church being the very cause of Christ, unavoidably dedicated to deliverance from evil, the liberation of the oppressed, and God's kingdom purposes being realized on earth, just as in heaven.

Thus, I would suggest that Ingraham's approach to the Bible is helpfully framed as a prophetic and liberative hermeneutic. As he weaves Scriptural references, images, and language throughout his own ruminations on life, faith, ministry, and family, Ingraham does not simply use the Bible as a means of affirming predetermined theological commitments, nor as a set of platitudes that might bring comfort in moments of challenge or uncertainty. Rather, he immerses himself in a Scriptural vision that prompts him to name and confront the evil he witnesses and to commit himself to the abolition of its source and its effects. Commenting on the work of Ingraham and his associates, Estrelda Alexander explains, 'Their activism was the inevitable embodiment of their theological convictions, which were nourished and sustained by vital practices of worship and devotion'.[24]

It is not difficult to see elements of correspondence between Ingraham's concern that the church in his day might 'awake' to the realities of dehumanizing violence and injustice based on constructed racial hierarchies, and analogous concerns articulated in a contemporary context that the church might awaken itself to the ways in which

---

[23] See further, Richard S. Briggs, 'These are the Days of Elijah: The Hermeneutical Move from "Applying the Text" to "Living in Its World"', in *Journal of Theological Interpretation* 8.2 (2014), pp. 157-74.

[24] Estrelda Y. Alexander, 'Conclusion: A Prophetic Past', in Daniels et al. *Awakening to Justice*, p. 168.

elements of those very same distorted ideological commitments (white supremacy) and resultant practices (systemic patterns of injustice, perpetuated and reinforced by racial prejudice) tragically persist.[25] Unfortunately, the tendency among many communities of evangelical and charismatic Christian faith in America today has been to view the metaphor of *awakening* either as hopelessly beholden to an inherently 'secular' agenda that is somehow antithetical to the concerns of the Gospel and thus to be resisted, or else as a feature of a reductive form of revivalism from which a corresponding concern for the pursuit of God's justice is noticeably absent.

For Ingraham, by contrast, it is not advocacy for social justice within a supposedly 'secular' culture that reveals a worrisome diabolical agenda; rather it is the Body of Christ itself that is in need of prophetic critique so as to awaken from its slumbering complicity in the work of the devil. Moreover, it is not merely in terms of evangelism and charismatic fervor that the church is in need of awakening or revival; instead, the Body of Christ needs an apocalyptic disclosure of the true cost of its continued acquiescence to, involvement in, and economic benefit from the systematic exploitation and diminishment of precious human lives, and a reinvigorated commitment instead to the holy cause of restoring and establishing justice for the vulnerable and the oppressed.

In my view, attentiveness to Ingraham's engagement with the Bible offers resources for us today that might contribute to a renewed vision for the church as concerned with not only revival but also repentance, nor merely with preservation of personal piety and communal holiness but also with the costly effort to 'leverage' whatever privilege any individual or community might enjoy for the purpose of standing against injustice and bearing faithful witness to the Kingdom of God.[26]

---

[25] For a detailed argument making the case that historical patterns of racism and injustice have not been eliminated or resolved but rather have adapted, and thus persist today, see Jemar Tisby, *The Color of Compromise: The Truth About the American Church's Complicity in Racism* (Grand Rapids, MI: Zondervan, 2019).

[26] On the scriptural theme of leveraging privilege in the service of pursuing racial justice, see Dominique Dubois Gilliard, *Subversive Witness: Scripture's Call to Leverage Privilege* (Grand Rapids, MI: Zondervan, 2021).

13

UNCHAINED HALLELUJAH: DECOLONIZING BLACK PENTECOSTAL WORSHIP

CLIFTON CLARKE[*]

Introduction

Pentecostal Christianity has emerged as a formidable force in the global Christian landscape, drawing millions of adherents from continents and cultures around the world.[1] Characterized by spirited music, exuberant Praise, and heartfelt prayer, the movement has secured a strong foothold in global Christianity, captivating believers from

---

[*] Clifton Clarke (PhD, University of Birmingham, UK) is Research Fellow at Queens Foundation for Ecumenical Theological Studies and Adjunct Professor at Lee University, Cleveland, TN.

[1] Numerous books attest to this phenomenon, including the following: J. Kwabena Asamoah-Gyadu, *Contemporary Pentecostal Christianity: Interpretations from an African Context* (Oxford: Regnum Books International, 2013); Peter L. Berger, and Paul Freston (eds.), *The Desecularization of the World: Resugent Religion and World Politics* (Grand Rapids, MI: Eerdmans, 2003), Chapter 3; Simon Coleman, *The Globalization of Charismatic Chrisitanity: Preading the Gospel Worldwide* (Cambridge: CUP, 2000); Carlos Cortés, *Pentecostalsim in Latin America: Its Growing Influence* (Maryknoll, NY: Orbis Books, 1996); Harvey Cox, *Fire From Heaven: The Rise of Pentecostal Spirituality and the Remaking of Religion in the Twenty-First Century* (Reading, MA: Addison-Wesley Publishing Company, 1995); Philip Jenkins, *The Next Christendom: The Coming of Global Christianity* (Oxford: Oxford University Press, 2002); Ruth Marshall, *Political Spiritualities: The Pentecostal Revolution in Nigeria* (Chicago: University of Chicago Press, 2009); David Martin, *Tongues of Fire: The Explosion of Protestantism in Latin America* (Oxford: Basil Blackwell, 1990).

Brazil to Nigeria, South Africa to the United States, and beyond Europe to Asia. Notably, Africa and African diasporic expressions of Christianity have proven highly amenable to Pentecostalism, a receptiveness often attributed to an epistemological outlook that upholds the enduring reality of the supernatural.[2] This perspective creates fertile ground for a vibrant communal worship, reinforcing core Pentecostal distinctives such as divine healing, prophecy, and Spirit Baptism, and fueling an ever-growing trend that transcends cultural and geographical boundaries. Within the burgeoning growth of Black Pentecostalism, worship occupies a place of pride, and black worship expressions have indelibly shaped the spiritual contours of modern Pentecostal spirituality.[3]

The Black Worship Tradition

It is important to remember that Black worship traditions, even before the emergence of modern Black Pentecostalism, have deep roots in the spirituals sung by enslaved Africans. These early expressions of Black spirituality, born out of suffering and a longing for freedom, laid the foundation for the passionate worship, call and response, and emphasis on the power of the Holy Spirit that characterize Black Pentecostal worship today.[4] The gift of black Pentecostal worship to the global Christian community arises, therefore, in part, from its

---

[2] See Asamoah-Gyadu, *Contemporary Pentecostal Christianity*, pp. 45-62, and Marshall, *Political Spiritualities*, pp. 78-95. Marshall's ethnographic work illustrates how Pentecostalism in Nigeria taps into existing beliefs about spiritual power, witchcraft, and divine healing, offering a framework for understanding and engaging with the supernatural. Allan Anderson, *An Introduction to Pentecostalism: Global Charismatic Christianity* (Cambridge: Cambridge University Press, 2004), pp. 157-83.

[3] Walter J. Hollenweger, *Pentecostalism: Origins and Developments Worldwide* (Peabody, MA: Hendrickson Publishers, 1997), pp. 18–20, 69–88. Anthea Butler, *Women in the Church of God in Christ: Making a Place for Ourselves* (Chapel Hill: The University of North Carolina Press, 2007), pp. 45–68, makes a similar point. Butler's study of women in the Church of God in Christ further underscores the vital contributions of Black individuals, particularly women, to the development of Pentecostal worship styles. Their leadership in music, testimony, and prayer meetings solidified expressive and participatory forms of worship as central to the Pentecostal experience, influencing its global spread. Iain MacRobert, *The Black Roots of Pentecostalism: African American Pentecostalism in the Twentieth Century* (Cardiff: University of Wales Press, 1988), pp. 105-28, directly addresses the foundational role of African American religious traditions in the development of Pentecostal worship.

[4] Melva Wilson Costen, *African American Christian Worship* (Nashville: Abingdon Press, rev. edn, 2007), p. 18.

formation in the crucible of historical experiences of colonialism, enslavement, and postcolonial resistance.[5]

Over time, however, this 'beautiful expression of human experience' that gave rise to the black church worship tradition, including black Pentecostalism, increasingly began to bear the vestiges of colonial power, racial hierarchies, and Eurocentric theological frameworks that continue to influence its religious experiences, theological imagination, and worship practices. In his book, *The Rise to Respectability: Race, Religion and the Church of God in Christ*, Calvin White, Jr., notes.

> After emancipation, generally, rural blacks tended to cling more tenaciously to older customs and traditional forms of worship, but in southern cities [such as Little Rock and Memphis], with the growing numbers of educated African Americans, their interest also grew in a more rationalized, uniform religious experience.[6]

Colonial epistemology and religious sensibilities not only increasingly influenced Black Pentecostal worship but have also, at times, silenced indigenous expressions, marginalized certain voices, and perpetuated the myth that 'proper' worship must privilege European and North American liturgical norms.[7] Consequently, the reclamation of core elements – such as spontaneity, African orality, communal bonding characterized by ubuntu, and embodied Praise that lie at the heart of African-descended spirituality – is at risk of being diluted, obfuscated, or tamed into what can only be described as the gentrification of Black Pentecostal worship.

The issues highlighted above raise a set of important inquires that has provoked this chapter: How have colonial power dynamics

---

[5] Hollenweger, *Pentecostalism*, p. 18-20.

[6] Calvin White Jr., *The Rise to Respectability: Race, Religion, and the Church of God in Christ* (Fayetteville: The University of Arkansas Press, 2012), p. 3.

[7] For further discussions on the impact of colonial respectability on black worship styles, see Elias Bongmba, '"Decolonizing Theology"': Reflections on African Theology in the Twenty-First Century', *Journal of Religion in Africa* 37.1 (2007), pp. 82-88; Ogbu U. Kalu, *African Pentecostalism: An Introduction* (Oxford: Oxford University Press, 2008), pp. 285-308; Anderson, *An Introduction to Pentecostalism*, pp. 157-83; Tinyiko S. Maluleke, 'Black and African Theologies in the New World Order: A Time to Drink from Our Own Wells', *Journal of Theology for Southern Africa* 108 (2000), pp. 7-12; Clinton N. Westman (ed.), *Pentecostalism and Indigenous Culture in Northern North America* (*Anthropologica*, Special Issue, 2013), pp. 15-35.

shaped contemporary Black Pentecostal worship styles and theology? What practices and theological motifs must be reclaimed in order to decolonize the black worship tradition? How can worship function as an act of cultural affirmation and communal resistance? Historically, Black Christian faith in general and black Pentecostal expressions more specifically emerged as more than a religious movement; it offered a liberating spiritual praxis for those navigating colonial legacies, racial hierarchies, and systemic inequalities. By recentering African-derived orality, community solidarity, and embodied worship expressions, this chapter underscores how Black Pentecostal worship can stand as a theological and cultural refusal of oppressive norms.

Key Terms and Concepts

Before we delve into this discussion, defining some key terms is necessary for clarity. To begin with I am using the term 'Black' to signify those of African descent: namely African, African Caribbean (including people of Caribbean extraction in the UK and Europe), and African Americans.[8] While acknowledging the distinct histories, traditions, and cultures of these groups, this classification recognizes shared characteristics rooted in the historical and ongoing impacts of the African diaspora and racialization. From a historical perspective, this categorization is understood through the lens of shared particulars arising from a universal experience of racialization. The 'universal' in this context is the historical and systemic experience of being categorized and treated as 'Black' within societies shaped by colonialism, slavery, and their enduring legacies of racial hierarchy. This shared experience of racial othering has resulted in a set of particular cultural, social, and political commonalities. The Black communities of the African diaspora, specifically those of African American, African Caribbean, and African, are therefore bound by a shared

---

[8] In this context, the term 'Black' refers broadly to individuals of Black African descent across the globe, including – but not limited to – Black Africans, Black Caribbeans (including those within the UK), and African Americans. While this usage acknowledges the breadth and diversity of Black identity – including Afro-Latin American, Afro-European, Afro-Arab, Afro-Asian, and other Indigenous or diasporic Black communities who share in the historical, cultural, and political legacies shaped by African heritage – this particular framing emphasizes the shared historical trajectory of Black Africans, African Americans, and Black Caribbeans through the transatlantic slave trade. This triadic focus is not meant to exclude, but to highlight the common thread of displacement, resistance, and cultural continuity that binds these communities together in the context of this work.

historical context forged in the crucible of the Transatlantic Slave Trade. This history has also shaped shared experiences of identity formation, as these communities have navigated societies that often devalue Blackness, leading to distinct yet related forms of Black consciousness and cultural expression, and fueling collective political action and resistance against racial injustice.

Therefore, while fully recognizing the distinct particularities of Black African, Black Caribbean, and Black American cultures, the use of 'Black' as an identifier in this context, I would like to argue, is justified by the shared universal experience of racialization and its consequent shared particulars in history, social experience, cultural expression, and political consciousness. This framing allows for the unity and the diversity within the black diaspora. Paul Gilroy's thesis in his widely acclaimed book, *The Black Atlantic*, which delves into the dynamic and ever-evolving nature of black identity within the expansive context of the Black diaspora, is instructive here.[9] He contends that the cultural landscape of the Black Atlantic is continuously shaped by the movements of people across various regions, resulting in a complex and multifaceted identity that transcends traditional racial categorizations. Gilroy argues that black identity within the black Atlantic is fluid and in constant flux which negates the idea of a static monolithic culture. Rather, it emphasizes the diverse range of experience and perspective within Africa and the Black Diaspora. Gilroy's assertion that this identity is fluid and in constant flux challenges the notion of fixed racial essences. It emphasizes the diverse range of experiences and perspectives within Africa and the Black diaspora.[10]

The terms 'Pentecostal' and 'Pentecostalism' often evoke diverse interpretations, uniting individuals under an elusive meaning.[11] With Dr. Allan Anderson, I adopt an inclusive definition of Pentecostalism as a term that describes globally 'all churches and movements that emphasize the working of the gifts of the Spirit, both on phenomenological and theological grounds'.[12] I define black Pentecostalism as a vibrant and dynamic Christian movement within the broader

---

[9] Paul Gifford, *The Black Atlantic: Modernity and the Double Consciousness* (Cambridge, MA: Harvard University Press, 1993).

[10] Gilroy, *The Black Atlantic: Modernity and the Double Consciousness,* p. 15.

[11] See Wolfgang Vondey, *Pentecostalism: A Guide for the Perplexed* (Bloomsbury T&T Clark, 2013).

[12] Anderson, *Introduction to Pentecostalism*, p. 13.

Pentecostal movement, characterized by its deep roots in the experience, culture, and spiritual expression of the black communities worldwide. My usage of the expression 'black Pentecostal worship' incorporates the core cultural and epistemological principles of black worship traditions that extend from the black experience in the black Atlantic among Africans, Caribbean, and African Americans.

Methodology

This work adopts a Postcolonial Liberative Theological Methodology. A detailed discussion of this methodological approach is beyond the scope of this chapter; therefore, four core statements that characterize this approach will suffice. This postcolonial approach critically engages the enduring legacies of colonialism on Christian theology, religious practices, and cultural expressions. It operates through several interconnected tenets: first, by critiquing colonial legacies embedded within theological frameworks, exposing their role in perpetuating power imbalances and marginalization.[13] Second, it involves reclaiming indigenous traditions and knowledge, recognizing them as vital and authoritative sources for theological reflection, often suppressed or dismissed by colonial dominance. Charles Long, a historian, has criticized African American and African religious scholars in their dependence on Eurocentric methodologies and theological categories. Long encourages black religious scholars to use the signs, symbols, and images to construct meaning for black faith. He maintains that theological discourse is itself an imperialistic enterprise because it is encoded in Eurocentric expressions.[14] Building upon Long's critique with utmost care, this work aims to cultivate an authentic expression of Black Pentecostal worship grounded in the symbols, signs, and meaning-making frameworks native to African peoples. It intentionally shifts away from Eurocentric modes of

---

[13] Proponents and works that take this approach include Frantz Fanon, *Black Skin, White Masks* (New York: Grove Press, 1967); Frantz Fanon, *The Wretched of the Earth* (trans. Constance Farrington; New York: Grove Press, 1963); Edward W. Said, *Orientalism* (New York: Pantheon Books, 1978); Edward W. Said, *Culture and Imperialism* (New York: Alfred A. Knopf, 1993); Gayatri Chakravorty Spivak, 'Can the Subaltern Speak?', in Cary Nelson and Lawrence Grossberg (eds.), *Marxism and the Interpretation of Culture* (Urbana: University of Illinois Press, 1988); Homi K. Bhabha, *The Location of Culture* (London: Routledge, 1994).

[14] Charles Long, *Signification: Sign, Symbols, and Images in the Interpretation of Religion* (Philadelphia: Fortress Press, 1986), p. 6.

theological thought and practice, which have long shaped dominant discourse, in order to open space for Afrocentric voices and wisdom traditions – especially as they inform Black worship. At its heart, Postcolonial Liberative Theology views theology not as abstract theory, but as a vital force for liberation – one that confronts injustice, resists domination, and seeks the full flourishing of those long wounded by empire.

This methodological framework is informed by postcolonial thought, including the seminal analyses of Franz Fanon in *The Wretched of the Earth* on the psychological and societal impacts of colonialism, Edward Said's *Orientalism* which exposes the construction of the 'Other' through Western discourse; Sylvia Wynter's call, in 'We must learn to sit down together and Talk about a Little Culture: Decolonizing Essays' for a decolonization of knowledge and being; Édouard Glissant's exploration of creolization and relationality in *Caribbean Discourse*, Noel Erskine's direct engagement with *Decolonizing Theology*; and James Cone's foundational work in *A Black Theology of Liberation*, which exemplifies a theological commitment to the liberation of the oppressed, to name but a few.[15] Although a more detailed integration of these works is reserved for a more extensive work, their postcolonial message and insights have profoundly impacted this work.

Colonial Legacies and Black Pentecostal Worship

Prior to the emergence of distinct Black worship practices, worship traditions deeply rooted in African spirituality provided an essential source of sustenance for enslaved African communities. From those captured and forced to sing songs of solace while awaiting transport on slave ships, to the communal work songs on Caribbean

---

[15] See Fanon, *The Wretched of the Earth*; Said, *Orientalism*; Sylvia Wynter, 'We Must Learn to Sit Down Together and Talk About a Little Culture: Reflections on the Foundations of a Movement', in George Jerry Sefa Dei and Leeno Luke Karumanchery (eds.), *The Humanities and the Curriculum: The African-American Struggle for Educational Equity* (New York: Peter Lang, 2004), pp. 1–25; Édouard Glissant, *Caribbean Discourse: Selected Essays* (trans. J. Michael Dash; Charlottesville: University of Virginia Press, 1989); Noel Leo Erskine, *Decolonizing Theology: A Caribbean Perspective* (Maryknoll, NY: Orbis Books, 1981); and James H. Cone, *A Black Theology of Liberation* (Maryknoll, NY: Orbis Books, 1970).

plantations, and the 'Hush Harbors' frequented by enslaved African Americans, these clandestine gatherings – described by historian Albert J. Raboteau as 'invisible institution'[16] – functioned as crucibles of both spiritual empowerment and social defiance.[17] Through ring shouts and call-and-response singing, enslaved African people enacted a theology of liberation that contested dominant narratives of racial subjugation. In doing so, they combined African religio-cultural traditions with biblical motifs of Exodus, creating a subversive worship context at the heart of their collective spiritual life.

Slavery, Colonization, and the Black Worship Tradition

During the dehumanizing experience of the slave trade music, signing, and dance were lifegiving activities as a means of expressing joy, lament, and resistance. [18] Along the coast of West Africa, as captives awaited transport in slave dungeons or made forced treks to coastal forts, oral histories hint at the indigenous laments they sang – songs charged with desperation and entreaties to ancestral spirits. Scholars such as John Mbiti and J.H. Kwabena Nketia note that these laments often contained pleas to family clan spirits, puzzled appeals to the ancestral spirits, and expressions of shock at the sudden loss of freedom.[19] One Twi-based recollection, for instance, mentions the words: 'Yɛrekɔ a yennim kwan / M'ase nyinaa y'awɔ nnipa anaa? / Meda so frɛ Nana / Na ɔmfa me ntor bra,' which loosely translates to, 'We are

---

[16] Albert J. Raboteau, *Slave Religion: The 'Invisible Institution' in the Antebellum South* (Oxford: Oxford University Press, Updated Edition, 1978).

[17] See Vorris L. Nunley, *Keepin' It Hushed: The Barbershop and African American Hush Harbor Rhetoric* (Detroit, MI: Wayne State University Press, 2011). While this book uses the barbershop as a central metaphor, it delves deeply into the concept of the hush harbor as a space of safe expression and knowledge generation for African Americans. It explores how these 'hush harbor' spaces functioned historically and how that tradition continues to shape African American communication and culture. It is a valuable resource for understanding the rhetorical and cultural significance of these spaces within the African American community. See also Albert J. Raboteau, *Slave Religion*. This is a foundational work in the study of African American religious life under slavery. Raboteau thoroughly examines how enslaved people created their religious world, often in secret, and how the hush harbor was central to that. It provides crucial historical context for understanding the origins and importance of these practices.

[18] See, William Francis Allen et al, *Slave Songs of the United States* (New York: A. Simpson & Co., 1867).

[19] John S. Mbiti, *African Religions and Philosophy* (London: Heinemann, 1969); J.H. Kwabena Nketia, *African Music in Ghana* (Accra: Longmans, Green and Co., 1962).

being taken away to a place unknown / Is my entire life now in the hands of strangers? / I still call upon my Ancestor / May they guide me through this trial'.[20] Although fragmentary, such verses suggest perplexity at captivity and a fervent desire for ancestral guidance, underscoring the sense of spiritual confusion and faint hope that accompanied the journey to the coast.

Farther across the Atlantic, on Caribbean plantations, work songs emerged as both a rhythmic aid to labor and a covert means of preserving camaraderie under the vicious, merciless scourges of white colonizers. These songs varied depending on the specific island's language and cultural influences – Jamaica, Haiti, Barbados, Trinidad – but often featured call-and-response patterns and veiled messages that transcended a simple work chant. One Jamaican fragment invokes, 'Bruck de stone, bruck de stone, / Sun hot, massa cannot see;/ Some day we be free, / Lawd, some day we be free'.[21] On the surface, it underscores the monotony of labor ('Bruck de stone'), yet it also implies a fleeting reprieve from the overseer's gaze due to the sun's intensity. Refrains such as 'Some day we will be free' could be heard as harmless optimism or, more deeply, as an affirmation of eventual liberation. In a similar vein, Haitian Kreyòl songs – like 'O, travay la di / Men nou pa ka lage / O, Bondye, mennen nou sove / Nou tout se frè ak sè' – carried the promise of divine intervention and communal unity, quietly challenging the notion that plantation hierarchies were immutable.[22]

In the United States, where enslaved communities gathered in hush harbors to worship beyond the scrutiny of plantation owners, spirituals often became coded anthems of defiance and resistance.[23] 'Steal Away to Jesus,' for example, could be interpreted as

---

[20] For a collection of slave songs sung by Africans who were stolen from their land see Ute Röschenthaler (ed.), *African Voices on Slavery and the Slave Trade* (Woodbridge, UK: Boydell & Brewer, 2018).

[21] See Martha Warren Beckwith, *Jamaica Folklore* (New York: American Folklore Society, 1928), p. 94.

[22] See Elizabeth McAlister, *Rara! Vodou, Power, and Performance in Haiti and Its Diaspora* (Berkeley: University of California Press, 2002). See also Michael Largey, *Vodou Nation: Haitian Art Music and Cultural Nationalism* (Chicago: University of Chicago Press, 2006), for more on the role of music in Haitian cultural resistance.

[23] James H. Cone, *The Spirituals, and the Blues: An Interpretation.* (Maryknoll, NY: Orbis Books, 50th Anniversary edn, 2022), p. 30.

a call to slip away for secret worship or an outright escape. Its lyrics – 'Steal away, steal away, steal away to Jesus, / Steal away, steal away home; / I ain't got long to stay here' – expressed a yearning for spiritual communion as well as a literal plan for flight to a better world. Other spirituals, like 'Go Down, Moses,' drew a bold parallel between enslavers and Pharaoh, turning the biblical account of Exodus into political theology. By invoking the words, 'Tell old Pharaoh, 'Let my people go!'' enslaved singers subtly professed that God's authority outweighed that of any earthly master. Meanwhile, 'Didn't My Lord Deliver Daniel' articulated a broader plea for equality, illustrated in the line, 'An' why not every man?' – a probing question that implicitly rejected the notion that certain human beings deserved bondage while others enjoyed freedom.[24] W.E. Du Dubois captures the power and beauty in the spiritual in his reflection on the African American experience.

> Little of beauty has America given to the world save the rude grandeur of God himself stamped on her bosom; the human spirit in this new world has expressed itself in vigor and ingenuity rather than in beauty. Thus, by fateful chance, the Negro folk-song – the rhythmic cry of the enslaved person – stands today not simply as the sole American music, but as the most beautiful expression of human experience born this side of the seas.[25]

These song traditions – whether drawn from African lament, Caribbean work calls, or hush harbor spirituals in the American South – reflect the dynamic blend of African religio-cultural retentions and biblical motifs of liberation that flourished in enslaved communities. Their melody and verse resounded with the overlapping themes of sorrow, resistance, and an unbending belief in freedom. With every refrain uttered and chorus sung, a defiant spark flickered beneath the smoldering heat of oppression that was a reminder of their sense of agency and faith in God.

---

[24] For interpretation of various 'Spiritual' see, Pedrito U. Maynard-Reid, *Diverse Worship: African American, Caribbean & Hispanic Perspectives* (Downers Grove, IL: InterVarsity Press, 2000), pp. 76-81.

[25] W.E.B. Dubois, *The Souls of Black Folk* (London: Longmans, Green and Co Ltd, 1965), pp. 160-61.

Navigating Colonial Respectability: Tensions in Worship Practices

By the early twentieth century, however, mainstream church structures and Western missionary worship forms in African, African American, and Caribbean communities increasingly aligned with Victorian notions of propriety, often to gain legitimacy within a racially hostile environment.[26] This shift influenced even the nascent Pentecostal movement, even though early revivals – such as the 1906 Azusa Street Mission in Los Angeles – were initially characterized by ecstatic worship, interracial fellowship, and a dismantling of rigid hierarchies.[27] As James Goff notes in *Fields White Unto Harvest: Charles F. Parham and the Missionary Origins of Pentecostalism*, certain Pentecostal pioneers endured harsh scrutiny: white Protestants dismissed them as 'primitive', while Black churches worried about social stigma.[28] In their quest for acceptance and willingness to conform against the religious diatribe of colonial rule, black leaders gradually adopted colonial acceptable worship styles and patriarchal leadership norms.

Gentrification of Black Pentecostal Worship

To receive more favorable treatment in the Jim Crow era, black congregations that were once known for their vibrant dance, polyrhythmic music, and spontaneous testimony, began to modify their

---

[26] Lamin Sanneh, in this book, *Translating the Message*, examines how African Christianities were shaped through European missionary translation and frameworks, often internalizing colonial ideologies even as they adapted Christian teaching in local languages; see, *Translating the Message: The Missionary Impact on Culture* (Maryknoll, NY: Orbis Books, 1989). Elsa Tames, in *The Bible of the Oppressed*, explored how Christian biblical interpretations in Colonial and postcolonial Latin American and the Caribbean often mirrored colonial hierarchies and values, especially in its ecclesial structures and theology; see, Elsa Tames, *The Bible of the Oppressed* (trans. Matthew J. O'Connell; Maryknoll, NY: Orbis Books, 1982). Rita Roberts in his book, *Evangelicalism and the Politics of Reform in Northern Black Thought*, provides a strong argument that many African Americans religious leaders, while advocating for abolition and reform, also internalized white evangelical norms in theology, moral outlook, and church practice; see Rita Roberts, *Evangelicalism and the Politics of Reform in Northern Black Thought 1776-1863* (Baton Rouge: Louisiana State University Press, 2010).

[27] Estrelda Alexandria, *Black Fire: One Hundred Years of African American Pentecostalism* (Downers Grove, IL: IVP Academic, 2011), p. 121.

[28] Goff, James R., Jr. *Fields White Unto Harvest: Charles Parham and the Missionary Origins of Pentecostalism* (Fayetteville, AR: The University of Arkansas Press, 1988), p. 123.

worship expressions in exchange for colonial respectability norms. While the Holy Spirit's active presence remained central, cultural markers such as drumming and African oral traditions were frequently minimized or even disavowed. Consequently, the once-subversive vitality of hush harbor worship – where oppressed communities encountered a liberating God – was in many contexts subdued by Victorian ideals of 'dignity' and 'order'. Ebony Marshall Turman, in *Toward a Womanist Ethic of Incarnation*, further contends that respectability politics not only weakened African diasporic worship forms but also reinforced patriarchy and other colonial assumptions regarding who is permitted to lead or shape liturgy.[29] In this regard, the gentrification of Black Pentecostal worship not only tamed its radical spiritual exuberance but also silenced its prophetic voice, sacrificing ancestral memory and liberative potential on the altar of pious and social respectability.

A detailed analysis of the impact of colonial sensibilities on black worship traditions and their subsequent gentrification in the transatlantic space is beyond the scope and word length allocated for this chapter; however, below are several illustrative examples. These colonial sensibilities created tension between African-informed expressions and Western-centric propriety in the following ways:

Prayer and Preaching styles: The spontaneous call and response preaching style, in which the preaching hour would be punctuated with shouts of 'Amen' and 'Hallelujah', was gradually replaced by more controlled and 'orderly' responses. It was not usual to see church leaders discouraging spontaneous emotional outbursts and fervor of traditional African Pentecostal style preaching, fearing it would be deemed 'unrefined' by white colonial religious gatekeepers.[30]

---

[29] Ebony Marshall Turman, *Toward a Womanist Ethic of Incarnation: Black Bodies, the Black Church, and the Council of Chalcedon* (New York: Palgrave Macmillan, 2013), p. 59.

[30] Cheryl Sanders addresses how traditional Black Holiness-Pentecostal preaching, known for being impassioned and Spirit-led, was sometimes labeled as 'embarrassing 'or 'underdisciplined', particularly when compared with white evangelical models (see Cheryl Sanders, *Saints in Exile: The Holiness-Pentecostal Experience in African America and Its Cultural Significance* (New York: Oxford University Press, 1996), pp. 76–80.

Muted Community Participation: The interjected exclamations, testimonies, and songs during worship were a hallmark of the dialogical and synergistic interplay between the preacher and the congregation. However, to project 'dignity' and propriety, this practice was increasingly discouraged, aligning with Eurocentric standards of decorum.[31]

Musical Styles and Preferences: The African practice of drumming and syncopated rhythms that fueled ubuntu communal bonding and spiritual connections was downplayed and, in some cases, completely banned in specific black congregations. To ward off accusations of stereotypes of 'African heathenistic practices,' worship services replaced drum-driven Praise and worship with piano or organ music, which was seen as more acceptable by Western norms. Congregational songs that rang out with polyrhythmic clapping and 'blue notes' symptomatic of African tonalities were often replaced by hymns and choral music. Even though these adaptations gave birth to a rich black choral tradition, they also diluted the spontaneity and communal improvisation inherited from African worship traditions.[32]

Bodily Expressions and Orderly Liturgy: Black worship tradition integrated dance as an expression of worship, which included ring shouts and other dance forms that mirrored African worship traditions. As western rationalist sensibilities modeled through Victorian respectability took hold, demonstrative expression of

---

[31] Melva Wilson Costen discusses the African oral and communal traditions in worship and how these were suppressed to conform to Euro-American liturgical standards, see *African American Christian Worship* (Nashville: Abingdon Press, 1993), pp. 15-25. Estrelda Alexander discusses respectability politics and the marginalization of emotional, participatory worship in favor of decorum; see *Black Fire*, p. 113. Albert J. Raboteau describes the African influences in Black worship and how white observers critiqued these practices as uncivilized, leading some churches to temper their worship style; see *Canaan Land: A Religious History of African Americans* (New York: Oxford University Press, 2001), pp. 88-93.

[32] Mellonee V. Burnim explains how early African American religious music was rich in polyrhythmic drumming, oral transmission, and call and response patters inherited from West African musical traditions were replaced with piano/organ as a direct response to colonial and racialized religious sensibilities, which viewed African instruments and rhythms as 'pagan' or 'undignified'; see, Mellonee V. Burnim, 'Religious Music', in Mellonee V. Burnim and Portia K. Maultsby (eds.), *African American Music: An Introduction* (New York: Routledge, 2006), pp. 45–72.

worship like dancing, leaping, clapping, or prostration was further discouraged.[33]

Shortened Services and Rigid Agendas: Where worship once flowed organically, building on Spirit-led testimonies, many churches instituted set times for prayer, announcements, singing, and preaching. This more regimented schedule not only limited opportunities for extended praise or spontaneous testimonies but also lessened the communal synergy that had been a defining feature of African-informed worship.[34]

Community Fellowship vs. Individual Piety. Emphasis on Private Devotion: In some contexts, African-based communal fellowship – centered on shared meals, collective problem-solving, and confession – became secondary to personal piety practices (quiet meditation, individual Bible reading). This shift mirrored Western evangelical models that prized the solitary believer's relationship with God over communal rites.[35]

Reduced Call – and – Response: Call and response is a robust, interactive, and communal means of African communication. This is expressed in prayers, songs, and music that embody African Christian faith expression. The adoption of Western ideals of worship diminished this potent collective vocal engagement, unintentionally marginalizing worshipers who found communal participation spiritually essential.

---

[33] See Maureen Warner-Lewis, *African Continuities in the Religious Culture of Trinidad* (Kingston: University of the West Indies Press, 2003), chap. 6, 'Christianity and Associated Religions', pp. 150–65; Noel Leo Erskine, *Decolonizing Theology: A Caribbean Perspective* (Maryknoll, NY: Orbis Books/Africa World Press, 1998), chap. 3, 'Colonial Christianity and African Retentions', pp. 70–85; Sylvia Wynter, 'The Ceremony Found', in Katherine McKittrick (ed.), *The Re-Enchantment of Humanism* (Durham, NC: Duke University Press, 2015), pp. 20–23

[34] Carter G. Woodson describes how 'progressive negroes' favored 'serious and classical music (organ or piano) and structured sermons. He notes how worship moved away from extended testimonies and impassioned gatherings towards timed, refined formats; see Carter G. Woodson, *The History of the Negro Church* (Washington, DC: Associated Publishers, 1921; repr., Project Gutenberg, 2005), pp. 255–56.

[35] See Du Bois, *The Souls of Black Folk*, ch. 10; and Woodson, *The History of the Negro Church*, pp. 255–56.

Collectively, these examples highlight the tensions between communal, African-informed expressions – rich in oral tradition, embodied movement, and collective energy – and Western-influenced standards that prize decorum. Collectively, these examples highlight the tensions between communal, African-informed expressions – rich in oral tradition, embodied movement, and collective energy – and Western-influenced standards that privileged formality and decorum, sentential liturgical order, and restrained emotional activities.

Colonial Residues in Contemporary Black Pentecostal Worship

Moving now to more contemporary worship styles and formats, modern Black Pentecostal worship, while a vibrant expression of faith, exhibits enduring traces of colonial hierarchies that manifest in several key areas, including musical expression, bodily practices, leadership structures, and theological language. These residues, though often subtle, continue to shape and, in some cases, constrain the full articulation of Black Pentecostal identity and experience.

One significant area of musical conformity that is worship illustrating is Contemporary Christian Music or CCM. This very popular music genre has overshadowed traditional African diasporic musical elements such as complex rhythms, call-and-response patterns, and improvisation. Robert Beckford, a black Pentecostal British scholar, observes in his book, *Decolonizing Contemporary Gospel Music Through Praxis: Handsworth Revolutions*, that this preference for Western compositional methods can lead to a hierarchical aesthetic within the church, where Afro-diasporic praise forms are implicitly or explicitly deemed less 'reverent' or sophisticated.[36] This can undermine the rich musical heritage of African-derived worship. The tension between African based aesthetics and conforming to Western church decorum is discussed by Melva Wilson Costen. She observes that black churches have often wrestled with this creative tension that often leads to the African expression being 'toned down' in an effort to appear more dignified.[37]

---

[36] Robert Beckford, *Decolonizing Contemporary Gospel Music Through Praxis: Handsworth Revolutions* (London: Bloomsbury Academic, 2023).

[37] Melva Wilson Costen, *African American Christian Worship* (Nashville: Abingdon Press, rev. edn, 2007), p. 18.

The attempts to suppress embodied worship go beyond eradicating a particular worship style, but the communal memory of how African people respond to God through embodied practices, language, and cultural forms. While African rhythmic modes of worship were being exchanged for more European worship sensibilities, colonial patriarchal structures were also embedded within the ecclesiastical culture of colonial leadership. An important and counter-cultural practices within the early Pentecostal movement was the inclusion of prominent women preachers and evangelists in ministry. Although this was not without its challenges, if demonstrated a level of gender inclusivity that was rare at the time.[38] The replication of colonial power dynamics often relies on selective biblical interpretations that reinforce male authority and marginalize indigenous models of female leadership and spiritual authority. These respectability norms have not only diluted African diasporic worship forms but also reinforced patriarchy and other colonial assumptions about who is permitted to lead or define worship within Black Pentecostal communities.

An additional point worth noting pertains to language and theology. The denial of the realities and legitimacy of African ontologies, labeling them as 'pagan' or 'demonic' amounted to the devaluation of the African spiritual outlook. This perpetuated a shallow understanding of faith that overlooks the holistic and socially engaged dimensions of African spirituality. The works of James Cone, particularly in his classic text, *The Spirituals and the Blues*, also speak to this point. Cone argues that these musical forms, arising from the suffering of enslaved Black people, represent theological assertions of God's presence and amid oppression and the power of faith-coupled-with resistance to transform reality. These songs, Cone contends, are more than mere artistic expression; they embody a prophetic tradition that intertwines sorrow with defiance, struggle with hope, and lament with liberation.[39]

---

[38] See, Estrelda Alexander, *The Women of Azusa* (Lanham, MD: Seymour Press, revised edition, 2023).

[39] James H. Cone, *The Spirituals and the Blues: An Interpretation* (Maryknoll, NY: Orbis Books, 1991), p. 27.

Decolonizing Black Pentecostal Worship

A decolonization of Black Pentecostal worship is a multifaceted endeavor that requires an intentional and sustained effort to purge Black Pentecostal worship of the vestiges of colonial influence and indoctrination. In this final section, I will highlight several key factors that I believe are essential for recentering worship as a distinctly African expression – one that connects us deeply to the Supreme God while allowing us to remain grounded in our cultural identity; allowing us to affirm the richness of our heritage, practices, and communal values as integral to an authentic spiritual encounter.

A Return to the Drum

A crucial first step in recentering African and Afro-diasporic traditions to the heart of our encounter with God is a return to the drum. In African traditional thought, the pounding of the African drum is the mimic beating of the heartbeat of God. The drum's tonal 'call' beckons us to respond, much like a child attuned to the supreme, its rhythm and voice instinctively drawing us into dance and attention. Steven Feld perceptively notes, 'The drum speaks like a child. Like Kaluli children, drums must be "fed" with prechewed food so that their language "hardens" to a well-formed and grammatical pattern'.[40] It is the vibration of the rhythm of life that is captured in the words of the Akan (Ghanaian) language known as 'Twi', 'Gye Nyame'.[41] The drum, with its varied tonalities and rhythms, is the ultimate 'call' to whose vibration we are called to 'respond' as children dancing in the shadow of the Supreme. The response to the drumbeat is not a perfunctory acknowledgement or a tacit intellectual assent but a fully embodied immersion into the presence of the divine numinous. A decolonized Black Pentecostal worship, therefore, is a return to embodied worship, where the Holy Spirit's anointing is experienced through full-body participation – dancing, clapping, and improvisation – an echo of hush-harbor worship. To embrace embodied worship is to affirm the theological premise that the Holy Spirit inhabits the entire body, freeing congregations to re-establish

---

[40] Steven Feld, 'Sound as a Symbolic System: The Kaluli Drum', in David Howes (ed.), *The Varieties of Sensory Experience: A Sourcebook in the Anthropology of the Senses* (Toronto: University of Toronto Press, 1991), p. 79.

[41] *Gye Nyame* is an Akan idiomatic phrase meaning 'Except God'. The full expression of this phrase is 'I can do nothing except God helps me'.

African-derived movement and communal joy in worship, countering colonial respectability norms that once deemed African bodily worship as undignified.

Anti-colonial and Justice-oriented Values

Beyond the reclamation of embodied worship, a decolonized Black Pentecostal worship is characterized by its alignment with anti-colonial and justice-oriented values. It necessarily decenters Eurocentric theologies that downplay systemic injustice, affirming the biblical emphasis on God's preferential concern for the oppressed – a concern that resonates deeply with Black lived realities. An important function of worship is the elevation of the soul beyond the existential limits of human experience. One must be cautious however, that worship does not function to induce spiritual exuberance as a means of anesthetizing black suffering but empower us to interpret and face structures of oppression and death. While Contemporary Christian music is a powerful medium that elevates the souls of worshipers in corporate ecclesial worship moments, it however often fails to engage and to dismantle oppressive systems actively through words and music. The spirituals, brush arbor songs, and Caribbean work songs, however, powerfully intertwine liberation and existential hope.

Challenging Patriarchal and Hierarchal Structures

An effort to decolonize Black Pentecostal worship also entails actively challenging patriarchal and hierarchal structures that limit the participation of women, youth, and elders in the church service and leadership roles. Instead, it rather embraces the critical Pentecostal belief in the priesthood of all believers, which affirms that the Spirit's presence and power are democratically distributed as record in Acts 2. This involves recognizing and placing value on the spiritual gifts and expressions of everyone, regardless of age, gender, or social standing, as evidence through prophecy, dreams, and vision, just as the Scriptures in Joel 2.28 proclaims. In her book, *The Spirit of the Lord: Renewal Spirituality, Biblical Justice, and the Prophetic Witness of the Church,* Pentecostal Womanist scholar Esrelda Alexander opines,

> Despite the prophetic witness of [these] early leaders, many were woefully short in shaping a lasting, liberative word towards women with the church and society. Too often the struggle for racial or

economic justice was the myopic focus of the moment, so they did not see failure to grant full liberty to women in the church and society as a form of injustice. Indeed, many espoused a biblical warrant for the second -class status they imposed on their sisters.[42]

Furthermore, a decolonized Black Pentecostal Worship practice must recognize the relationship between worship and social activism, public advocacy, and community engagement. In this regard, embracing worship as warfare should be extended beyond the bounds of the physical universe to the principalities and powers that works through political and system injustice and oppression. Worship as warfare must also be an activity in the public square where the principalities and powers are manifested through the oppressive structure of society. Social activism is also spiritual activism, and scripture is replete with copious examples of where worship functioned as a form of warfare or resistance against injustice, oppression, or evil powers.[43] These examples demonstrate how worship, praise, prayer, music, lament, and prophetic declaration act as spiritual and societal disruptions. Decolonized worship requires a reimagining of worship song writing, where songwriters write songs that could be sung during spiritual activism such as prayer vigils, public fasting, anointing and blessings on sites of injustice, praise marches, street worship gatherings, lament walks, sit-ins, occupations, and boycotts. This requires introducing black prophetic voices into the creative space of songwriting to ensure that the cries for justice, the visions of liberation, and the prophetic pronouncements rooted in Black lived experience find their voice and rhythm within the contemporary worship experience. Engaging creative worship song writing in critical dialogue with black prophetic voices would foster a creative environment where the pain and resilience of the community can be articulated through worship, not as escapism, but as a catalyst for transformative action and a powerful expression of hope grounded in the struggle for justice. One can only imagine the potent impact of songs born from Black prophetic Christian voices echoing the liberating message of Lk. 4.18

---

[42] Estrelda Alexander, *The Spirit of the Lord: Renewal Spirituality, Biblical Justice and the Prophetic Witness of the Church* (Lanham, MD: Seymour Press, 2022), p. 118.

[43] Exodus 15.1-21; 2 Chron. 20.1-30; Ps. 149.6-9; Josh. 6; Daniel 3; Daniel 6; 1 Samuel 1-2; Exod. 5.1; Acts 13.25-26; Revelation 5 and 6.

within the vibrant and expressive tradition of Black Pentecostalism cannot be overstated.

Art as Prophetic Resistance

In addition to music, decolonized Black Pentecostal worship also recognizes the role of artistic and symbolic resistance, such as mural and street art,[44] Spoken word and gospel protest music, prophetic theater, or reenactment, to name but a few examples. Building upon the recognition of artistic and symbolic resistance, one could argue that they serve as powerful visual and auditory declarations echoing the historical and contemporary struggles for liberation just as the Black Lives Matter murals during the George Floyds protest became potent symbols of resistance and a collective cry for justice, envisioning murals infused with the spirit of Lk. 4.18, visually manifesting the spirit of liberation employing color, imagery, and sacred text to forge a compelling experience that ignite resistance, proclaiming God's transformative power, and fostering critical dialogue within the worshipping community.

Worship as Vernacular Expression

In addition, a decolonized Black Pentecostal worship integrates vernacular expression into every facet of its worship, practice, prayer, and preaching. It includes everything from the stirring songs and biblical interpretation. This approach counters the colonial thinking that 'worship' must be given in the language of the colonizers, restoring

---

[44] Visual declarations of resistance were effectively used during the George Floyd protests, such as the Black Lives Matter murals. One can envision murals with Lk. 4.18,

> The Spirit of the Lord is upon Me,
> Because He has anointed Me
> To preach the gospel to the poor;
> He has sent Me heal the brokenhearted,
> To proclaim liberty to the captives
> And recovery of sight to the blind,
> To set at liberty those who are oppressed;

finding a natural home within the expressive tradition of Black Pentecostalism. Just as Black Pentecostal worship embraces embodied expression, these murals would embody the spirit of liberation, using color, imagery, and biblical text to create a powerful visual experience that inspires resistance and proclaims God's transformative power.

profound cultural authenticity to the worship experience by embracing the rich lexical diversity of the Afro-diaspora. Building upon the enduring legacy of Negro spirituals, born from the depths of the enslaved experience, the secretive yet spiritually potent hush harbor tradition, and the inherently resistant rhythms pulsating through Caribbean work songs, the vibrant energy of carnival music (soca, calypso), and the spiritually conscious vibrations of Reggae music, worship can be truly earthed in the everyday language and lived realities of the Black experience. Think about prayers that can be deeply felt and connect someone to God using Black English vernacular (BEV). Consider sermons that would incorporate the unique and rhythmic storytelling traditions of the community and spoken in a language that evokes culture to explain religious texts. Envision worship songs that use traditional styles blended with gospel and contemporary slang along with modern phrases to the point where it is both personal and accessible. Imagine the decolonized reading of sacred text by using Afrocentric viewpoints, considering the biblical story in its cultural context from within the cultures that gave rise to it, rather than from western perspectives. Additionally, the diaspora's inclusion of proverbs and folktales along with specific vernaculars from various Black cultures, enriches the worship service, affirming the value and significance of these lively expressions, which are rooted in the encounter with God.

Worship and Urban Vernacular
The reclamation of the vernacular into the worship space must also extend to Black urban cultures, where worship can meaningfully connect with diverse 'subcultural' forms and artistic expression across the USA, UK, and the wider diaspora. For instance, incorporating the lyrical brilliance and social critique expressed in spoken word poetry or rap cyphers can transform testimonies into prophetic urban declarations. Beats rooted in hip-hop, trap, or neo-soul would enrich praise and worship, creating a sonic landscape where young people recognize their own voice and rhythm in the holy sanctuary. In such a service, preachers might reference contemporary street slang or cultural icons in their preaching, not as gimmickry or a desire to come across 'streetwise' but as theological bridges that connect sacred truth to everyday experience. In this way, the pulpit becomes both altar and

cipher, the sanctuary a space where the streets are not silenced but sanctified.

A decolonized worship reaffirms the black urban life, with all its complexity, beauty, and pain, as a valid and vibrant site of divine encounter. Worship infused with reggae rhythms and patois not only bridges cultural memory but also brings prophetic consciousness into the sanctuary. In the UK, grime music – with its raw lyricism, urban grit, and spiritual thirst – offers another avenue for a decolonized contextual worship. In addition, sermons and prayers might adopt grime's cadence and directness, allowing God's Word to speak into the realities of post-industrial neighborhoods, systemic injustice, and youth alienation. Similarly, Afroswing, drill, and spoken word poetry reflect the lived realities of third or fourth-generation African and Caribbean youth in urban London, Birmingham, and Manchester. When these forms are integrated into worship, they affirm that the Spirit can indeed speak in many tongues through the vernacular prophetic utterances of our sons and daughters.[45]

Worship as Visual Aesthetics

A corollary extension to the use of the vernacular, a decolonized Black Pentecostal worship intentionally incorporates African diasporic visual aesthetics to create a sacred space that reflects the cultural identity and spiritual heritage. This involves a conscious reclamation of sacred and liturgical expression through several key elements. Sanctuaries are adorned with decoration that draw upon African artistic traditions and motifs. Afrocentric religious art and symbols, rich in meaning and history are freely displayed to create a visually resonant environment. Furthermore, worship garments are chosen or designed to reflect Pan-African colors and styles, visually connecting the worshipper to their shared heritage, and affirming the beauty and dignity of their cultural identity within the context of worship. In addition, cultural iconography – such as murals and

---

[45] For a detailed exploration of the literature that promotes this perspective in detail, see Alejandro Nava, *Street Scriptures: Between God and Hip-Hop* (Chicago: University of Chicago Press, 2022); Caleb Thomas Kudlo, *New Urban Liturgy: Making a Lane for Hip-Hop in Multicultural Worship* (DWS diss., Liberty University, 2021); Andre E. Johnson (ed.), *Urban God Talk: Constructing a Hip Hop Spirituality* (Lanham, MD: Lexington Books, 2013); Daniel White Hodge, *The Soul of Hip Hop: Rims, Timbs and a Cultural Theology* (Downers Grove, IL: IVP Academic, 2010).

stained-glass windows that depict biblical figures with African features, attire, and setting – serves a sacred imagery that challenges the 'whitening' of all things biblical through centuries of Renaissance and Enlightenment iconography and images. This deliberate use of visual aesthetics serves to decolonize the worship space, making it a true reflection of the community's spiritual and cultural roots.[46]

Authenticity against Performance and Commercialization

Moreover, a decolonized Black Pentecostal worship prioritizes authenticity over polished, performance-driven, and commercially marketed presentations. This involves resisting the trend of modeling services' profit-focused or celebrity-oriented CCM trends. This is a troubling trend in which worship submits to capitalist impulses that commodify praise and transform genuine spiritual expression into a consumer product. This process of decolonizing worship entails restoring worship as a collective, Spirit-led act instead of a commodified product. A decolonized Black Pentecostal worship gives primary importance to authenticity and challenges colonial notions that worth is tied to outward display, favoring performance-driven and commercialized beauty. This choice is troubling in that it seeks to mimic worship services on profit-centric, celebrity Contemporary Christian Music (CCM) services which is a form of capitalism intruding into holy places.

This encroachment commodifies praise and transforms genuine spiritual expression, a deeply personal and communal encounter with the Divine, into a mere consumer product. Such a decolonized worship process is a deliberate act of reclaiming agency, re-establishing worship as a collective, Spirit-led act of communal participation and authentic encounter, rather than a passively received product. By divesting from these commercially driven models, Black Pentecostal worship actively decolonizes its understanding and practice, centering the lived experiences, cultural expressions, and the unfiltered

---

[46] In his essay, 'Afrocentric Spirituality in Christian Faith', Archbishop Chase stresses the transformative power of integrating African artistic traditions, symbols, and vibrations of prayer and dance within Christian liturgy. He highlighted the way the redeeming qualities of Afrocentric Spirituality may serve as an act of contextual reclamation in worship; see, Archbishop D.E. Chase, 'Afrocentric Spirituality in Christian Faith', in *Afrocentric Spirituality in Christian Faith*, Metropolitan Cathedral (2024).

voice of the Spirit within the community itself, free from the dictates of a market-driven, often Westernized, spiritual aesthetic.

Implications for Global Pentecostalism

The decolonization of Black Pentecostal worship holds critical implications for global Pentecostalism. By resisting the cultural globalization of worship that increasingly reflects Western cultural aesthetics and cultural sensibilities, a decolonized Black Pentecostal worship is advocating and embracing a more inclusive and culturally authentic approach to worship. This decolonization will foster a more profound sense of ownership and empowerment among Black Pentecostals across the world. In this regard, Black Pentecostals will contribute their unique gifts to the broader Christian oikos. A model of decolonization of worship, such as presented here for black Pentecostal worship, may serve as a model for other Pentecostal communities seeking to reclaim their worship practices that have been infused with colonial sensibilities.

Undoubtedly, Pentecostalism is a global phenomenon that has taken root on various continents, particularly the global south. Despite this global footprint, there remains a dominant Western paradigm that continues to shape Pentecostal theology and practice. A recentering and reclamation of Black Pentecostal worship in its various Afro-diasporic traditions challenges global Pentecostalism to engage in a critical reflection and examination of its own biases and presuppositions. This process of decolonization and reexamination of bias can lead to a deeper and more diverse understanding of the working of the Holy Spirit in the world, one that acknowledges and celebrates the diverse ways in which God is encountered and experienced through worship across cultures.

A decolonized Black Pentecostal worship is therefore not merely a stylistic preference; it is the very bedrock upon which a robust and authentic practice of worship as resistance is built. This understanding moves beyond a superficial engagement with spiritual practices, recognizing that true liberation cannot be found in a worship culture designed to anaesthetize the oppressive pain of its worshippers.

Such a culture, despite its good intent to provide momentary relief and conform or emotional catharsis, inadvertently decouples affection from liberation. It might offer an escape, a temporary respite from the harsh realities of systemic injustice. However, it fails to equip individuals with the tools or the resolve to dismantle those oppressive structures. On the contrary, a decolonized Black Pentecostal worship is deliberately designed to invite God's presence directly into human spaces, not as a distant, abstract deity, but as an immanent force that engages with the lived joys and cries of his people. This epistemic shift recognizes the inherent, undeniable relationship between worship and resistance. It posits that a genuine encounter with the divine, when unburned by the weight of colonial imposition, naturally ignites a spirit of defiance again injustice. God's presence, when truly welcome into the 'skin', languages, and cultures' of Black people, empowers them to see their inherent worth and to challenge any system that denies it.

Conclusion

The quest to preserve and value our unique worship experience, therefore, is not based upon a nostalgic longing to return to the past, but a radical act of self-affirmation and spiritual survival. It is a longing for God to encounter us precisely as we are – in our Black skin with our rich vernacular, through our distinctive cultural expressions, and within our unique epistemologies. This is profoundly significant because it prophetically challenges the longstanding and often unspoken assumption that proximity to the divine requires assimilation into dominant cultural forms. This harks back to a past when colonial religious practices presented God as more accessible through European aesthetic, languages, and theological frameworks, implicitly or explicitly devaluing African and African-diasporic spiritualties. A decolonized worship, is therefore, not just about expressing a preference; it is about asserting one's ontological claim to a divine encounter that is deeply personal and communal. This encounter becomes a wellspring of resilience and resistance that it explains because it speaks on a soul level; it affirms their pain, their joy, their history, and their very raison d'être. This decolonized worship fosters a spirituality that is not a desire to escape from present realities but be fully engaged in current struggles as whole people, providing the spiritual fortitude to confront oppression head-on with courage and strength. The music, the shouts of hallelujah, the embodies expressions such as dancing and clapping, and the sermonic cadences of the preacher, all become a vehicle for a Black Pentecostal liberation theology of worship that is lived and breathes, a testament to the power of a God who meets us not in a sanitized, alien form, but in the fullness of who we are. This active preservation becomes an ongoing act of resistance against the cultural erasure and spiritual subjugation that have historically characterized the Black experience.

The real cruelty and tragedy of denying people the opportunity of worshipping God through their own culture, vernacular, and epistemology is that it denies the very humanity of the worshipper, implying that their cultural expressions are somehow less capable of mediating the divine through their soul. Black people often experience a cognitive dissonance in worship, where one must make an uncomfortable choice between authentic selfhood or spiritual exuberant solidarity. This type of epistemic dissonance often leads to a diluted faith experience, perpetuating a colonized gaze within the sacred and reinforcing the idea that God is more accessible through dominant colonial forms, which hinder the profound and transformative encounter that a truly decolonized worship offers. It is nothing short of spiritual violence that amputates a people from their ancestral roots and the unique pathways through which their community has historically experienced the sacred – an erasure that muffles the drumbeat of memory, silences the tongues of fire and renders mute the cries of an *Unchained Hallelujah*.

14

ECHOES OF ECOLOGY: UNPACKING THE ECOLOGICAL THEMES IN SELECTED AKAN PENTECOSTAL HYMNOLOGY

EMMANUEL AWUDI[*]

Introduction

It is increasingly becoming evident that the role of religion, especially Christianity, in the conservation of biodiversity, especially in Africa, cannot be overemphasized. In my PhD thesis, I discussed how some indigenous churches in Africa have explored the continuities in their primal cultures and the OT to formulate their own 'green theologies'.[1] Rather than demonizing and condemning their primal cultures, these churches 'converted' and found affinities between them and the OT eco-values toward the development of their own ecotheologies. For Samson Gitau, 'If Christians were to treat the environment as they possibly treat the Lord's Supper, that is, with faith and awe, the battle against environmental degradation would become less

---

[*] Emmanuel Awudi (PhD, Akrofi-Christaller Institute) is a lecturer at Pentecost University in Accra, Ghana.

[1] These churches include the Ethiopian Orthodox Tewahedo Church, the Zionist Church in Zimbabwe, the Musama Disco Christo Church, and the Ossa-Madih Church in Ghana. See Emmanuel Awudi, 'Beyond Eco-Pneumatology: An Examination of Scripture with "Green Eyes" and The Eco-Praxis of Some Indigenous African Churches towards the Development of an African Pentecostal Ecotheology' (PhD Thesis, Akrofi-Christaller Institute, 2023), pp. 44-78.

menacing'.[2] This statement is a truism as seen in the liturgy of the indigenous African churches mentioned early on.

In attempting to find theological responses to the loss of biodiversity, Veli-Matti Kärkkäinen advises Pentecostals:

> The task of an ecological constructive Christian theology is twofold: on the one hand, it has to clarify and help avoid ways of thinking and speaking of nature as creation that are detrimental to her survival and well-being. On the other hand, it also has to search for resources – theological insights metaphors, approaches – that can help foster the flourishing and continuing shalom of Gods' creation.[3]

Kärkkäinen is of the view that aside from carefully drawing lessons from Scripture, Christian teachings on nature, if not carefully handled, can rather lead to exploitation of nature. Such teachings include the 'prosperity gospel' which encourages amassing of wealth without regards for the lives of the other members in the ecosystem.

I pointed out in my thesis that the ecclesiology of African Pentecostals is yet to integrate ecology fully.[4] Perhaps, one of the most critical aspects of Pentecostal worship that requires greater ecological emphasis is music. David Nyansah Hayfron contends 'Next to the Bible, a hymn is probably our most important aid in the worship of the Almighty God.[5] This article argues that Pentecostals must move beyond merely singing of these hymns to appreciating the practical implications of these songs for caring for the environment. In other words, several Ghanaian Pentecostal worship songs touch on creation care, yet their potential to foster ecological stewardship remains largely unexplored. Pentecostals have a long history of oral or unwritten theology. Perhaps what accounts for this is the fact that many of the precursors of Pentecostalism especially in Africa, were unlettered. Amos Jimmy Markin affirms this: that the founders of the

---

[2] Samson Gitau, *The Environment Crisis: A Challenge for African Christianity* (Nairobi: Acton Publishers, 2000), p. 3.

[3] Veli-Matti Kärkkäinen, 'The Greening of the Spirit: Towards a Pneumatological Theology of the Flourishing of Nature', in A.J. Swoboda (ed.), *Blood Cries Out: Pentecostals, Ecology and the Groans of Creation* (Eugene, OR: Pickwick Publications, 2014), pp. 83-93 (88).

[4] Awudi, 'Beyond Eco-Pneumatology', p. 4.

[5] David Nyansah Hayfron, *A Sound from Heaven: The Life and Singing Ministry of Mrs. Eunice Johnson of Ghana* (Accra, Ghana: Pentecost Press Limited, 2019), p. 1.

three classical Pentecostal churches in Ghana had little or no formal education or theological training.[6] Some of these unwritten theologies including songs, poetry, and prayers may relate to ecotheology but remain unexplored. Thus, though there is inadequate scholarly works on Pentecostalism and ecology, these oral expressions may speak to God's care and love towards creation and how creation in return render praise to him. This study, therefore, examines six Pentecostal worship songs popular in Ghana, unpacking the ecological themes that emerge from their lyrics and exploring their implications for environmental responsibility.

Overview of the Akan Culture and Pentecostal Hymnology

The Akan culture is arguably one of the most receptive cultures to the Pentecostal brand of Christianity in Ghana. Perhaps a major reason for this receptivity is that the three major Classical Pentecostal Churches (CPCs) that emerged in Ghana – Christ Apostolic Church (CAC), the Apostolic Church (TAC), and the Church of Pentecost (CoP) started from within the Akan communities. Kwabena Asamoah Gyadu argues that the level of acceptability of Pentecostalism among Africans is partly due to the offering of forms of spirituality that connect with what Africans have traditionally considered as important in religion.[7] In most local CPCs in Ghana, Akan is the dominant language. One can conclude that the growth of the CPCs in the Akan communities in Ghana is largely due to the compatibility between the Pentecostal tradition and the Akan culture.

The move of the Spirit in the early days of the Pentecostal tradition in Ghana witnessed the manifestation of some pneumatic experiences including the gifts of the Spirit, prophecies, and the composition of 'prophetic songs'. Emmanuel Larbi indicates that before individuals started to 'receive' or 'compose' their own songs in the CPCs, Timothy Albertson Aidoo, a member from the early days of

---

[6] Amos Jimmy Markin, *Transmitting the Spirit in Missions: The History and Growth of the Church of Pentecost* (Eugene, OR: Wipf & Stock, 2019), p. 248.

[7] J. Kwabena Asamoah-Gyadu, 'Drinking from Our Own Wells: The Primal Imagination and Christian Religious Innovation in Contemporary Africa', *Journal of African Christian Thought* 11.2 (December 2008), p. 35.

the Pentecostal movement, translated some English songs which were sung at meetings.[8] Later, local choruses began to emerge which resonated well with the continuities of their primal faith and the gospel.

Notable 'authors' of some Akan songs that are widely sung among Pentecostals in Ghana include Eunice Addison, Eunice Johnson, and Opoku Onyinah of the CoP, and Ebenezer Ampiah of the CAC. The majority of the songs that were written by these composers were 'prophetic' – either spontaneously received through pneumatic experience or the songs carry prophetic messages. These songs range from praise, adoration, petition, and encouragement. Some of them speak to how God cares for his creation while others speak to how creation in turn sings God's praise. The next sections have been dedicated to analysing the contents of six Akan Pentecostal songs and how they communicate environmental stewardship even though the 'composers' themselves and their churches might have not paid much attention to the messages they carry. This study argues that these songs can become significant starting points for the emerging African Pentecostal ecotheology.

God is the Creator and Sustainer of the Universe

Pentecostals acknowledge that God is the Creator of the universe as seen in *The Tenets of the Church of Pentecost*, 'We believe in the existence of the One True God, Elohim, and Maker of the whole universe; indefinable, but revealed as Triune Godhead – Father, Son and Holy Spirit – one in nature, essence and attributes'.[9] Similarly, the statement of faith of the Assemblies of God states, 'The One true God has revealed himself as the eternally self-existent 'I AM', the Creator of heaven and earth and the Redeemer of Mankind'.[10] Not only does

---

[8] Emmanuel Kingsley Larbi, *Pentecostalism: The Eddies of Ghanaian Christianity* (Accra, Ghana: Centre for Pentecostal and Charismatic Studies, 2001), p. 119.

[9] Emmanuel Anim, 'The Doctrine of God', in Opoku Onyinah (ed.), *The Tenets of the Church of Pentecost* (Accra, Ghana: The Church of Pentecost, 2019), pp. 95-112 (95).

[10] Assemblies of God, *Constitution and Bylaws* (Avenor Junction, Accra: Assemblies of God Press, ND), p. 6. The position of the CAC on the doctrine of God is '[a]. God is one in three persons: The Father, the Son and the Holy Spirit (Jn 10.30; Matt. 28.18-20; Luke 3.22). [b]. God is Eternal, Omnipresent, Omniscient and Omnipotent, among others (Psalm 90.1-2). [c]. God created the whole universe out of nothing (Gen. 1.1)', See Christ Apostolic Church International (CAC), *Constitution* (Accra, Ghana: Christ Apostolic Church International, 2019), p. 6.

the CPCs in Ghana acknowledge God as the Creator of the universe in their tenets but their songs clearly demonstrate this.

Ɔsoro yɛ Wo de	The heavens belong to you
Asase yɛ Wo nan ntiaso	The earth is your footstool
Na emu nneɛma yɛ Wo de	Its inhabitants belong to you
Yɛ Agya Onyame, yɛda W'ase (x2)	Our Father God, we thank you
E. K. Asamoah[11]	*Translation mine*

This song echoes the psalmist's declaration, 'The earth is the Lord's and the fullness thereof, the world and those who dwell therein, for he has founded it upon the seas and established it upon the rivers'.[12] Scripture is clear on how the universe came into existence. The phrase, *Bereshit Elohim* (in the beginning God), answers several puzzles surrounding the creation narrative maybe including God's location at the time he was creating the heavens and the earth, or Adam's age at the time of his creation. Thus, the intention of the author was not to give a vivid description of what transpired but to draw attention to the fact that everything in the universe began with God.[13] For Emmanuel Asante, 'First this statement assumes that God has always existed, even though everything else has a beginning. Second, creation owes its being to God, who is the Creator, the absolute Originator, of everything'.[14] The phrase therefore, draws attention to the fact that first, God exists; second, he existed before creation; third, he is the main character in the creation narrative; fourth, he did what no one could ever do; and fifth, he did what pleased him.[15] These thoughts are clearly demonstrated in some Akan Pentecostal hymns.

---

[11] The Church of Pentecost, *Pentecostal Songs Book – English and Twi* (Accra: Pentecost Press Limited, 2018), p. 350. There are several other songs among the Akan Pentecostals that carry the same message.

[12] Psalm 24.1, ESV.

[13] Awudi, 'Beyond Eco-Pneumatology', p. 17.

[14] Emmanuel Asante, 'Ecological Crisis: A Christian Answer', *Trinity Journal of Church and Theology* 4.2 (December/January 1994-1995), pp. 8-19 (13).

[15] Awudi, 'Beyond Eco-Pneumatology', p. 17.

In the Akan culture, God is revered as *Onyankopɔn* (Great Friend) with other common attributes like *Ɔboade* (Creator) and *Borebore* (Carver, Excavator, Originator, Inventor, or Architect).[16] Scholars like J.B. Danquah and J.S. Pobee note that the Akan understanding of God as the Creator and Sustainer underscores their deep respect for the universe and its governance.[17] Thus, for the African, knowledge about God as the Creator is not debatable as the Akan sages go, '*Obi nkyerɛ akwada Nyame* ('No one teaches a child about God'). For the Akan, knowledge about God as Creator and the one who sustains the universe is inborn. The adage, ' *sɛ Awurade nkum wo a, ɔteasefoɔ yɛ kwa* ('If God does not kill you, man tries in vain'), also highlights their primal religious conviction that life belongs to God alone. The adage implies that the Akan primal religious person believes that every single life belongs to God and he alone can take it back.

The Akan Pentecostals' conviction in God as Creator and Sustainer not only influence their worship but also informs their valuation of creation, encouraging a sense of care and preservation. This, in turn, shapes their perspective on the environment and their role within it. It implies that the Akan people are inclined to protect God's creation, valuing its inherent life and sustaining power. By extension, this understanding fosters a sense of responsibility towards God's creation. It also reminds them that the Creator is not an absentee God but actively present within his creation, watching over and protecting it. Human beings can know him through his creation with the understanding that he first made himself known through his creation.

Creation Reveals God's Attributes

As far back as AD 57, the Apostle Paul reminded believers in Rome 'For what can be known about God is plain to them, because God has shown it to them. For his invisible attributes, namely, his eternal power and divine nature, have been clearly perceived, ever since the creation of the world, in the things that have been made. So they are without excuse.'[18] Reflections on the mysteries behind nature, and the

---

[16] J.B. Danquah, *The Akan Doctrine of God: A Fragment of Gold Coast Ethics and Religion* (Frank Cass & Co. Ltd, 1968), p. 30.

[17] Danquah, *The Akan Doctrine of God,* p. 195. See John S. Pobee, *Toward an African Theology* (Nashville: Parthenon Press, 1979), p. 46.

[18] Romans 8.19-20, ESV.

awareness of human limitations are some of the pointers to the existence of God within most African cultures. It is generally accepted among Christians that creation is a source of revelation of the transcendent. This knowledge is quite profound among African Pentecostals due to the continuity within the primal understanding than creation connects humanity to the Supreme Being.[19] This view is demonstrated clearly in the Apostolic Church hymn as follows:

Onyankopɔn	God Almighty,
abɔde kyerɛ ne tumi kɛse	creation reveals your might
Ɔde ne tumi bɔɔ wɔn	He created them with your power
Dekyerɛ sɛnea ɔte.	To show his nature.
Onyankopɔn wo so	Great are you Lord
Wo korɔn wɔ soro hɔ	You are great in the heavens
Wo korɔn wɔ asaase so	You are great on the earth
Wote saa wɔ soro hɔ[20]	You remain the same in heaven
Author unknown	*Translation mine*

John Mbiti earlier posits that African traditional religionists admit that God is Supreme, transcendent, and immanent among his creation.[21] These continuities are seen within the African Pentecostals. Aside from God revealing himself through other means, his creation is one of the ways through which people can know him. Similarly, J.J. Ongong'a posits that creation not only speaks of the presence of the divine, but it is also a manifestation of his character.[22] He states, 'For an African, nature does not only reveal God as a Cosmic Engineer but as an Engineer, who is actively involved in his creation so that whatever happens is believed to be a deliberate manifestation of the

---

[19] Robert Owusu Agyarko, 'God of Life: Rethinking the Akan Christian Concept of God in the Light of Ecological Crisis', *The Ecumenical Review* 65.1 (2013), pp. 51-66 (62).

[20] The Apostolic Church-Ghana, *Apostolic Twi Hymnal* (Accra: The Apostolic Church – Ghana, 2008), p. 28.

[21] John Mbiti, *African Religions Philosophy* (New York: Anchor Books, 2nd edn, 1970), pp. 29-38.

[22] J.J. Ongong'a, 'Towards an African Environmental Theology', in Mary N. Getui and Emmanuel A. Obeng (eds.), *Theology of Reconstruction: Exploratory Essays* (Nairobi: Acton Publishers, 1999), pp. 50-69 (55).

Engineer'.[23] Though God is actively involved in his creation, not all natural phenomena are ascribed to him in African cosmology. Ill health, catastrophes, and natural disasters are credited to the anger of the gods or the ancestors.[24] Samson Gitau seems to side with Ongong'a when he contends that

> The environment seems to speak a religious language to mankind and above all, those who believe. For instance, the Sun, the Moon, the Stars, mountains, lakes, seas and rivers, thunder and lightning, earthquakes, forests, plants, and animals can all speak to humans about the beyond.[25]

For the African Christian, such understandings come with ease because of the primal worldview that '… the physical realm is meant to be patterned on the model of the spiritual world and beyond'.[26] Pobee is emphatic when he argues, '… the Creator God did not leave the world without his stamp as asserted by the theology of natural revelation'.[27] Even before the advent of the Gospel of Christ in Africa, nature arguably revealed the nature and attributes of God to people. Creation therefore can be likened to a book of revelation of the transcendent and the immanent Creator and his nature. Thus, for the Akan Pentecostals, creation has intrinsic value that requires humanity to treat it with respect.

God's Creation is Wonderful

The creation narrative shows a deliberate and thoughtful process, with the Creator carefully created each element of the universe.[28] This mirrors the Akan concept of God as *Borebore* as in *Borebore a ɔbɔ adeɛ no* ('The skilled Carver who meticulously fashioned things'). This understanding highlights that creation is intentional, purposeful, and orderly, with every element having its inherent value and meaning. In

---

[23] Ongong'a, 'Towards an African Environmental Theology', p. 66.

[24] Peter Sarpong, *Ghana in Retrospect; Some Aspects of Ghanaian Culture* (Accra-Tema: Ghana Publishing Corporation, 1974), p. 53.

[25] Samson K. Gitau, *The Environment Crisis: A Challenge for African Christianity* (Nairobi: Acton Publishers, 2000), p. 3.

[26] Harold Turner, 'The Primal Religions of the World and their Study', *Australian Essays in World Religions* (Bedford Park: Australian Association for the Study of Religions, 1977), pp. 27-37 (32).

[27] Pobee, *Toward an African Theology*, p. 103.

[28] Awudi, 'Beyond Eco-Pneumatology', p. 179.

other words, nothing in the universe came by accident as every creation has its own intrinsic value and purpose.

However, it is important to note that the value of creation is not defined by human perception or aesthetics; rather, it stems from its value and purpose.[29] Thus, whether humanity knows the value of a creature or not, the Creator knows it. Pentecostals acknowledge this widely as it is articulated in some Akan Pentecostal songs as the one below:

Wo nsa ano ndwuma nyina ara	All that you created
ɛyɛ nwanwa	Are wonderful
Wo nsa ano ndwuma nyina ara	All that have created
ɛyɛ nwanwa	Are wonderful
ɛyɛ nwanwa (2x)	It's wonderful (2x)
Wo nsa ano ndwuma nyina ara	All that have created
ɛyɛ nwanwa	Are wonderful
Author unknown	*Translation mine*

This song not only aligns with scripture but speaks to the value embedded in every creation of God. To underscore the beauty, mystery, and wonder of God's creation, the narrative highlights a recurring divine affirmation: 'it was good,' repeated five times, with in the ultimate declaration, 'it was very good' (Gen. 1.31). This divine seal of approval underscores the inherent value and perfection of creation. This 'very good' creation reflects the character of a benevolent God. In other words, a good creation can only come from a good God. The Apostle James affirms this when he says, 'Every good gift and every perfect gift is from above, coming down from the Father of lights with whom there is no variation or shadow due to change' (Jas 1.17). 'God's creation is not only good but wonderful, perfect, and orderly.'[30]

The creation narrative highlights God's process of bringing order to the universe through three key acts of separation: distinguishing day from night (Gen. 1.3-5), separating the sky from the land (Gen.

---

[29] Awudi, 'Beyond Eco-Pneumatology', p. 179.
[30] Awudi, 'Beyond Eco-Pneumatology', p. 180.

1.6-8), and dividing the waters from the land (Gen. 1.9-10). These separations established the framework of space and time that governs creation. With this foundation in place, God then brought forth life, creating plants (Gen. 1.11-13), animals (Gen. 1.20-25), and then human beings (Gen. 1.26-31). Psalm 104 celebrates the wonders of creation, with the psalmist marveling at the mysteries behind God's handiwork, many of which remain beyond human understanding. This perspective invites Christians to approach creation with reverence and respect, moving beyond a view that commodifies or assigns monetary value to every creation on earth. Instead, it encourages a deeper appreciation for the intrinsic value, awe, and wonder behind God's creation.

All Creation Praises God

Tom Regan argues that the original purpose of creating animals was not for human consumption as in the 'steaks and chops, roasts and stews' that most people are used to in recent times but for both to live in harmony and render praise to their Maker.[31] A careful analysis of Scripture not only reveals this truth about animals but all that exist, for the Creator's praise.

Like the Torah and the Prophets, the Writings contain valuable lessons that Christians can glean as responses to ecological challenges in modern times. The Psalms contain songs that sing the glory of God's creation, those that point to God's love and care for his creation, and how creation in return, renders praise and worship to the Creator. For example, the stanzas 3 to 9 of Psalm 8, praise the wonders of God's creation. Looking at the great and wonderful creatures around him, the psalmist could not fathom how God could give humanity the role to reign over the rest of creation. Humanity is elevated to this status as near-equals to the Creator to enable them to participate in the governance of the universe as viceroys. Similarly, Psalm 19 declares that the heavens tell of God's glory while the skies proclaim the works of hands. Like the above psalms are some Akan Pentecostal songs that declare that God's creation declares his praise. The following lines from one popular Akan Pentecostal song states.

---

[31] Tom Regan, 'Christianity and Animal Rights: The Challenge and Promise', in Charles Birch, William Eakin and Jay B. McDaniel (eds.), *Liberating Life: Contemporary Approaches to Ecological Theology* (Eugene, OR: Wipf and Stock Publishers, 1990), pp. 73-87 (73).

Wo nsa ano adwuma	The things you made
trontrom Wo	adore you
Ɔsoro abɔfo sɔre Wo	The angels in heaven bow before you
W'ahotewfo, yɛto dwom sɛ	Your saints sing with one accord
Nhyira nka Wo din	Blessed be your name
nhyira nka Wo din	blessed be your name
Eunice Johnson[32]	*Translation mine*

The song also acknowledges that not only humanity or the inhabitants of the earth praise God, but also the angels in heaven. As mentioned earlier, the Akan Pentecostals, by this song, acknowledge that all creation renders praise to God. Though one cannot readily tell if the primal worldview influenced the composition of this song but can be sure that the composer was influenced by her understanding of Scripture. This confirms Rev. 4.11 that all creation,[33] acknowledges that God is worthy of glory and honour and power because he created and sustains all creation. It shows that both humans and other-than-human creation render praise to God. It also validates the fact that creation exists not to sustain human life, but for the Creator's pleasure. Similarly, the song below also confirms how the non-human species praise God. It goes as far as mentioning individual creation that render praise to God including birds, the sea, storm, and the wind.

Nnomma de wɔn nnwomto yi N'ayɛ	The birds sing praise to him
'Po nso de n'asɔrekye kamfo no	The oceans also praise him by their storm
Ahum de n'ahumtu da N'ase	The wind renders thanks to him
Ɔno n'ɔsɛ ayeyi	He alone deserves the praise

---

[32] The Church of Pentecost, *Pentecost Song Book*, p. 382.

[33] Onesimus Ngundu, 'Revelation', in Tokunboh Adeyemo (ed.), *Africa Bible Commentary* (Nairobi, Kenya: WorldAlive Publishers, 2006), pp.1568-1605 (1581).

Onyame fata ayeyi	God deserves praise
Onyame fata ayeyi	God deserves praise
PAN(T) 1094[34]	*Translation mine*

This song aligns with Psalm 148 which calls for a universal praise – praise from all creation in the universe. The palmist mentions the heavens, sun, moon, stars, angels, fire, hail, snow, clouds, mountains, trees, animals, and humans to praise the Lord. It is therefore not out of place to say that the exploitation and the wanton destruction of creation denies the Creator the praise due Him. Though these songs clearly show how creation renders praise to their Creator, they are seen by some as metaphorical. Jürgen Moltmann's position summarizes it all.

> God created the world for his glory, out of love; and the crown of creation is not the human being; it is the Sabbath. It is true that as the image of God, the human being has his special position in creation. But he stands together with all other earthly and heavenly beings in the same hymn of praise of God's glory, and in the enjoyment of God's Sabbath pleasure over creation, as he saw that it was good.[35]

Thus, according to Jürgen Moltmann, God's creation is motivated by love aimed at his glory, with the Sabbath being the pinnacle of creation, rather than humanity. This perspective challenges the common temptation to view humans as the zenith of God's creation. Instead, the apex of creation is the seventh day, when God rested and delighted in the beauty of his creation.

The creation narrative does not end with God's admiration of his very good creation but his rest on the seventh day. It shows that though creation of the universe and its inhabitants was within six days, the seventh day climaxes the entire creation.

God Cares for All His Creation

The Bible highlights God's care and provision for his creation, emphasizing the intricate relationship between Creator, humanity, and the natural world. God's care extends beyond human beings to the

---

34 The Church of Pentecost, *Pentecost Song Book*, p. 309.

35 Jürgen Moltmann, *God in Creation* (London, SCM Press, 1985), p. 31.

other-than-human species in the ecosystem. In the OT, the law of harvest made provisions for the poor, strangers, and both domestic and wild animals. For example, farmers were forbidden from thoroughly gleaning their fields or picking up every leftover after major harvests, allowing the poor, strangers, and animals to benefit from the remains (Exod. 23.11; Lev. 19.10). During sabbatical years, no sowing, pruning, reaping, or harvesting was permitted, enabling the poor, strangers, landless, and animals to feed on the growth of the land (Lev. 25.5-7). Additionally, leftover food in the fields was intended to nourish birds and wild animals, demonstrating God's care for these creatures.

Jesus reinforced this idea in his Sermon on the Mount, noting that God provides for birds that do not sow or reap (Mt. 6.26) as mentioned in the song below.

Monhwɛ nnomaa a wokyin wɔ wim	Look at the birds in the air
Wɔnnɔ wɔmpam, wɔmmu nhyɛ asan	they neither weed, sow, nor gather into barns
Agya Oyname, ɔkyɛ a ɛso wɔn so	Our Father who shares and give them
Na ɔma wɔn daa daa aduan	But he always gives them their daily food
Eunice Addison[36]	*Translation mine*

This highlights God's provision for all creation, regardless of their ability to work or store food. This understanding is not unique to Christianity; the Akan people of Ghana express similar sentiments in their proverbs, such as *Aboa onni dua no, Onyame na ɔpra ne ho* ('It is God who drives away flies from the tailless animal'), illustrating God's love and care for all creatures.

Towards Akan Pentecost Ecological Hymnology

This study has demonstrated that there are several ecological lessons in Akan Pentecostal hymnology as there are in the OT Psalms that

---

[36] The Church of Pentecost, *Pentecost Song Book*, p. 298.

can be gleaned towards the development of a theology on the environment in the Pentecostal tradition. However, many Pentecostals are yet to see the value in these songs and how they connect to creation care. These lessons include God as the Creator and the sustainer of the universe. This agrees with several portions of Scripture (Gen. 1.1-30; 2.1-15; Deut. 10.14; Job 38-40; and Ps. 24.1) and also show the mystery, awe, and beauty behind God's creation. Such songs also demonstrate that the creation came from a good Creator who carefully designed each one of them.

The songs show that creation reveals the character and the attributes of God – he is omnipotent, omnipresent, and omniscient. He is all-powerful, capable of providing for all that he has created. His omnipresence reveals that he has not absconded from his creation but is involved in the day-to-day management of the universe. His omniscience is a testament that he knows the location of every single creation of his. Just as he is compassionate, gracious, slow to anger, abounding in love (Ps. 145.8-9) he implores humans to demonstrate same traits in their care for nature.

The songs do not only reveal that God is the final authority and overload of the universe but also the understanding that humans are not the owners of creation but caretakers. Humanity's role in creation, as described in Gen. 1.28 and 2.15, is not one of exploitation but rather of service and care. According to Flavius Josephus, God commanded humans to care for the plants in the Garden of Eden.[37] This responsibility extends beyond flora and fauna to the entire earth and its inhabitants. Scholars like Samson Gitau and Claus Westermann interpret the terms 'dominion' and 'rule' from the Hebrew words *kābaś* and *rādā* as implying shepherding, nursing, and protection of God's creation, rather than exploitation.[38] Though their original meanings may imply violence and abuse as some scholars suggest,[39] they rather imply benevolent care and stewardship. Asante defines *kābaś* as caring, preserving, conserving, cultivating, and

---

[37] See Flavius Josephus, *The Works of Josephus* (trans. William Whiston; Peabody: Hendrickson, 1987), p. 29.

[38] Claus Westermann, *Genesis* (New York: T&T Clark International, 1964), p. 11.

[39] See Norman L. Geisler, *Christian Ethics; Contemporary Issues & Options Second Edition* (Grand Rapids, MI: Baker Academic, 2010), p. 325.

protecting creation, excluding subjugation and exploitation.[40] This mandate requires humans to use the environment for survival while also guarding it against destruction.

There is the tendency also to place humanity at the centre stage of God's creations. However, it is important to know that the image of God in humanity is just a prerequisite for partnership with God in caring for creation – God is rather at the centre of care for creation. Calvin B. DeWitt outlines four principles for humanity in caring for creation: First, the conservancy principle – reciprocal service between humans and creation; second, the safeguarding principle – protecting creation as God safeguards humans; third, the fruitfulness principle – enjoying creation's fruit without destroying its fruitfulness; and fourth, the Sabbath principle – providing for creation's rest.[41] These principles demonstrate that humanity's role is one of conservation, not exploitation. He writes

> Service from the garden to us is implicit; service from us to the garden is explicit. What is expected of Adam, and of us is return the service of the garden with service of our own: a reciprocal service – a con-service, a conservancy, a con-servation.[42]

Prefixing the service with the Greek word, *con,* which means 'together',[43] implies serving together. In other words, humans are viceroys, exercising authority over creation on behalf of the Sovereign King. The concept of viceroyalty, as described by Desmond Tutu and Gitau, emphasizes humanity's delegated responsibility to care for creation.[44] Thus, humanity's role in creation is one of service, care, and stewardship, rather than exploitation and dominance.

---

[40] Emmanuel Asante, *Topics in Old Testament Studies* (Accra, Ghana: SonLife Printing, 2005), p. 131.

[41] Calvin B. DeWitt, 'To Strive to Safeguard the Integrity of Creation and Sustain and Renew the Life of the Earth (i)', in Andrew Walls and Cathy Ross (eds.), *Mission in the 21st Century: Exploring the Five Marks of Global Mission* (Maryknoll, NY: Orbis Books, 2008), pp. 84-93 (88-89).

[42] DeWitt, 'To Strive to Safeguard the Integrity of Creation', p. 89.

[43] Online Etymology Dictionary, 'Con-', Accessed 31 May 2020, https.//www. etymonline.com/word/con-.

[44] Desmond M. Tutu, 'Religious Perspectives on Religious Human Rights: Religious Human Rights and the Bible', *Emory International Law Review* 10 (1996), pp. 63-68 (65).

The songs also show how the Creator loves his creation and demonstrates his love and care towards all. Since the creative love of God embraces all creation, the value of all creation needs to become explicit in the teachings and the mission strategies of churches. Thus, nothing came by accident as every creation has its own intrinsic value and purpose. As mentioned earlier, the value of creation may not lie in aesthetics, whether human beings know the value or not, the Creator designed it for a purpose.

Conclusion

This study has demonstrated that the Akan Pentecostals have several hymns that sing about the value of God's creation, but these lessons are yet to be gleaned by Pentecostals toward the development of their ecotheology. It has shown that Pentecostals in these churches need to go beyond the enjoyment of the instrumentations behind these songs and draw the ecological lessons in these songs as they are in the Psalms. Such songs like the Psalms and other writings in the OT have valuable lessons for Christians towards environmental stewardship. They are not just metaphoric as some see them to be but clearly show that the praise of God is universal as his care and love.

CONCLUSION

WORSHIP THAT MOVES UPWARD, INWARD, AND ONWARD

PHILIP A. STRUYK*

Introduction

In this concluding chapter, I wish to offer a resource to worship leaders and pastors who have a hand in the direction of their church's worship ministry. While I will speak from my own social location/Pentecostal-charismatic perspective and though I purposefully direct my thoughts primarily to church leaders in my own tradition, I suggest that the following reflections might also have relevance to those who lead worship in other traditions within the broader framework of Christianity. The impetus for this conclusion comes from my experience at the recent Society for Pentecostal Studies Conference held in Kirkland, Washington in March 2025 where I had the privilege of attending as a member of a cohort of worship leaders. The SPS conference was both an inspiration and a challenge at many levels, especially the deep intellectual, spiritual, and socio-ethical dimensions it touched upon. The conference theme, 'More Than a Song: Scholarship as Worship in the Church, the Academy, and the Public Square', brought about a diverse array of session presenters and chapter topics for our consideration. Out of the many thought-provoking sessions dispersed over the course of three days, a few key

---

* Philip A. Struyk (PhD, Fuller Theological Seminary) teaches at Heritage Christian School in California.

recurring themes rose to the surface and became the topics of the subsequent conversations we had in our cohort meetings. It is out of these lively conversations that the content of this conclusion has emerged.

Amidst the turbulent political climate of our day and the increasing digitization of society so heavily influenced by social media and artificial intelligence, this chapter discusses three important dimensions of worship that church leaders ought to keep in mind as they plan and implement worship services. For worship to be 'more than a song' I claim that it must be intentionally theocentric, spiritually-driven, and missionally-minded. To use a directional metaphor, I maintain that worship should move upward, inward, and outward. By an upward trajectory I mean the kind of worship that truly seeks to bring worshipers before the throne of the holy Triune God. By inward formation I refer to worship ministries that are genuinely interested in the spiritual transformation of worshipers and not preoccupied with their temporary enjoyment or entertainment. By outward orientation I envision worship services that inspire and facilitate holistic missional activity mindful of our prophetic vocation in this world – a divine call not only to proclaim the verbal gospel of Jesus Christ but also to contend for social justice in his name. To make my case I draw from various biblical resources in conversation with the contributions offered by selected conference speakers, namely, Leah Payne, David Taylor, Lester Ruth, and Jacqueline Grey.

Reflections on Leah Payne's Historical Analysis

The tone for our conference was set on its opening night by Leah Payne who presented a paper based on her book, *God Gave You Rock & Roll* – an insightful and interesting history of Christian music in the United States. Payne's main point was that the socio-economic factors that produced the Contemporary Christian Music (CCM) industry (which exploded onto the scene in the 1980s as a 'safe' alternative to secular music) have given rise to what is now the mass-marketed performance-driven worship music machine. Payne has shown how decades ago white suburban evangelical moms effectively exerted influence on the production of Christian music since they were the primary consumers who bought albums at Christian bookstores for their adolescent and teenage children. This 'cool Christian music' was deemed essential lest their children fall prey to 'the devil's music' popularized by MTV and secular radio. Once frowned upon by the church, Christian rock music was not only embraced as a better option for youth to listen to recreationally but it quickly became the predominant style of instrumentation for worship in the majority of Pentecostal-charismatic and evangelical churches.

As Payne demonstrates in her book, CCM has lost momentum over the past several years for various reasons but worship music as a marketable genre has now taken center-stage. Presently, there is pressure to give the church-goers (aka, the entertainment-loving consumers) exactly what they want in high-energy and visually-appealing performance-driven worship services (aka, concerts). In light of these social realities, as Spirit-filled worship leaders we must stop and ask ourselves some important questions: Are we remaining focused on magnifying the holy Triune God? Are we truly being led by the Spirit of God as we worship God? Are we still making space for the operation of the gifts of the Spirit in our churches? Is there room for genuine spontaneity in our worship services anymore? Have we confined ourselves with click tracks, pre-planned lighting changes, and other features of tightly-run made-for-streaming productions. If we plan our worship services down to the minute how can we welcome the movement of the Spirit in our midst? By asking these questions I suggest that making space for the Spirit's spontaneity is itself a move towards theocentricity – not personal subjectivity.

It is not a ground-breaking concept to say that God ought to be the center of our worship; however, since the human heart is a perpetual idol-factory (to borrow Calvin's famous words) it is necessary to stop and to examine our hearts regularly and also the priorities and practices of our worship ministries. Along these lines, the psalmist reminds us when he declares, 'Not to us, LORD, but to your name be the glory, because of your love and faithfulness' (Ps. 115.1 NIV). It can become easy to exalt the self if a worship ministry becomes more focused on either generating a particular feeling or satisfying the tastes of a congregation rather than striving to bring our people before the throne of the Holy God. This is not to say that once worshipers encounter God's Presence in worship they should not experience deep emotions. Communion with God will often produce intense feelings of overflowing love, joy, and peace. Orthodoxy and orthopathy ought to go hand-in-hand. Nevertheless, we must rely on the *Spirit's* work in generating these affections and emotions rather than seeking to manipulate them. Our primary role as worship leaders is to lead the congregation to a place of *divine* encounter. The author of Hebrews is instructive on this theme: 'Therefore, since we are receiving a kingdom that cannot be shaken, let us be thankful, and so worship God acceptably with reverence and awe, for our 'God is a consuming fire' (Heb. 12.28 NIV). As we reflect deeply on who God is in all of his matchless glory, our worship cannot help but take on a more upward orientation.

As we prioritize the lifting of our hearts, minds, and bodies upward to God in worship for the praise of His glory we find that our lives are changed *inwardly* by the Spirit in the process. As worship ministers we have the sacred duty to pray for, facilitate, and foster moments of inward transformation for the people of our congregations. Paul's well-known words are worth repeating about this theme.

> Therefore I urge you, brothers and sisters, in view of God's mercy to offer your bodies as a living sacrifice holy and pleasing to God. This is your true and proper worship. Do not conform to the pattern of this world but be transformed by the renewing of your mind. Then you will be able to test and approve what God's will is – his good, pleasing, and perfect will (Rom. 12.1-2 NIV).

As we model and encourage fully surrendered worship for our churches, let us remember that if we bring ourselves to the Lord in sacrifice, then God will send down the fire of the Spirit on our offering. Just as fire always brings change to the natural environment so the Spirit always brings change to the abandoned soul.

As I have been arguing, it is impossible for someone who has truly encountered the Presence of God to walk away unchanged. Dramatic biblical examples of God's transforming power abound. Think of Moses when he faced the burning bush or when he saw God's glory atop Mount Sinai. Consider Isaiah's vision of God in the Temple or the effect of the Transfigured Christ on Peter, James, and John. Think of the way the apostle Paul was utterly changed when he met Jesus on the road to Damascus or the way that the early church in Jerusalem was supernaturally empowered on the day of Pentecost. With these examples in mind, have you considered Paul's description of the operation of the spiritual gifts in the context of corporate worship when he writes to the Corinthians?.

> [T]ongues, then, are a sign, not for believers but for unbelievers; prophecy, however, is not for unbelievers but for believers. So if the whole church comes together and everyone speaks in tongues, and inquirers or unbelievers come in, will they not say that you are out of your mind? But if an unbeliever or an inquirer comes in while everyone is prophesying, they are convicted of sin and are brought under judgment by all, as the secrets of their hearts are laid bare. So they will fall down and worship God, exclaiming, '*God is really among you*! (1 Cor. 14.22-25 NIV)

Spirit-initiated charismatic activity cultivates a deep sense of the Presence of God amidst the congregation as well as a powerful reminder of God's desire to provide a living testimony of Godself to people both inside and outside of the church. As powerful as the preached Word of God is towards the transformation of lives, as worship leaders we must never forget that God's manifest Presence can revolutionize a life in an instant.

Returning now to further reflections on Leah Payne's book (as summarized in her conference presentation), the author not only implicitly calls for worship that is God-centered (upward) and genuinely spiritual (inward) but she also brings a sense of our socio-ethical responsibility (outward) as worship leaders. In other words, we must be mindful of the social contexts in which we are worshiping. There is indeed a time and a place at church for energetic celebratory worship at a high volume complete with elaborate instrumentation. Our praise should be glorious as is befitting of our glorious King. That said, we should also make space for times of silence, contemplation, solemnity, and lament within the liturgy in response to the social ills and injustices that exist around us. Admittedly, if a worship leader decides to be socially-conscious in the process of leading and planning worship sets, certain doubts and fears may arise. How will the church react if time is given to pray about things like rampant homelessness, merciless deportations, or environmental degradation (to name just a few of many possible concerns)? Will there be complaints of being 'too political?' Will people begin to complain that worship isn't inspirational enough if we pray and/or sing prayers of lament? There are indeed strong market-driven forces that impinge upon the worshiping church ever ready to capitalize on the appetites of worship music consumers. Many worship leaders feel a certain pressure to incorporate only the kind of upbeat and inspirational worship music popular on Christian radio or the CCLI top 10 list. At times, however, our congregations need to sing songs of confession, repentance, and lament. An awareness of the church's liturgical calendar and the (re)incorporation of traditional liturgical elements into our weekly services may be the antidote to the kind of pervasive commercialism of which Payne warns her readers.

Reflections on David Taylor and Lester Ruth's Notion of Scripted Spontaneity

Along these lines, another excellent general session was delivered by David Taylor entitled, 'The Spirit of Spontaneity'. Taylor's chapter calls worshipers to find a balance between the scripted and spontaneous aspects of Christian worship. His aim is to challenge those who may tend to gravitate towards one extreme or the other in their preferred liturgical form to see the value of embracing the Spirit's work both in the past and the present. By the Spirit's *past* work, Taylor refers to the fixed elements of liturgical/traditional worship including prescribed prayers. By the Spirit's *present* work, Taylor means the free working of the Spirit in the liturgical space. Taylor bookends his remarks with the story of a man in his old Vineyard church (Taylor is now an Anglican priest) who would inevitably break into spontaneous worship dance at some point in the service yet in such a way that his movements never seemed anything less than Spirit-led and God-glorifying. This 'scripted spontaneity' may be compared to jazz music which has a basic form yet allows for skilled musicians to improvise within certain moments during the performance of a particular piece of music. This analogy is helpful to Pentecostal-charismatic worshipers who often equate true worship with a dramatic encounter with the Spirit. Taylor's point is that these encounters still should have some sense of continuity with the broader corporate gathering if they are to fit within the community's offering of worship. Otherwise one wonders why the 'spontaneous worshiper' needs to be at church at all to have such an experience with God!

Another excellent presentation that brought together the 'scripted and the spontaneous' was offered by Methodist liturgical scholar and historian of Pentecostal-charismatic worship, Lester Ruth. In his chapter, 'A Eucharist that is Truly Eucharistic', Ruth, offers thought-provoking ideas for a more robust 'Pentecostal eucharistic practice'. The musings presented in Ruth's chapter were sparked by his study of the recent interest among key Pentecostal theologians in the Eucharist and sacramental theology.[1] Ruth begins his chapter by showing that many of the ancient eucharistic prayers capture a sense of exuberant (and even extemporaneous) praise and thanksgiving at the Table itself. Justin Martyr's famous liturgical instructions and Basil's liturgy are historical examples of this 'truly eucharistic' celebration. As Ruth notes, thankful overflowing praise fits quite nicely with the ethos of Pentecostal Praise & Worship.

In my view, the value of Ruth's chapter is found in its generous spirit and practicality. Certainly, couching the Eucharist within celebratory times of musical Praise & Worship or times of extemporaneous prayer could inspire meaningful and S/spirited worship. In response to Ruth's creative contribution I have no critique; however, I do have one concern worth noting. Since Pentecostal-charismatic worshipers already expect to experience the Presence of God at other times in their liturgy (such as in the musical Praise & Worship or the 'altar time'), I would hope that the moments of quiet awe-struck remembrance and peaceful contemplation so often afforded by Holy Communion would not be lost altogether in Pentecostal-charismatic congregations if they were to adopt Ruth's model. Thus, I argue that Ruth's model of Eucharistic celebration would serve better as an occasional or semi-regular practice among Pentecostal-charismatic believers. Worshiping congregations of any Christian tradition should seek a healthy balance between times of joyful exuberance and peaceful reflection in their liturgical cycle.

---

[1] As an aside, I am honored by Ruth's acknowledgement of my recent PhD dissertation on this topic which served as a catalyst for his own research and experimentation (I wrote on the topic of methods of Pentecostal liturgical theology).

Reflections on Jacqueline Grey's Prophetic Call

Jacqueline Grey's chapter 'Miriam's Worship as Prophetic Action' provides another helpful example of the *outward* dimension of Pentecostal worship. Grey interprets Miriam's jubilant activity after the crossing of the Red Sea as an act of prophetic worship. Her actions of playing a hand drum, singing, and dancing may be seen as embodied forms of prophetic communication that convey the freedom of worshiping God in juxtaposition to living as slaves of Egypt. As an ancient worship leader, Miriam's actions communicate to the people a vivid message: God's people have been set free in order to worship the Lord with their bodies. Miriam's celebration of God's rescue of their bodies out of slave labor under Pharaoh's oppressive leadership into the joyful freedom of salvation points ahead to new covenant realities we now enjoy in Christ. A prophetic imagination will help the reader of Exodus receive and appropriate the visionary communication resident within this worshipful moment. In Grey's words, 'Imagine Miriam and the dancers shaking off the slavery. Imagine them using their bodies in new ways that resist the containment of Egypt. Together, as they dance, their whole beings are free to love God and worship God' (Grey, p. 32).

Like our Pentecostal forebears, Miriam testifies to us in our day that worship is not meant to be passive nor purely cerebral; rather, worship should engage the body and may even serve, at times, as an act of holy rebellion. On this point, Grey makes an interesting connection with historical Pentecostal worship whose origin may be traced in part back to the worship style of the African-American slaves. She writes, 'The expression of dance at this time by Afro-Pentecostals can be considered a prophetic activity as it communicated a message of freedom and justice to give hope for the future of the African-American community' (Grey, p. 34)'. Thus, 21st century worship leaders do well to take note of Miriam's prophetic leadership as we offer our whole bodies in worshipful celebration of our freedom in Christ – both in a spiritual and social-ethical sense. Since Pharaoh symbolizes oppression, Miriam's song can be re-appropriated in our day and age to inspire songs of freedom in the face of various forms of oppression and injustice. Miriam's dance is a prophetic act that expresses in a bodily form the true liberation found in Christ.

Similarly, worship in the church today may use dance and other forms of physical expression to convey God's truth, justice, and freedom.

Conclusion

The 2025 Society for Pentecostal Studies Conference was impactful for me at many different levels. The biggest take-away for me had to do with the relationship between the Spirit, worship, and political theology. As a conservative-leaning person, I was reminded at the conference – through many of the sessions and also through fellowship with our cohort – of how antithetical so many of the attitudes and actions promoted by the current American government are to the values of the Kingdom of God. My heart was refreshed and recalibrated by the prophetic Spirit to be ready to side with the poor, the marginalized, and the disenfranchised in our community and our world. This spiritual realignment was needed since I work in a predominately white evangelical space that has been heavily impacted by the forces of Christian nationalism. Sadly, this troubling political movement is fueled in America by a significant number of Pentecostal-charismatic Christians who operate under the influence of the far right-wing elements of the New Apostolic Reformation movement (see Matthew Taylor's excellent book, *The Violent Will Take it By Force*, for more on this topic).[2] Thus, I am praying for the discernment and the courage needed to use my position and my voice to speak, write, and lead prophetically in the power of the Spirit.

In conclusion, the 2025 Conference theme of 'More Than a Song: Scholarship as Worship in the Church, the Academy, and the Public Square' has called Pentecostal academicians and church leaders to seek forms of corporate worship and public witness that are simultaneously theocentric yet mindful of our socio-ethical mandate to pray for, advocate for, and fight for justice and shalom. Our worship cohort walked away from the SPS conference reminded that corporate worship should be structured yet spontaneous, priestly yet prophetic. True worship the Father seeks must be anointed by the Spirit yet bounded by the guardrails of biblical truth. We were reminded that loud voices from the political sphere and powerful forces from

---

[2] Matthew D. Taylor, *The Violent Take It by Force: The Christian Movement That Is Threatening Our Democracy* (Minneapolis, MN: Broadleaf Books, 2024).

the economic sphere have joined forces and are creating a consumerist and sometimes narcissistic brand of public worship ('the worship machine'). Our worship music and worship services therefore must resist the powerful forces which market neatly packaged yet often shallow expressions of praise. Conversely, may our pastors and worship leaders strive to foster worship services marked by robust upward, inward, and outward dimensions. As we remain mindful of each of these trajectories of worship we can offer God (and our congregations) worship services that are truly 'more than a song'.

www.ingramcontent.com/pod-product-compliance
Lightning Source LLC
Chambersburg PA
CBHW070556100426
42744CB00006B/296